3-
12+

Concerning JUVENILE DELINQUENCY

HENRY W. THURSTON

Concerning JUVENILE DELINQUENCY

Progressive Changes in Our Perspectives

IN LITTERIS
LIBERTAS
1754·1893

1942 · *Columbia University Press* · *New York*

PREFACE

THIS BOOK does not discuss the techniques of case work with the individual juvenile delinquent.

It tries to make clear that perspective as regards both cause and treatment is essential for successful case work with juvenile delinquents. In so far as he is familiar with the whole range of opinions on the causes of juvenile delinquency—has historical perspective—the case worker will be helped to understand the causes of delinquency in each juvenile delinquent whom he knows, and to see him as a total personality in a total situation. And the case worker and the community will be helped to choose and to provide successful methods of treatment for each juvenile delinquent to the degree to which they are familiar with the whole range of treatment processes hitherto used.

In short, as a guide to our own next steps in service to juvenile delinquents, I have tried to describe some of the beginnings and some of the processes of change from old to new perspectives that have already been made. Both as individuals and as communities, in order to do our best to understand, to treat, and to prevent juvenile delinquency, we need an evolutionary time-perspective.

In the words of Walt Whitman in *Passage to India,*

For what is the present after all, but a growth out of the past?
As a projectle formed, impelled, passing a certain line, still keeps on,
So the present, utterly formed, impelled by the past.

If Whitman is right, each today will be a part of the past to impel each tomorrow. Each today should do more and more to impel a tomorrow that will have less juvenile delinquency.

Acknowledgments

In my efforts to make the progressive changes in our perspectives concerning juvenile delinquency as clear as possible, I have made many quotations from newspapers, magazines, organizations, publishers, and press departments of universities and from the words and writings of individual men and women many of whom are no longer with us but whose words are still alive and working for a more abundant life for juvenile delinquents. For each of these quotations I have tried to show my appreciation by giving in a footnote the publisher, the publication, and the author. As consents by publishers have usually included permission to quote from the speakers and writers involved, I have not made personal contact with some of the persons whose words I have gratefully used. A special written consent has been given me by each of the following:

Newspapers: Boston Herald, Chicago Daily News, Chicago Tribune, New York Herald Tribune, New York Sun, New York Times, New York World-Telegram, Philadelphia Inquirer, Philadelphia Record.

Magazines: American Magazine, Annals of the American Academy of Political and Social Sciences, Current History, The Family, Opportunity, The Survey.

Publishers: D. Appleton-Century Company; Charles Scribner's Sons; Harcourt, Brace and Company; Little, Brown and Company; The Macmillan Company; McGraw-Hill Book Company; New Republic; Stratford Company.

Social Organizations and University Presses: Judge Baker Guidance Center, National Probation Association, Russell Sage Foundation, University of Chicago Press, Harvard University Press, University of North Carolina Press, Yale University Press.

Individual Men and Women: Dean Edith Abbott, Dr. Clairette P. Armstrong, Dr. Amos F. Baker, Dr. Sophonisba P. Breckinridge, Dr. Augusta F. Bronner, Editor William L. Chenery, Charles L. Chute, Henry E. Drewry, M.D., Professor Thomas D. Eliot, Joseph Fishman, Dr. Eleanor T. Glueck, Dr. Sheldon Glueck, William J. Harper, Shelby M. Harrison, Dr. William Healy, J. Edgar Hoover, Karen Horney, M.D., Commissioner Austin H. MacCormick, Professor J. B. Maller, Columnist Westbrook Pegler, Dr. James S. Plant, George H. Preston, Edgar Rickard, M.D., Dr. Frederick M. Thrasher.

For coöperation with me in the planning, writing, and editing of this book, I am especially grateful to these persons:

Leonard W. Mayo, Dean of Applied Social Sciences, Western Reserve University, Cleveland, Ohio, who not only wrote Chapter XIII but also helped me, while we were both in New York School of Social Work, in my first tentative plans for writing a book in this field.

Paul T. Beisser, Secretary and General Manager, St. Louis Children's Aid Society, who studied my manuscript and gave me detailed critical and constructive advice as to final formulation and sequence of chapters and as to purpose and scope of the book as a whole.

Miss Mabel P. Ashley, New York School of Social Work, for critical reading of galley proofs; and Miss Mildred Prinzing, Editorial Department, Columbia University Press, who helped make my sentences and their sequences express my ideas with greater clarity.

In these days of increasing maladjustment in social relations, all the way from the family to the world, there is danger as never before in our times that increasing numbers of our youth will experience such frustrations as to make them juvenile delinquents unless they have our help in all communities. It is a time for each one of us to do his best to understand, to treat, and to prevent such frustrations.

HENRY W. THURSTON

Montclair, New Jersey
July 22, 1942

CONTENTS

x　　　　　　　*Contents*

Part One: DELINQUENCIES AND
THEIR CAUSES

Chapter I: JUVENILE DELINQUENCIES FROM MISCHIEF TO MURDER

T HE PROBLEM of understanding, treating, and preventing juvenile delinquency is only the first part of the positive and larger problem of helping youth to be good citizens. The Fourteenth Amendment to the Constitution of the United States declares that "All persons born or naturalized in the United States, and subject to the jurisdiction thereof, are citizens of the United States and of the State wherein they reside." By this authority boys and girls are citizens; they do not need to wait until they are twenty-one. Many persons confuse "citizen" with "voter," and sometimes even noted speakers who are giving advice to young people when they are graduated from the elementary or high schools use the expression "when you become citizens" when they mean "when you become voters." It is important that, as we face the problems of juvenile delinquents, we remember that we are facing the problems of young citizens who will one day be voters.

For a historical perspective on the treatment of juvenile delinquents I cite here these sentences pronounced by judges in England in 1819 and 1821: on a fourteen-year-old boy who stole a cotton gown, value two shillings, "Seven years transportation"; on a thirteen-year-old girl for stealing a hat, "To be imprisoned six months"; on two boys, eleven and thirteen, accused of stealing about seventeen shillings, "Guilty—Death." [1]

For perspective on the range of delinquent acts of our youth there is a decided advantage at the outset in keeping our eyes open to the things done frequently by boys and girls in our own homes, on our own streets, and elsewhere in our own towns. Some ways in which we may do this are: to observe and ponder the meaning of the ques-

[1] Wilbur M. Stone, "Juvenile Crime a Century Ago," *New York World,* January 28, 1929.

tionable behavior of boys and girls in our own homes and neighborhoods; to talk with teachers, recreation leaders, policemen, probation officers, and others about what they know concerning bad citizenship in youth; and also to read in the daily papers printed reports of unsatisfactory citizenship activities of boys and girls in different parts of the country. Most of the examples which follow have either been observed by me or have been mentioned in the New York papers which I habitually read. So far as my travels have permitted, I have also sampled, for brief periods, the daily papers of other sections of the country; for example, New England, the Chicago area, and our northwestern coast. Activities similar to those of boys and girls in the Eastern area have also been found described in these sections. Furthermore, if it be objected that such casual personal observation and such limited newspaper stories may lack some scientific detail, this fact is readily admitted; but at this stage of our discussion the use of stories of unsatisfactory citizenship activities of boys and girls, based on personal observation and newspaper accounts, is defended on two grounds: first, that such sources of information are open to everybody; secondly, that there is in a vast majority, even of newspaper stories, sure indication of behavior of youth that challenges parents, teachers, and other citizens to ask *why* children behave thus and *how* they can be helped or taught to behave differently.

It is my hope that all my readers will feel a sacred obligation, personally and collectively, to help meet the challenge of the youthful behavior that probably lies behind the stories which follow even though these narratives are somewhat impressionistic and may possibly include some errors in statement of actual details. My mistake, if any, at this point, is not that I accept the evidence of my own observation and believe that there is at least some basis in fact for most of the newspaper stories of the unsatisfactory behavior of young citizens, but that I have stopped with the mere observation and casual reading or, at most, have said in effect "Well, it is just too bad, but what can we do about it?" Whether or not such newspaper stories as follow are accurate to the last detail, their effect on us should be to stimulate us to more persistent questions, such as, "What, in full detail, did these children actually do?" "Why did they do such things?" "How can they and other children be taught better citizenship activities?"

The activities of the young citizens now to pass in rapid review before the reader range from thoughtless mischief to individual and group murder. Other illustrations will be given in Chapter VII. It is hoped that the questions "What?" "Why?" and "How?" as used above will be continually in the reader's mind as he sees these boys and girls in action.

Children Throw Stones before Passing Automobiles

The first story to be told is one of thoughtless mischief. On a hot summer afternoon I was looking through the window of my own house on a residential street in Montclair, New Jersey. I saw, sitting in the shade, on the curbstone before the front door, an eleven-year-old girl and an eight-year-old boy, picking up loose stones, some of them as large as hens' eggs, and throwing them just in front of the wheels of many automobiles that were passing swiftly. The street is of hard, smooth asphalt, slightly rounded toward the center, but there were some stones in the gutter. Already at least two dozen stones lay scattered over the street. It would have been very easy for a wheel to skid far enough on one of these stones to cause one car to graze or sideswipe another.

Boys Throw Stones at Passenger Trains

The following story comes from a city newspaper. A city superintendent of schools recently reported that eighteen passengers had been severely injured in three months by stones thrown at trains which passed to and from the center of the city. A three-year-old girl had lost an eye. The superintendent also reported that considerable damage was done to plate-glass windows by the use of air rifles and guns.[2]

A Pensacola Janitor's Report

A clipping from a paper, without date or reference, kept by me for many years, quotes this letter (spelling is as in the clipping):

[2] *New York World Telegram*, May 13, 1934.

"Dear Sir: I regret the circumstance which insinuates a duty, to report an irregularity, that has assumed abnormal toleration, and threatens a stampede among the tenants at the East Side apartment. In short; room 24 has two boys who are instructed that they have as much right on the premises as anybody else, and they measured up to the peaceful relationship that exists among tenants. Some of the causes, that I personally know, are the pounding of the floor with hammers; scrapping with other children; tearing up the toilet paper; occupying the bath up to the point of indurance; and leaving the room in a compromising condition, punching holes through the bottom of old chairs; howling in a boisterous way; putting things on the railway tracks; leaving of bread and trash in the main passway, and before other tenants doors. I submit these prerogatives to you for regulation; personally I have no kick to make, Janitor and trash makes a job. Yours truly. . . ."

High School Students Throw Pies and Tomatoes at Police

A newspaper account of activities of high school boys reads in part:

"About 1500 students went 'raw bottom' yesterday at the . . . High School . . . St., and . . . Ave. and a dozen policemen who tried to quell them were routed with a barrage of pies, apple cores, pop bottles and ripe tomatoes.

"The disturbance started when police shooed away a group of boys eating lunch on the steps of . . . West . . . Ave., the residence of Mrs. E. It seems that Mrs. E. objected to dripping of mayonnaise on her front steps.

"The boys retreated, but only to the school yard where they slammed the gates and went to work on the police. A Keystone comedy didn't have a thing on the ensuing scene, and quiet was restored only when the ammunition gave out. Then the boys filed back to classrooms to resume their study of *civil government*." [3]

[3] *Philadelphia Record*, June 7, 1934. Will the reader please note that this reference to the study of Civil Government (education in citizenship) is made by the newspaper reporter, and not by me?

Gunplay by Boys in the Streets

I have personally seen dramatized gunplay almost under the shadow of two great universities. The first occasion was in the summer of 1931, near the State University in Seattle, Washington. I was looking out of my window toward a church on the opposite side of the street. This church had outside steps leading to the basement, and the curbing above was covered with ivy. Suddenly a boy about ten years old came running from the east, looking back over his shoulder from time to time as he ran. When he reached the area steps he jumped down and, crouching behind the ivy, brought a three-foot toy gun to his shoulder and snapped the trigger. I saw no boy in pursuit, but evidently the boy was satisfied that his shot had killed his pursuer, for he came quickly out of the area and walked away.

The second incident occurred in Chicago. Early in October, 1931, I walked from Dorchester Avenue west on Fifty-eighth Street to and through the grounds of the University of Chicago. It was Saturday morning, and I saw three separate groups of boys with toy guns playing shooting games—in each case against a visible enemy of one or more boys. There was attack, retreat, pursuit, hiding behind flower beds, hedges, corners of houses, and so forth. One boy, who had fled across Fifty-eighth Street from the north, was brought down by an imaginary fatal shot by his pursuers. He lay as if dead until two boys from the firing line came across the street and turned him over, limp and lifeless. When they had gone away, the "dead" boy got up and walked off.

Whether, and to what degree, the current craze for wearing holsters with pistols in them and for carrying various types of gun is an evidence of good or bad citizenship in youth is a pertinent question for every reader.

Youth Activities near the "L" on the South Side, Chicago

A columnist in a New York newspaper thus describes some of his own youthful activities on the South Side in Chicago. This is valid testimony.

"I grew up in a moderately crowded neighborhood of Chicago on a street of three-story apartments, where most of the families had freckled, buck-toothed ordinary children. The 'L' ran behind the row and the young blades of the neighborhood, up to the age of, maybe, 14, got up as early as four o'clock in the morning to go running in short pants and undershirts, training for the next Marathon race of the Illinois Athletic Club. Marathon racing was the fad of the moment, and you could see leggy little brats, built like mosquitoes, staggering around and around Graceland Cemetery, at least three miles per lap, I should say, early on summer mornings, building up their wind, as they thought, and close onto rupturing their hearts, training for the twenty-six-mile Marathon of the I.A.C.

"After training thus, a man naturally would find himself tired and without immediate occupation, the family being not yet awake and life not yet astir in the town. The milkmen went around, however, cat-walking up and down the wooden back stairs on their sneaker soles, setting down a quart of Grade A here and a few cents worth of cream for the coffee on the kitchen steps. And the pie wagons from the wholesale bakeries were making the rounds of the neighborhood delicatessens in the dawn, dropping stacks of pies and bushel sacks of cinnamon rolls and coffee rings into wooden lock boxes, which stood on the sidewalks in front.

"The young bucks used to follow the milkman around, a few minutes behind, and steal the milk and drink as much as they could and wantonly smash the other bottles against the pillars of the 'L,' and presently, somehow, a stencil of the master key to the pie boxes fell into our hands and we followed the pieman around, too, swiping, which is a euphemism for stealing, merchandise of value.

"We had other vices. We would hop on the streetcar and ring up ten or a dozen fares on the poor conductor, while he was inside poking coal into the stove, and hop off and run. We rigged the slots of gum-vending machines with paper wads, a trick too marvelous to explain in detail, to steal a few pennies per machine per day, and we were pretty bad characters weight for age.

"There were two pioneer automobile thieves in our set, who used to steal Ramblers and Sampsons and chain-drive Queens in the evening and drive them until they gave out. Some of us could have been taken in sin for going along with them a time or two on these exploits." [4]

Activities of Youth on Jones Street, in New York

The activities of New York city youth in a slum area are also described in a newspaper article written long ago by the present editor of *Colliers,* William L. Chenery. This also is the valid testimony of a competent eyewitness. His description reads in part thus:

"My place of observation is Jones Street. A blacksmith shop, a piano factory, not to mention numerous small stores and decrepit tenement houses, are my neighbors. In these last, hundreds of children are gathered. The Jones Street gang has quite a reputation in our neighborhood. Whenever a howling mob of dervishes is heard rushing toward some errand of destruction, the old denizen shakes his head and mutters, the Jones Street gang again.

"I first became aware of the group early one morning. As I left my lodging I saw two little chaps of six or seven on the door stoop. They were shooting craps. They invited me to join in the game. On my assertion that I didn't know how to play, they offered to explain the rules. They did. It would have been hard to find a gang of wandering Negro laborers who were more expert at 'African golf.' At seven my neighbors are proficient gamblers. . . .

"I do not think less of them for it. Rather I think more. It shows how unconquerable is their spirit. New York can distort it, but it cheerfully lives on. From early morning well on to midnight, fair weather and foul, the Jones Street kids are driven by circumstances to gamble. When they have pennies, these are the stakes. When they have no money, but are not quite bankrupt, Liberty Loan buttons will serve the purpose. If they are below the poverty line of childhood, the tin tops of beer bottles take the place of coin. But whatever the medium and whatever the game, they gamble.

"So universal is it that none familiar to the scene notices it. Policemen usually do not interfere. Parents approve lest something worse be done. In truth the entire adult neighborhood would view with re-

---

[4] Westbrook Pegler in *New York World Telegram,* January 29, 1934.

gret any effort to end children's gambling, for it would undoubtedly mean trouble. Windows would be broken, the percentage of fights would be higher. Street accidents would increase, street noises would be noisier, depredations would be more numerous, life would be even less tolerable in that squalid section where poverty and art make so vain an attempt to hide ugliness which nothing less than the demolition of great areas could truly cleanse.

"Gambling is, in fact, practically the least noxious of the avocations of youth from the cursory point of view of the adult world; craps and pitching pennies keep children quiet. The preoccupation of a legislator playing poker can be seen on the faces of children absorbed in this supreme pastime. All the good qualities, and they be many, which betting games bring out are undoubtedly developed. In particular, there is the great deftness, the skill, produced by much handling of dice, much slinging of pennies and shuffling of cards. A cunning artistry to a degree is thereby attained. A capacity for quick judgment may be stimulated. The boys of Jones Street and their comrades of the lower West Side are, perhaps, using the best opportunity which New York gives them when they gamble. Yet it is not from preference that they pitch pennies hour after hour. They try other devices only in the end to be balked. . . .

"With the opportunities at hand, they do show real imagination. They attain true adventure. For example, a half dozen may be seen disputing with an express wagon or a motor van the right of way through some side street. It takes courage to stand in the way of a motor truck until the driver is uncertain whether or not he will kill a boy. Sometimes, tragically, that agility fails. Fluency is needed to continue a satisfying conversation with the driver when the lad escapes. The Jones Street gang can and does do that, but it is hazardous and after a time it palls. Dodging is wearisome, the stream of traffic is endless, but the strength of certain children does not hold out forever; besides, even profanity has its limitations as a diversion. A boy can exchange oaths for ten minutes with a righteously angry driver, but words fail when the next car comes. Shooting craps is better than that. There are other things, of course, which a boy's or a girl's imagination will discover. Making unusual noises is one of the most entertaining, to those performing the feat. The Jones Street gang knows how to beat the thin boards taken from orange boxes in such a way that the exploding ebullition of old-fashioned firecrackers seems, in comparison, but a feeble chirrup. It is a great sight to gaze on a block of youngsters whacking the sidewalk with those thin boards so furiously that subway, motor cars, blacksmith shops and factories are drowned in the din. Such an outburst of energy is admirable; it bodes well for the future of the race. The possession of the temperament which demands expression even at such a cost is a noble thing. It is none the less, a melancholy comment that veritable babes should be driven to such violence in order to attain pleasure. As a man hears it, gambling is better. But the yearning of the young is incessant. It stops not with such endeavors. The Jones Street boys, and more particularly the girls, have learned to howl in unison. That is a special accomplishment. Exhibitions are given when it is desirable to discipline some meddlesome adult. I have heard forty children howl down a woman indiscreet enough to order the gang to depart from her domicile for their own.

"A marvelous quality is to be heard in this mass howl. Naturalists describe a monkey in the Amazon upper jungles which is said to have the most terrible sound of any living creature. I do not believe these scientists have listened to the charms of Jones Street when its members have been excited to the utmost of derision. Possibly it would be profitable for some futurist musician eager to learn strange novelties to attend such a concert. He would hear wild sounds undreamed of where life flows in more placid channels. From the explosions which thus come when the current of youthful emotion is dammed are produced vibrations uncharted by the old masters. From a certain standpoint, however, gambling is preferable. . . .

"As individuals, too, the members of the Jones Street gang have acquired many varieties of strange skill. Much of this is devoted to escaping the consequences of adult irritation. The duel of the boy and the grocer is all too typical. In a contest of this kind, the boy is the first aggressor. When he has teased the grocer past endurance by disarranging the vegetables, the game begins. As I have seen it played, the grocer kicks and the boy retreats. But not far. The boy usually is able to estimate the trajectory of the grocer's kick to a nicety. He, bent over something after the manner of a swordsman, faces his grown-up adversary. The grocer tries to kick him in the stomach, that being esteemed especially successful, if the blow is landed. But I have never seen it land.

"The boy jumps back a few inches at a time. The rhythm of kicking so masters the man that he must perforce continue kicking, even though a change of tactics would be more successful. As the boy jumps, he yells, it matters not what he says. The grocer understands that abysmal contempt is being uttered. I have never witnessed a derision more complete. This joust usually attracts a large crowd, and sympathy seems ever with the boy. When the man, who is ordinarily fat, finally fatigues himself to a point where a change of attack is essential, the boy runs away and is lost in the crowd. An event of this kind is very amusing in Jones Street. Its visible aftereffects persist for some time. I am not certain, however, that it is to be chosen in place of gambling.

"The one overwhelming fact is that New York's children were not taken into account when the city was allowed to grow. New York fancies that children are objects to be ignored. It cannot be done.

"It would be hard to conceive of a more abnormal world than that in which dwell the children of Greenwich Village and similar sections in New York. Hardly a single decent instinct of childhood is permitted wholesome expression. If a little girl craves the companionship of a doll, it is the street, somebody's door stoop or a recess in some old house that is the only available refuge. If a boy wants to build a playhouse, he must trespass. I have seen small-boy houses built against the barred windows of slightly used factories. Their pathetic little structures are thrown up, to endure until some contemptuous adult kicks them down. It is not strange that children turn to gambling. That at least is not annoying enough to warrant the interference of the grown-up world. There at least is quiet undisturbed and peace for children.

"Babies are scarcely born on Jones Street before they learn to wail on the highway. Uncomfortable tenements drive mothers to deposit their helpless babies at the edge of the uncomfortable street. There

the mingled cries of children of all ages compose a medley unap-
proached as a warning of distress. The shrill yells of infants of various ages merge to notes harassing to consider. Then toddlers crawl
about the dirty gutters competing sometimes with gaunt cats for the
right of scrutiny into a stray accumulation of waste. The older and
upright, tender children are forced to learn all the infamy which
chaotic neglect amid overcrowding can teach. But nevertheless these
are the people in whose hands the future of this city rests. These
unthought-of municipally undesired children of today are they to
whom the responsibility of the future must be committed. What says
statesmanship of this? Does no one care for the New York that is
to be?" [5]

Young Citizens and a Policeman in the Street before the House of Paul Revere

To give a glimpse of a recent street scene in Boston to accompany
those cited from Chicago and New York, I now include verbatim a
description given me by my Montclair pastor.[6]

"One day last summer, August 3, 1939, I stopped in front of the
old house of Paul Revere in Boston. Not far away was the Old North
Church where the lanterns had been hung to send Paul Revere on
the famous ride which has become symbolic of the American struggle for liberty. But Paul Revere would have had long thoughts had
he stepped from his front door that hot August afternoon. The square
was swarming with Italian boys who had nowhere to play. A street
fight was in progress, and one lone policeman had seized one boy as
a sort of hostage for the good behavior of the crowd. After a profane
tongue-lashing, he released the boy, who ran across the square shouting back taunts at the officer, culminating in the defiance, 'You can't
do nuttin' to me—my fader pays taxes!' A spectator could not help
looking at the house of Paul Revere, and asking, 'Is this the freedom
for which Paul Revere rode through the night?' These boys were
not free to become good citizens—the community was not giving

[5] *New York Times,* September 14, 1919.
[6] Dr. Morgan Phelps Noyes, Pastor of the Central Presbyterian Church, Montclair,
New Jersey.

them a fair chance. This idea that the paying of taxes is the price one pays for doing as he pleases—is that the American idea of freedom? These squalid homes which house an immigrant population which was admitted when labor was needed and now represents America's surplus labor supported by relief—is this the best that a free country can do with its economic problem? We obviously need changes in the world we live in. The good news of the Kingdom of God is our assurance that they can be in the direction of a more fraternal, more coöperative, and more satisfying life for all men."

To what degree could the reader of the foregoing descriptions of youth activities and community conditions in Chicago, New York, and Boston now find such activities and community conditions in his own town or some near-by city?

Cheating by Boys at the Subway Turnstile

Not many years ago I went with two boys, eleven and ten years old, respectively, from Montclair, New Jersey, into New York city to go up to the top of the Empire State Building, visit the Museum of Natural History, eat luncheon at the Automat, and so forth. As the boys passed through a turnstile to take a subway train in the city, one boy put a nickel in the slot while the other boy crowded under the turnstile ahead of him. When I challenged their action they exclaimed, as with one voice, "Oh, that's all right. We can *get by* easy!" Has the reader ever seen other illustrations of this getting-by behavior in young or adult citizens?

A Negro Boy Tries to Go to Dixie Land in a Borrowed Boat

In June, 1934, when the United States fleet was in the Hudson River, the press told this story of a Negro boy's reaction to parental discipline:

"At two o'clock, Tuesday morning, a fifteen-year-old boy had had a falling out with his mother, who lives at . . . West . . .th St. Then and there he decided to leave home forever, and go for a protracted visit to his kinfolk in Virginia.

"To the boy's fleet-conscious mind there could be but one means of transportation to the Old Dominion and that was by boat. Proceeding to the 155th Street dock, he picked himself out a rowboat and rowed into the main stream, where his fancy fastened on a boat with sails and an auxiliary motor. He recognized this as a superior means of locomotion to elbow grease and oars.

"After making the transfer, he set his course for the Narrows. Unable to raise the sails, he just drifted. Hunger attacked him before he had gone very far, and, abandoning navigation, he went below where he found the galley well stocked. It was while he was thus off duty that the craft he skippered struck Destroyer 113 amidship. He was taken on board and then to the children's court. The judge asked him 'Are you sure you weren't out to attack the Fleet?' 'No, Sir, I was going to Virginia.' " [7]

Police Overtake Three Boys in a Stolen Automobile

An adventure of three boys of fourteen or fifteen in a stolen automobile is thus told in a daily paper.

"Three muffled figures darted from the theatre throng at . . . Ave. and . . . St., last night, sprang into a parked car and drove off. Detectives gave chase.

"The fugitives swerved in and out of the long lines of traffic at . . . Ave. and . . . St., the detectives brandished their pistols, shouting that they would shoot. The fugitives stopped. The detectives covered the car and out stepped the three boys. The tallest was four feet tall, the driver was only three feet eight inches." They were taken for juvenile delinquency to the Childrens' Society Shelter.

"Later Mr. M. of H. P. walked into the police station and reported that his car had been stolen. 'We know it,' said the detective, 'we just got it back from the kindergarten.' " [8]

Three Adolescent Brothers Buy a $2,000 Car with a Forged Check

"A sixteen-year-old boy, who, with his twin brothers fifteen years old, bought a $2000 car with a forged check, got the car stored and serviced in a garage on credit and drove about the city for seven days, one day to a town twenty-five miles away, before they were

[7] *New York Times*, June 14, 1934.
[8] *New York World Telegram*, October 23, 1933.

caught. The boys were well dressed, and with stiff choir-boy collars which surmounted their coats, they impressed the dealer to whom they represented themselves as the beneficiaries of a nine-million-dollar trust fund. When the judge asked the oldest boy why he had done what he had, he replied without hesitation, 'I have a complex for automobiles.' " [9]

A Gang of Boys Finds It Difficult to Play Pirates on Land

"The discovery of two supposedly human skeletons on the city dumps several weeks ago by five local boys gave them the idea of establishing a pirate's den in which they conducted a secret organization dedicated to the proposition that Captain Kidd was a grand old gentleman who could do no wrong.

"Their imaginations ran away with them, it seems, and all five wound up in another den (not a pirate's) charged with arson, larceny and breaking and entering. They were released today in the custody of their surprised parents and will reappear tomorrow morning in the Juvenile Court to explain a few things like the theft of $50 in school supplies, the burning of two bath houses and the attempt to burn two empty houses.

"On most occasions when the boys, whose ages range from 9 to 13, started out from the pirate's den they would wear grotesque masks, a holdover from Hallowe'en. On their way to a house of potential plunder they would sneak along the highways and byways, darting into alleys and doorways to avoid detection.

"Before starting out they were imbued with a certain degree of false courage by standing for long periods gazing intently at the two skeletons hanging up in the den. The skeletons, one complete and the other minus a leg, were placed together by string and wire by the boys.

"The den was in the second story of an old barn. It was decorated with pirate pictures, newspaper photographs, and its only furniture was a soap box and bench. A lone candle provided the illumination when the pirates met in nocturnal session to plot the next move.

[9] *New York Herald Tribune,* December 21, 1931.

"In the two empty houses, one on L . . . Avenue, and the other on T . . . S . . . Avenue, near the den, police found that efforts to burn the structures had been made by setting fire to mattresses in the middle of floors.

"The boys told the police they did not like the idea of being land pirates, anyhow. With a ship, they indicated, they could have accomplished something." [10]

[NOTE.—For other varieties of gang activities see *The Gang,* by Frederic M. Thrasher, Ph.D., the University of Chicago Press, 1927. And for youthful adventure away from home see *Boy and Girl Tramps of America,* by Thomas Minehan, New York, Farrar and Rinehart, 1934.]

Youthful Robbers Who Lived in an Old Automobile

This story tells of the arrest of two fourteen-year-old boys who had lived for several weeks in an old automobile in a vacant lot at . . . Avenue and . . . Street.[11] A girl of eleven whom they had taken along with them to ring apartment doorbells was caught by the police and gave their hide-out away. Their procedure was to ring a bell and then, if no one answered, go up on the roof and enter the apartment through the skylight. The girl remained in the hall to notify the boys with a whistle if anyone came to the door later.

Looting by a Boy Gang for the Sake of Thrills

This story too is told in a daily paper.[12] Five boys, sixteen, thirteen, fourteen, fifteen, and thirteen, were turned over to the Children's Society in New York for arraignment in the Children's Court. The police accused them of looting fifteen homes in a residential section. The loot did not aggregate more than $1,000, and nearly all of it was found hidden in the cellars of the boys' houses. The homes robbed, the police said, were those of persons away on vacations, and in every case the boys entered by smashing windows or opening them with screw drivers.

[10] *New York Times,* February 6, 1935.   [11] *Ibid.,* February 15, 1932.
[12] *Ibid.,* August 31, 1933.

None of the boys was of criminal type, the police said. They blamed the robberies on the fact that the boys had too much time on their hands and were seeking thrills.

School Children Break into Schoolhouse during Vacation

An instance of the bad citizenship activities of school children comes from the newspaper of a New England city.[13] The report, as condensed for this chapter, runs thus:

A squad of police, with shotguns, bullet-proof vests, and tear-gas bombs, in response to a call from one of the near-by residents, had surrounded a schoolhouse from which scores of boys poured out through windows, doors, and basement entry. Most of the boys escaped, but two boys of seven, two of eight, and two of twelve were captured. A dozen windows had been broken, chairs were tipped over, a piano was wedged in the door, floors were littered with colored paper, chalk, and broken clay bubble pipes, and grotesque pictures with a slogan "No school tomorrow" were drawn on the blackboard.

Boy of Sixteen Recruits a Gang of Adolescents

Again from a paper I condense this story of a red-cheeked and dimpled boy of sixteen who, with an accomplice, was arrested and charged with assault and robbery.[14] He had been twice in a local reformatory before he was fifteen. He had escaped by sawing the bar of his cell and swimming a river. After getting a revolver and blackjack he recruited a gang of twelve, in their teens, but quarreled with them over the division of the loot and was repudiated as leader. He got another pal and stole a parcel-service pay roll of $1,140. He says he also alone robbed about fifteen other places. When arrested he and his pal had hired a keeper for their guns and blackjacks. This keeper was afterwards arrested and was found to have three revolvers and a blackjack in his possession.

---

13 *Boston Herald,* July 17, 1935.
14 *New York Times,* April 8, 1932.

Boy Smugglers of Liquor from Canada

Before prohibition was repealed, a newspaper carried this story of smuggling by Buffalo boys.[15] Four to six Buffalo boys from fifteen to twenty-one years old were repeatedly taken across the International Bridge from Buffalo to Fort Erie in an automobile driven by one of them. When darkness had settled down on the Niagara River, each of the boys returned to Buffalo rowing a boat with twenty-five cases of beer or their equivalent. The pay per load was said to be fifteen dollars. The boys were all from families of good reputation.

A Western Boy of Fourteen Threatens to Bomb a Man's Store

In a Western paper is an account of a fourteen-year-old boy who wrote this note to a jeweler: [16]

"Mr. D. Unless you place $300 dollars in ten dollar and five dollar bills your store will be bombed before August 3, 1931. Place money in a cigar box and then place in a newspaper box on the corner of . . . Avenue and . . . St. before eight o'clock—to be more exact, between seven-thirty and eight on the night of July 26th. If I fail to receive the money, your store will be bombed by dynamite. You remember the cleaning shop bombing quite a while ago. Yours will be the same, or your wife will be killed, or at least injured by a stray bullet, or maybe you. I think you'll know better than to tell the police. Four-out-of-work."

Boy of Sixteen Threatens to Kidnap a Man's Daughter

A boy of sixteen, in the South, confesses to having written a letter to a Northern businessman who owned a near-by farm, demanding that the man deposit $25,000 in a rural mailbox near by, or the man's fifteen-year-old daughter who is a student in a Southern school would be kidnaped.[17] The boy says that the reason he thus wrote was "to get even" with the Northern man, with whom he had had trouble

15 *Ibid.*, April 22, 1932.
16 *Post Intelligencer*, Seattle, Washington, July 27, 1931.
17 *New York Times*, May 31, 1934.

about a dog some months ago, when he and his foster parents lived on a farm belonging to the threatened man.

Two other extortion letters had been written from the same locality to two other wealthy people, demanding that large sums of money be deposited near the same spot near the boy's home.

High-School Girl of Thirteen Arrested for Threatening to Kidnap

A high-school girl of thirteen was arrested when she went to a certain garbage can to get a supposed $10,000, which she had written to a prominent physician to deposit there, on her written threat to kidnap his eleven-year-old daughter. The arrested girl was reported to be an excellent pupil in the high school.[18]

Boy of Twelve Shoots a Sheriff

In the summer of 1931, while I was in Seattle, I learned that a twelve-year-old boy shot and killed the sheriff of Asotin County, Washington, who had surprised the boy while he was burglarizing a store. The lad was tried for murder, convicted, and sent for life to the state prison at Walla Walla, Washington.

A Dillinger Impersonator Kills His Half Brother

A Southern boy of sixteen killed his half brother during a re-enactment of the shooting of Dillinger. The boy who was killed had impersonated Dillinger, and the gun which the other pointed at his stomach proved to be loaded.[19]

A Student Monitor Stabbed by a Schoolmate

A paper tells the story of a Negro boy, fifteen, who, because he was told to keep in line by a Jewish monitor in a public school, challenged him to a fight after school.[20] "During the fight the Negro was said to have taken a small pearl-handled knife from his pocket and stabbed the monitor, barely missing his heart."

[18] *Ibid.*, April 6, 1933.
[19] *New York World Telegram*, July 11, 1934.
[20] *New York Times*, June 15, 1934.

A Boy of Eleven Kills a Neighbor Boy

An Eastern boy of eleven shot and killed a fourteen-year-old neighbor boy in a dispute about the ownership of an apple tree that grew behind the double house in which they lived.[21] The account states that when the older boy began to climb the tree in defiance of a warning from the younger, the latter ran into the house, got a small rifle, and fired two shots. The first caused the boy in the tree to jump down, and the second struck him just below the heart as he was running away. He died within an hour.

A Boy of Thirteen Shoots a Pal

A thirteen-year-old Western boy shot an eleven-year-old companion because the latter threatened to tell that these two and another boy had robbed a schoolhouse.[22]

Youthful Robbers Carry Northern Loot South

This story is condensed from a newspaper report.[23] A sixteen-year-old Northern schoolboy and his friend, seventeen, were arrested in a Southern city when the elder boy was accidentally shot in the arm by an automatic pistol in the hands of the younger youth. Their story was that about a month earlier they had made their way via roof-tops to the penthouse apartment of a broker at E. . . . Street, . . . City. Mr. S. was not at home, but the youths made themselves so. They smoked his cigarettes, sampled his champagne, and, because the younger boy liked to hear corks pop, uncorked eight bottles. After a time the youths left the penthouse carrying two suitcases containing several bottles of liquor, a camera worth $400, some money, and odds and ends of jewelry valued at about $3,300, and with their loot they headed South by bus.

At M. a pawnbroker refused to accept the camera, and they robbed his shop "to get even." Among their spoils was an automatic pistol which happened to be loaded. The shooting followed, and M. detectives, sent to investigate the shooting, discovered the stolen North-

---

[21] *Ibid.*, July 24, 1934.
[22] *New York World Telegram,* August 6, 1934.
[23] *New York Times,* March 10, 1934.

ern property and notified Northern police. The boys' return to the Northern court followed, and they were held to the Grand Jury.

A Boy of Eight Kills His Father in Play with a Gun

Here is an account of an eight-year-old boy who, with a shotgun, shot and killed his father at the lunch table.[24] The gun had been in the rear shed for two years, and the boy had played with it. Only that day he had found a shell that would fit it. As there was no protruding lead as in a bullet, the boy thought it was a blank cartridge and intended only to frighten his father. The father and mother, with their three other children, had sat down to luncheon when the boy appeared in the door with the gun. The mother, without looking up, said, "Sit right down to your luncheon; you are late now." The boy put the gun to his shoulder and pointed it at various things in the room and then aimed at his father, saying, "Look, Pop." His father looked around in astonishment and was just about to get up from his chair to take the weapon away from the boy when there was an explosion, and the father fell.

Three Adolescent Boys Shoot a Sleeping Man

Two days after the above incident was written into this chapter, the writer saw in the daily paper the headline: "Boy slayers sent to reformatories." [25] The boys referred to were brothers thirteen and eleven years old and a third boy, thirteen, who stole a revolver from a policeman's outfit and, finding a jobless painter asleep on the ground in a vacant lot, woke him up and demanded money. When he refused and told them to go away, one of the brothers shot and killed the man.

Boy of Fifteen Shoots His Mother

The story of a matricide is an account of a fifteen-year-old boy in a Southern state, who confessed to the police that he shot and killed his mother while she was working in her flower garden.[26] He intimated that his mother insisted that he study English during the

[24] *Ibid.*, November 5, 1931. [25] *Ibid.*, July 19, 1935.
[26] *Ibid.*, July 3, 1933.

summer as he had failed in this subject during the last semester in school. "The police found a shotgun, given to the lad as a Christmas present, under a mattress in the bedroom of the father, a box of cartridges under a chair cushion and a discharged shell in another part of the house."

An Honor Student Kills His Mother

Another murder story runs thus: "A fifteen year old boy, only son and honor student in the local high school, killed his thirty-five year old mother with an axe as she lay ill in bed reading. He said that she had scolded him for not weeding the garden and 'this awful thing came into my head while I was cultivating the garden. I was hot and angry and my head hurt, I went into the woodshed, got the axe, and holding it back of me, went upstairs to my mother's room. She was reading a book or a magazine; I hit her three or four times.'

"He then covered the body with a blanket and took a half hour bicycle trip, came back 'discovered the crime' then called in the neighbors, the doctor and an uncle. His father was at work on a farm near the village. During the investigation his father asked him if he was hungry and what he would like. 'I'd like to have a piece of that cake mother made,' he replied." [27]

A Boy of Sixteen Kills His Grandmother with a Hammer

A story from the Middle West runs thus: "A sixteen year old boy had told his companions that he would furnish a car for a dance. He said that his parents were temporarily out of town and had left him with a car and a checking account. On the evening of the dance his grandmother refused him permission to use the car and in a surge of anger he took a hammer and struck her such blows as to cause her death, after which he threw her body in a cistern." [28]

Youth in Crime

Although relating to youths above sixteen years of age, but still legally minors, a few statements published with the above title [29] may

[27] *Ibid.*, July 2, 1933.   [28] *Ibid.*, November 24, 1932.
[29] The American Law Institute, Philadelphia, March, 1940.

well conclude, for this chapter, my illustrations of bad youthful citizenship.[30]

"Youths—our children from sixteen up to twenty-one—are only an eighth of our population over fourteen years old."

"But youths—from sixteen up to twenty-one—are a fifth of our criminals."

"Youths: 13 per cent of our population old enough to commit crimes; but 19 per cent of the convicts behind prison bars for serious crimes, which means just this: youths are responsible for 50 per cent more of America's crime than their number in the population makes reasonable."

[NOTE.—The word *crime* as used above is strictly a legal term. Many offenses, if committed by boys and girls under the juvenile court age (sixteen years in most states), are not called crimes and do not make the culprits subject to criminal court procedure. But they become crimes in a legal sense if committed on or after the day these boys and girls become sixteen.]

If, as suggested at the beginning of this chapter, the reader has found from observation, interviews, court records, and the press that there are youth in his own community who are sometimes delinquent—bad citizens—in one or more ways, he will be the more eager to ask with me the question "Why?" to which I devote the whole of Chapter II.

I believe that it is only by repeated and persistent search not only for the what but for the why of delinquency that we, both as individuals and as communities, can hope to give adequate treatment to youth who have already become delinquent and to coördinate or orchestrate our community activities so as to prevent delinquent behavior by other boys and girls.

[30] Further illustrations of juvenile delinquency will be found in Part Two, Chapter VII, and in Appendix B.

Chapter II: A FORUM DISCUSSION
OF CAUSES

AMONG social workers, parents, teachers, and all other thoughtful companions of youth, the question of *why* particular children behave the way they do must always hold a middle place between our observation and knowledge of *what* children do and the further question of *how* we can help them to substitute satisfactory behavior for their past unsatisfactory behavior and can prevent undesirable behavior on the part of other children.

Everyone who is trying to understand why a certain youth committed a particular delinquent act should hold in clear perspective the answers to at least these three basic questions:

1. Are the causal factors in juvenile delinquency and bad citizenship on the part of youth many or one?

2. If there is only one factor, what is that factor?

3. If there are many causal factors, what are some of the most important factors operative in the particular individual or group delinquencies with which we ourselves are called upon to deal?

To help my readers to find the right answers to the above questions, I shall now serve as chairman in a forum discussion by a wide variety of speakers who have had their opinions printed. I confidently believe that the apparent contradictions will in the end be largely cleared up and harmonized. It certainly is important that we get a clear perspective on the whole range of opinions as to causes of juvenile delinquency.

As chairman, I shall introduce the speakers, some of whom will give quotations not only from their own writings but from the writings of others. I shall also summarize and condense in my own words some of the statements made. I shall usually give reference to the newspaper article, monograph, report, or book in which the speaker's opinions may be read at greater length than is possible even in an extended forum discussion such as we are to have.

*Malnutrition, Often Caused by Poverty, as a Causal Factor in
Juvenile Delinquency*

Chairman.—J. B. Maller, who made a study of the rate of juvenile
delinquency in 114 neighborhoods in New York city, gives sub-
stantially these statements as to the prevalence of malnutrition:

In these 114 neighborhoods, delinquents who had been brought
into the juvenile courts were found to suffer from many more physical
defects than the child population in general. These defects included
defective vision, carious teeth, glandular disturbances, and, particularly, malnutrition. In areas of high delinquency, 42 percent of the
children were found by the Department of Health to be suffering
from malnutrition, compared with an average of 19 percent for the
city as a whole. Some areas were found to have a delinquency rate
(for children 5 to 16 years old) of 23 per 1,000, while the average
rate for the city as a whole was 6 per 1,000 and for some districts only
1 per 1,000. In economic status, the delinquency areas are low. In the
ten areas with the highest rate of delinquency, the average monthly
rental is $18.00. For the city as a whole, based on the 1930 census, the
rate is $50.00 per month.[1]

I shall call upon Mr. Maller later. As to the extent of malnutrition
among children in New York city, I find that in 1935 there was a
study of the health of elementary-school children in that city, made
during the last school year, which revealed the fact that malnutrition
of 135,000 of these children, one fifth of the enrollment, was so great
that they were unable to do satisfactory work in school.

I also note that Miss Grace Abbott, Chief of the Federal Children's Bureau, reported in an article on "Children and the Depression" that even before the depression these percentages of malnutrition were found among the children of New York city: in 1928, 13.6
percent; in 1929, 13.4 percent.[2]

---

[1] *New York Times,* April 15, 1934. See also "Juvenile Delinquency in New York
City," *Journal of Psychology,* November, 1939, and Mr. Maller's reports for the New
York State Legislative Committee on Juvenile Delinquency, *Legislative Documents
No. 75,* 1939, and *No. 62,* 1940.
[2] *New York Times,* December 18, 1932.

If one were to urge that malnutrition of children is itself caused largely by the poverty of parents, this further evidence of the presence of poverty in New York city is found in the press report of August 1, 1935, that the director of school relief and Bureau of Attendance found that more than 75,000 children in New York city faced the school year with inadequate shoes or clothing.

Relation of Poverty and Physical Defects to Delinquent Behavior

Chairman.—The next speaker is Dr. Edgar Rickard, Vice President of the American Child Health Association. Dr. Rickard, what connection do you report between physical weakness and delinquent behavior?

Dr. Rickard.—Poor health and bodily defects often result in feelings of inferiority, discouragement, and bewilderment and thus become a cause of delinquency. A difficulty quite common among boys is a heart defect which prevents their playing baseball. Many a boy compensates for the mortification concealed in the words, "Mama says I can't do that," by extraordinary acts which make him conspicuous and give him the right to boast among his fellows. Human beings, no matter how young, want position, a place in their world, the feeling that they are leaders.[3]

Chairman.—I suppose the police have more opportunity than most of us to see the varieties of juvenile delinquency. I would like to call now upon a former police commissioner of New York city. Mr. Mulrooney, how do you account for the increase of certain juvenile delinquencies that you have observed?

Mr. Mulrooney.—I have recently said to the captains and higher-ranking officers, as we have discussed crime prevention among youth, that there had been many complaints of an increase of holdups by gangs of boys around eleven and twelve years of age. Several boys of that age recently held up a youth of their own years in Central Park, slugged him, and stole fifty cents that he had in his pockets.

Reports have also reached my office that roving bands of tough

[3] *Ibid.,* May 1, 1932.

boys, such as roamed the streets twenty or thirty years ago preying on children in neighboring districts, are forming again. Thefts of sleighs, wagons, and other playthings seem to be the chief aim of these gangs.

It is my opinion that most of these juvenile crimes are prompted by a desire of children in the poorer tenement districts to gain possession of the toys and other belongings of the children of families better situated financially. Existing economic conditions probably have a lot to do with it. It is not a simple problem.[4]

Chairman.—For comparison with what Commissioner Mulrooney has just said about the effect of poverty upon juvenile delinquency, it will be interesting to hear testimony based on the lifetime observations of that veteran friend and defender of criminals, Mr. Clarence Darrow.

Mr. Darrow.—Practically all the inmates of prisons come from homes of the poor and have had no chance to become adjusted to conditions, neither were they taught any occupation or trade to fit them for the stern realities of the world, when they are beyond school age. The inmates of prisons are mostly the product of large cities, where as boys they had all sorts of companions. Their playgrounds were the streets and the alleys and such vacant spots as the poor of great cities can find. They enter unoccupied buildings and take out lead pipe which they sell to junk dealers. How else would such children get possession of a few coins for themselves? They do not know the meaning of an allowance. Their petty thefts furnish the excitement and emotion necessary to growing life, which they can get in no other way. On account of playing ball on the street and slight delinquencies, they have already made the acquaintance of the policeman in the neighborhood. Soon they are on the black list and taken into the police station and the juvenile courts. They want the things that so many other boys get in some other way. Their course is the straight and narrow path from the simplest misdeeds to the penitentiaries and electric chairs, and as inevitable as the course of the other boys who pass from grade schools to graduate from colleges. Who is to blame? To say that it is the fault of the one who

[4] *Ibid.*, January 24, 1933 [condensed].

goes the luckless way is a travesty upon logic, common sense, and the first elements of fair dealing.[5]

Chairman.—And how does this factor of poverty in relation to youthful delinquency look to Pauline Tripp, a psychologist in the New York House of Refuge?

Miss Tripp.—The children of poverty do not get enough to eat. They are worried about their parents' struggle for a living. Many of them find it hard to maintain an interest in school work. They feel its unreality. Most of these proletarian children are eager to drop school and go to work as soon as possible. It is a natural choice.[6]

Chairman.—Dr. Glueck, you and Mrs. Glueck have studied criminal careers of adults and delinquent careers of youth. I note that you spoke recently, to the members of the Federation of Big Sisters and Big Brothers at the Waldorf Astoria, New York city, of the economic factor as one of the causal influences in these delinquent lives. How important do you find this economic factor?

Dr. Glueck.—Reliable researches have demonstrated that there is an increase in certain offenses, particularly property crimes and vagrancy, during periods of economic stress. This shows that the individual's power of resistance has been overbalanced by the strength of other circumstances.

How society shall meet its basic obligation to strengthen the resistance capacity of many of its citizens by raising the level of economic security is the great question to be answered today.[7]

Chairman.—I am glad to have as a member of our forum Professor Sullenger of Nebraska. Professor Sullenger, did you find the economic factor at all important in your study of 1,145 juvenile delinquents who were brought into the courtrooms of Omaha, Nebraska?

Mr. Sullenger.—I found that poverty and dependency are conducive to juvenile delinquency, as they lower the physical and mental powers of resistance, increase temptations and physical disease

---

[5] Clarence Darrow, *The Story of My Life*, 1932, pp. 83–84.

[6] *New York World Telegram*, February 27, 1933; 1932 Report of the House of Refuge.

[7] *New York Times*, April 16, 1935. Dr. Sheldon Glueck is Professor of Criminology at Harvard University.

and place the family in poor neighborhood environmental conditions. The result of efficiently administered out-door relief shows a decided trend toward the prevention of juvenile crime.[8]

Chairman.—In this connection I would like to cite a statement made by the Director of Attendance for the public schools of New York in a letter to the Commissioner of Accounts, urging more money for the schools so that they could meet the needs of truant and indifferent children. In substance, the statement was: The shortcomings of poor homes and of the schools should be held largely responsible for truancy and juvenile delinquency, in which truancy is usually the first step. The economic factor is dominant; poverty and resultant unsatisfactory home conditions produce the child's maladjustment, and inadequacy of financing prevents the schools or other social agencies from effectively counteracting early environment.[9]

Before passing on to discuss in more detail certain other causal factors in delinquency that are often closely associated with malnutrition and poverty, I call upon Mr. Maller, whom I have already quoted as to malnutrition, to sum up his findings as to other correlations in the 114 New York city neighborhoods studied for the frequency of juvenile delinquency.

Mr. Maller.—Negative correlations were found between delinquency and such desirable characteristics as health, economic status, school progress, and intelligence. That is to say, delinquency was found to be *low* where such factors are ranked *high*. Conversely, positive correlations were found between delinquency and such undesirable characteristics as incidence of disease, density of population, death rate, and infant mortality. Where such characteristics were prevalent, so was delinquency.

Emotional and Mental Defects as Causal Factors in Delinquency

Chairman.—In another part of his report Mr. Maller emphasizes the fact that on tests for emotional adjustments, delinquents were found to be well adjusted less frequently than other children; that

---

[8] Thomas Earl Sullenger, Professor of Sociology at the University of Nebraska, *Causes of Delinquency in Nebraska.*

[9] George H. Chatfield, in the *New York World Telegram,* June 21, 1935.

the percentage of broken homes in the classification of delinquent children was 40, while in the normal school population the percentage was about 20; and, finally, that this disparity was especially marked in the case of delinquent girls.

Before continuing our discussion, I wish to call special attention here to a recent pamphlet.[10] The author emphasizes a certain form of physical, emotional, and mental abnormality in children. He states (page 22) that specific glandular defects are causal factors for various types of emotional instability, including behavior problems of a vicious nature and behavior of a feminine type in boys, accompanied by a bullying tendency as a compensatory mechanism.

This mention of the compensatory action of children suggests that I now call upon another student of this problem, Dr. Karen Horney, psychiatrist and psychoanalyst. Dr. Horney, you have been quoted in the New York press. Have you any instances of compensatory action in girls?

Dr. Horney.—Yes. In a study of thirteen "boy crazy" girls I found that a fear of not being normal is what makes girls "boy crazy." They reach out for love not because the other sex is attractive to them but because the adoration of a man serves to reassure them and alleviates their fear of not being normal. This fear manifests itself in a fear of not being able to have a child and in a general sense of insecurity.[11]

Intelligence Quotients

Chairman.—While we are talking of mental defects, I would like to cite early and authoritative evidence that a large percentage of all reported juvenile offenders are not feeble-minded. Dr. William Healy, from whom we shall hear later, reported on his studies of 2,000 recidivous delinquents, both boys and girls, in Chicago and 2,000 more in Boston. He summarized the characteristics of these repeaters in a table the facts of which I present in Table 1.[12]

[10] A. S. Blumgarten, M.D., F.A.C.P., Lenox Hill Hospital, New York city, *The Scientist Looks at the Unstable Child,* Child Research Clinic Series, Vol. I, No. 3, published by the Child Research Clinic, Woods School, Langhorne, Pa., 1935.

[11] *New York World Telegram,* December 26, 1933.

[12] Dr. William Healy, *Delinquents and Criminals: Their Making and Unmaking,* New York, Macmillan, 1926, Table 47, p. 273.

TABLE I. CHARACTERISTICS OF 4,000 DELINQUENTS

DIAGNOSIS	CHICAGO		BOSTON	
	% in 1st 1,000	% in 2d 1,000	% in 1st 1,000	% in 2d 1,000
Normal mentally	69.5	75.0	73.8	72.0
Clearly feeble-minded	13.5	12.5	12.0	16.2
Subnormal mentally	10.1	8.2	10.6	7.7
Psychoses	6.9	4.3	1.0	1.1
Psychopathic personality	—	—	2.6	3.0

I wonder how intelligence as a causal factor in crime looks to Dr. Amos T. Baker, a psychologist who has worked with adult criminals in Sing Sing. Dr. Baker, will you tell us what you said about this to your fellow psychologists in the American Orthopsychiatric Association in Baltimore, Maryland?

Dr. Baker.—Most criminals go wrong because of unfavorable home conditions, not because they are mentally deficient. The mentality of most criminals compares favorably with that of the law-abiding population. Only approximately two percent of convicts are insane, and approximately five percent are feeble-minded. The ethical level of the community in which one is reared is largely responsible for his becoming a criminal or not a criminal.[13] The modern gangster type of criminal has about the average mentality. Forgers average the highest mentality and convicts guilty of assault the lowest. Most murderers have a normal mentality.[14]

Parental Attitudes and Home Conditions

Chairman.—Physical and mental defects may be due partly to heredity or congenital influences; but we know that parental attitudes and home environmental influences may also cause physical, emotional, and mental deficiencies that in turn become causal factors in the delinquencies, or bad citizenship, of youth. For testimony upon this point, I first call upon Dr. David M. Levy of the New York Institute of Child Guidance.

Dr. Levy.—Of the parents, the mother contributes the more to the

---

[13] See Appendix B for further opinions upon adult examples as causes of juvenile delinquency.

[14] *New York Herald Tribune,* February 19, 1932.

delinquency of children. Excessive mother love, indulgence, and overprotection of the child produce personality traits which lead to delinquent behavior. Rebellion from the father is caused by these mother-child relationships. The father is an accomplice in this situation in that he fosters the development of these behavior difficulties by giving the mother free rein in the care of the child, thereby allowing the overprotection of the offspring to grow unchecked. When the father permits the situation to continue for a time and then tries to check it, rebellion on the part of the child almost inevitably follows.[15]

Chairman.—Another medical man, George H. Preston, has put his ideas of the influence of disagreeing parents upon the child into the following verses:

GUIDES FOR GROWN-UPS

Mother keeps me tied so tight
To her apron strings
That I never have a chance
To try my wings.

How can I pick right from wrong
Or guide my ways
If I always have to do
Everything she says?

Ought she not to teach me
How to crawl
While she still can pick me up
If I fall?

Daddy says I'm trifling,
Says I'm stupid, slow and mean
Says I never learn my lessons
And I'm never neat and clean.

"Sissy's" what he calls me,
Says my head is made of wood,
So I've just about quit trying
To be better, if I could.

[15] *Philadelphia Enquirer,* May 15, 1932.

If my Daddy says I'm worthless
Then it surely must be so
Cause my Daddy is the wisest man
In all the world, I know.

Father pulls me one way, Mother pulls another,
One says "yes" and one says "no"
Till I don't know where to go.

Father has "digestion," Mother has a "pain,"
And no matter what I play
It is always wrong today.

Father says it's Mother, Mother says it's Pa,
But they never seem to see
What their fussing does to me.

If they only would agree,
Make a plan in unity,
Always one instead of three,
What a happy child I'd be! [16]

Delinquent Attitudes

Chairman.—Closely connected with the factors of physical and mental defect and parental attitudes and home conditions is the factor of attitude of both youth and adults. I shall introduce a noted student of, and writer on, juvenile and parental delinquency, to say a word on attitudes. Dr. Miriam Van Waters, what did you say about this to the National Conference of Social Work in Toronto, Canada, in July, 1924?

Dr. Van Waters.—In any society there are certain individuals whose sense of human relations is undeveloped and who tend to offend against and challenge the prevailing standards of conduct. The number of these individuals vastly increases with civilization. They are recruited from every intelligence level and every social position. Some are strong and well, others weak and handicapped. They agree on one thing only—that it is useless, impossible, or foolish for them to do as their neighbors do in respect to authority, property, industry, chastity, or team play. The kind of response they will make to the

[16] *The Survey*, October 15, 1930.

ultimate demands of the community depends largely on the emotional attitude they assume. This attitude is very early conditioned by the emotional attitude of the parents, the school, shall we say also the church, the social agencies, and the juvenile courts. Bad methods produce the attitude of delinquency.

Youth is in conflict today very largely because the demands of our modern life are inappropriate to childhood. The only possible approach that a social worker is justified in making toward delinquency is the approach that one should make to normal childhood. Everything should be done to create the sense of human relationship, and the feeling of isolation should never be permanently fixed in any offender. I cannot refrain from repeating the profound saying of Santayana in describing fanatics: "Fanatics are those who redouble their efforts—when they have forgotten their aim." [17]

Chairman.—For further illustration, I now call upon another writer, Dr. Marian McBee of the Illinois Society for Mental Hygiene, who will sum up the result of an intensive clinic study that she made of eight high-school students in 1930 to find out how family attitudes affected their school behavior.

Dr. McBee.—In all these cases there has been a situation around which the problem develops; in no case can we say that the attitude of the family has been responsible for the problem. As in all situations in which we are studying human behavior, we find that we have a complicated interaction of personalities, attitudes, and physical and social situations with which to deal. The purpose of examining the cases presented was to study the way in which family attitudes affected the situation and the child's behavior. Although no generalizations may be made from so cursory an examination of so few cases, it can be safely said that in these eight typical situations of problems involving school behavior, the attitudes of the student's family were the determining factors in the child's adjustment to the problem.[18]

Chairman.—To continue along a similar line, I ask Miss Bertha C.

---

[17] *Report of the National Conference of Social Work,* 1924, p. 165. Also published in *The Family,* July, 1924.
[18] *The Family,* March, 1930.

Reynolds to tell us what she said, as Associate Director of the Smith College School of Social Work, in 1932 to the National Conference of Social Work in Philadelphia.

Miss Reynolds.—Most of the business of child-guidance clinics consists in helping parents to get free enough from their own affairs and twisted loves and hates to give their children such love and security as shall make it possible for them to grow up less afraid. How can you give the child the pattern for healthy love relationship when all the experiences of his own life are the reverse? [19]

Broken Homes

Chairman.—We hear a great deal about broken homes as a cause of juvenile delinquency. We have with us Mrs. Marjorie Bell, who for the National Probation Association has personally studied the conditions leading to delinquency in all sections of our country. We shall hear her general opinion, and we shall hear in more detail about two statistical studies of this factor made by others in Chicago.

Mrs. Bell.—Here in this report by Clifford Shaw [20] is a study which includes a group of 7,278 boys from 29 public schools in Chicago. These boys come from age groups comparable to those in the juvenile court, and the schools were further selected with reference to varieties in delinquency areas (residence) and to diversity of national groups. There was found to be a wide variation in the distributing of broken homes among the different national and racial groups, and, as was to be expected, the rate of broken homes increased with the age of the child. But—and it is a very important but—there was not found to be any significantly greater proportion of broken homes among the delinquents than among the nondelinquents. Also, an intensive study of a smaller group of 1,679 boys who were delinquents, according to the records of the Juvenile Court of Chicago, and a corresponding nondelinquent group of the same general com-

---

[19] *Philadelphia Record,* May 18, 1932.

[20] Clifford Shaw, *Wickersham Report,* Vol. II, No. 13: *Causes of Crime,* 1931. See also Shaw's *Delinquency Areas,* Chicago, University of Chicago Press, 1929; and, in contrast with Shaw, Sophia Moses Robison, *Can Delinquency Be Measured?* New York, Columbia University Press, 1936.

position sustained this conclusion. The rate of broken homes among the delinquents was 42.5 and that among nondelinquents was 36.1. It must be borne in mind also that the delinquent child from the broken home is more likely to be brought into court than the delinquent from a normal home whose problem may be otherwise adjusted. Without considering this, however, the difference between the two rates is not sufficiently great to indicate that the broken home is a significant causative factor.

We must therefore look deeper than the *external* [italics by H. W. T.] breaking of the home for the causes of delinquency. Family relationships and all the intricate interplay of family life may be potential causes of juvenile delinquency, but rupture of the normal structure of the home is less important than are other psychological factors.[21]

Racial Factors

Chairman.—Many persons believe that most of our delinquency and crime results from immigration and is especially prevalent among the native-born children of the foreign-born. We have with us one who has critical opinions on this phase of our problem: Dr. Clairette P. Armstrong, Psychologist of the Children's Court in New York city. Dr. Armstrong, how important do you consider the racial factor in juvenile delinquency?

Dr. Armstrong.—Juvenile delinquency on the whole results from the clash of civilizations. Low-grade, intellectually dull immigrants thrust into our complicated, highly organized civilization are unable to adjust their likewise intellectually dull offspring to the exigencies of such environment. The stupid child of such immigrants becomes somewhat Americanized through the school environment and association with other children. Then he is a misfit in his foreign home. Influenced also by other harmful factors, such as school misgrading, broken homes, and extreme poverty, he often becomes delinquent. Of course, inferior, low-grade immigrants generally flock together in crowded districts, giving rise to delinquency areas, where delin-

[21] *Probation,* October, 1931.

quency is not in the air but in the quality of the inhabitants, foreign from all points of view and in the inferior environment and standards which they furnish themselves.

Dull immigrant parents of delinquents of similar mental stature are incapable of training their children to adjust even in a limited way to the codes of our social scheme.[22]

Chairman.—And now, for the first of some opinions that differ with Dr. Armstrong's, I ask Mr. Earl R. Moses, who, as Director of Research, Chicago Urban League, made a special study of delinquency in the Negro community, to give us the gist of his conclusions.

Mr. Moses.—The "Black Belt" in Chicago is not a homogeneous area of Negro juvenile delinquency; I find "areas of disorganization," "areas in transition," and "organized communities" with corresponding variations in percentages of from 10.2 to 0.8 of Negro juvenile delinquents. In short, patterns of delinquency among Negroes show a similarity to the patterns of delinquency in non-Negro areas.

Since Negro boys do not become delinquent immediately upon arrival, the facts indicate the influence of community patterns of behavior in the development of delinquent careers. Delinquency, then, is not a problem of race but is more intimately bound up with settlement in areas of deterioration where delinquent patterns of behavior prevail and where crime, prostitution, and vice are rampant. Out of this situation the Negro delinquent emerges.[23]

Chairman.—The situation in Harlem, New York city, as reported in newspapers in 1941, we know is not alone a racial problem but has important social, economic, and political aspects; it presents a challenge to the whole city and, in fact, to the whole country to combat such causal factors as poor housing, lack of recreation, poverty, and racial discrimination.

For a discussion of the prevalence of crime among various racial groups, we should study the two volumes on causes of crime published by the Wickersham Commission. Winthrop D. Lane, once Director of the Division of Parole, State Department of Institutions

[22] *New York Times,* April 22, 1934.
[23] *Opportunity Magazine,* October, 1933, p. 307.

and Agencies, Trenton, New Jersey, summarizes the most important conclusions of the reports on the racial factor in delinquency and crime.

Mr. Lane.—Probably the most forthright conclusion from the Commission's study of crime and the foreign-born is that reached by Alida C. Bowler, who was then Research Assistant at the University of Chicago and is now associated with the Federal Children's Bureau. In proportion to their respective numbers, says Miss Bowler, the foreign-born commit considerably fewer crimes than the native-born. This is bound to prove surprising to many people, though not to social workers in large cities. Miss Bowler adds the following conclusions: The foreign-born approach the record of the native white most closely in the commission of crimes involving personal violence; in crimes for gain (including robbery, in which there is also personal violence or the threat of violence) the native white greatly exceed the foreign-born; in the commission of certain types of offense there is considerable variation among the different nationalities within the foreign-born group, but the detailed data as yet available are insufficient to warrant final conclusions; also, there is insufficient information to warrant any deductions as to criminal activity among the native-born of foreign parentage. Miss Bowler concludes that there would be a great advantage in continuing the study of such subjects over a period of at least five years and on a national scale.

Dean Edith Abbott, of the Graduate School of Social Service Administration of the University of Chicago, directed this study of the foreign-born and contributes a critical and historical survey of public opinion on crime and the foreign-born from colonial to modern times. There are also three studies of the incidence of crime among Mexicans in this country, from which it appears that Mexicans in Illinois and Texas do not run foul of the law any oftener than anybody else, but that the record is not quite so favorable with respect to Mexicans in California.[24]

Chairman.—We have heard from Dr. Sheldon Glueck on the economic factor as a cause of delinquency and crime; I now call upon Dr. Eleanor Glueck, his wife and partner in research. Mrs. Glueck,

[24] *Annual Report of the National Conference of Social Work,* 1932, pp. 558–59.

will you now tell us what you and your husband have found out, not only about the importance of the racial factor in delinquency and crime, but also about other factors, especially that of the school, which you mentioned in your address before the Harvard Teachers' Association at Radcliffe College, "The Family, the School, and Crime"? I note that you recited statistics showing how crime is bred in the minds of youngsters in school; how a child's environment affects its future; and how the child's mind can be diverted to the more elevating things of life by careful training in the school.

Mrs. Glueck.—A retracing of the life careers of 500 adult male and 500 adult female offenders reveals that from two thirds to four fifths of them first manifested delinquent behavior in childhood.

An intensive study of 1,000 juvenile offenders shows that the average age at the onset of delinquent behavior is nine years and seven months, so that obviously the indicia of delinquency must have been evident during the school years.

Who are juvenile delinquents and their families, as reflected in the group of 1,000 boys? Over four fifths of them are native-born, but seven out of every ten are native-born sons of foreign-born parents, a far higher proportion than is found in the general population.

They are children of large families, there being five children per family (and these were probably incomplete families). Half of the mothers of these young delinquents were under twenty-one years of age at marriage, which reflects the extent to which they were unprepared for the responsibilities of parenthood. Half the parents had no schooling.

Now what of their school history? Might these boys have been recognized as the criminals of tomorrow? One fourth of them left school in the sixth grade and only seventeen percent entered high school. Only one fifth of the boys were in the normal grade for their age.

It does not surprise us, therefore, to find that seventy-five percent of these boys were school truants and that another ten percent presented behavior difficulties of other kinds in the classroom, so that in a total of eighty-five percent of cases indicia of antisocial behavior were evident in school.

These facts certainly place at the door of the school the responsibility for the early recognition of delinquency and at least participation in a treatment program.[25]

Delinquency Areas and Adult Example

Chairman.—Several of our speakers have referred not only to economic but to various other living and neighborhood conditions. I ask Dr. Thrasher, the writer of "Gangs," whom we all know, to give us his summary of community conditions, including the bad example of adults, as causal factors in juvenile delinquency.

Dr. Thrasher.—We know without question two striking facts about delinquency and crime. In the first place, careful scientific studies indicate that serious criminal careers begin in childhood and adolescence and that they develop naturally as the result of the forces in the vicious environment of young men and boys. The second striking fact is that delinquents and criminals develop in certain typical areas in our cities.

These areas are characteristized by physical deterioration, decreasing population, high rates of dependency, high percentages of foreign and Negro population, and high rates of adult crime. Studies in New York and Chicago which show that the delinquency areas are to be found in the zone immediately surrounding business or industrial areas, or occupy other sections adjacent to business or industrial areas, have been corroborated by findings in fifteen other American cities. The report on six of these cities has already been published by the National Commission on Law Observance and Enforcement.

The slum is more important as a sociological than as a physical fact. It is a state of mind. There is nothing in poverty and bad housing in themselves which predestines their victims to delinquency or crime. The reason these districts breed crime and develop criminals is that delinquent habits and attitudes are inculcated on the streets, in play groups and gangs, in poolrooms and other hangouts, and in other unsupervised contacts.

The streets and the hangouts grant no degrees and give no diplomas, but they educate with fatal precision. It is here that the boy first ac-

[25] *New York Times*, March 17, 1935.

quires demoralizing personal habits and a premature sophistication which often leads him to cynical attitudes later in life. It is here that he comes into direct contact with the hoodlum, the street-corner tramp, the semicriminal, and the underworld and learns the technique of crime. He learns the methods of bootlegging and beer-running, the tricks of the racketeer and the corrupt politician, how to go through doors without keys, how to purchase guns and how to use them, how to "beat the rap," how to break the seals on freight cars and distinguish between a grain car and a merchandise car, how to sell stolen goods to "fences," and innumerable other details of criminal practice. The whole technique of vice, crime, gambling, and racketeering is the common parlance of the district.

Furthermore, the boy in these areas acquires a philosophy of life which ideally fits him to participate in criminal activities—a philosophy of fatalism or "taking a chance." He acquires an attitude of independence and learns to stay away from home for long periods of time. He learns how to rely on himself rather than on others. He acquires disrespect for law and authority because he is in a position to see the law frequently flouted by corrupt politicians and "fixers." The machinery of society which is designed to correct the young delinquent has no terrors for him. Oftentimes it is necessary for him to be sent to a correctional institution before he may become a full member of his gang.

With these traditions of delinquency, it is not surprising that crime is bred and criminals are developed in areas of this type. The foreign-born rarely commit crime, and in so far as they have control of their children, their children grow up to be law-abiding citizens. It is the breakdown of family control and the fact that the boys live on the streets of the disorganized American community which result in the delinquency of the American-born child of the foreign-born.

In a very real sense it might be said that Americanization is one of the chief causes of crime, because the child in these areas comes into direct contact with all that is vicious and demoralizing in American life without having an adequate opportunity to participate in the finer cultural heritages which we consider most characteristic of America.

The fact that large numbers of boys are subjected to these influences in the slums of our towns and cities has been conclusively demonstrated by scientific study. It has been estimated that between 25,000 and 30,000 young men and boys in Chicago are subject directly or indirectly to the influence of delinquent gangs, and the number in New York is proportionately greater. This indicates the real source of the crime problem of this country. The delinquent youth of these areas constitute an increasing supply of criminals as well as a market for crime which is self-perpetuating and helps to create a demand for the criminal lawyer, the political fixer, the corrupt bail bondsman, and other obstructors of justice.[26]

Chairman.—I have the great honor now to call upon Jacob Riis to speak to us of the "Street Arab."

Mr. Riis.—Not all barriers erected by society against its nether life, not the labor of unnumbered societies for the rescue and relief of its outcast waifs, can dam the stream of homelessness that issues from a source where the very name of home is a mockery. The "Street Arab" is as much an institution in New York as Newspaper Row, to which he gravitates naturally, following his Bohemian instinct, crowded out of tenements to shift for himself, and quite ready to do it. He meets there the host of adventurous runaways from every state in the Union and from across the sea, whom New York attracts with a queer fascination, as it attracts the older emigrants from all over the world. A census of the population in the Newsboys' Lodging House (founded by Charles L. Brace) on any night will show such an odd mixture of small humanity as could hardly be gotten together in any other spot. It is a mistake to think that they are helpless creatures, to be pitied and cried over because they are alone in the world. The unmerciful "guying" the good man would receive who went to them with such a program would soon convince him that that sort of pity was wasted and would very likely give him the idea that they were a set of hardened little scoundrels, quite beyond the reach of missionary efforts.

But that would be his second mistake. The "Street Arab" has all

[26] Signed article by Dr. Frederic M. Thrasher, "Gangs, the Gangster—Why?" *New York Times Magazine*, March 17, 1935.

the faults and virtues of the homeless life he leads, vagabond that he is, acknowledging no allegiance to anybody or anything. With his grimy fist raised against society whenever it tries to coerce him, he is as bright and sharp as a weasel, which among all the predatory beasts he most resembles. His sturdy independence, love of freedom, and absolute self-reliance, together with his rude sense of justice that enables him to govern his little community, *not always in accordance with the municipal law or city ordinance* [italics by H. W. T.], but often a good deal closer to the saving line of "doing to others as one would be done by"—these are strong handles by which those who know how can catch the boy and make him useful.[27]

Inadequate Schools and Teachers

Chairman.—The school is an important part of the child's environment as it affects delinquency, and we hear many voices lifted in criticism of our schools. I ask one of these critics, Miss Esther Zwaifler, of Brooklyn, New York, to speak to us now.

Miss Zwaifler.—We have an oversupply of undereducated teachers—yes, undereducated in the social and political and international problems of today. Indeed, those words alone make many of them blush with fear—fear due to ignorance, to higher-ups, and to change.

Teachers here work five days a week and about 190 days a year, and have ten-day vacations at Easter and Christmas time, and ten weeks' vacation in the summer, and work insurance in the form of pensions; why haven't they been in the foreground fighting for these better working conditions for the rest of our country's workers?

Why don't teachers recognize the crime problem and contribute one afternoon a week to run school clubs, game rooms, athletics, etc.? Why should not a platoon system be adopted whereby teachers would serve one summer in five years in some social capacity in the schools? Why haven't teachers revised more drastically the course of study? Why keep on teaching, year after year, subject matter that is utterly useless to the child when he is out of school? The schools are not preparing our children to meet changing conditions in a continually

[27] Jacob Riis, *How the Other Half Lives,* New York, Scribner, 1890, p. 196.

changing world and are not creating attitudes of openmindedness, tolerance, and receptivity to change.

Crooked politicians, religious and racial bigots, delinquents, criminals, sex perverts, petty racketeers, exploiters of the poor and ignorant —these are all products of our public schools. And what do school people say to this problem? They lay the blame on the home, the parents, the community.

Granted that we are all partly to blame for these conditions, the schools are not meeting their responsibility, and a change in teachers' attitudes is the first requisite.[28]

Toy Pistols

Chairman.—Henry Edward Warner, of Baltimore, Maryland, is eager to be heard on the subject of toy pistols. Mr. Warner, what is on your mind about the use of toy pistols?

Mr. Warner.—My three-year-old grandson has just been given, by his father, a pistol and a belt full of toy cartridges. He was told to show it to his grandmother, which he did by drawing it and pointing it at her head, his baby feet set fiercely, all ready to kill if she didn't stick 'em up and deliver. Cute, you might call it!

All over the country, babies even younger are given toy pistols and cartridge belts. In the back yards, in the vacant lots, and on the streets, boys older than babies are strolling with their toy implements of banditry and murder, training themselves in bandit games to be quick on the draw. I have seen them dodging in and out among parked cars, behind telegraph poles and trees, some of them so expert that I believe with a real weapon they could kill a cop before he could draw, just the way the machine gunners slaughtered seven officers in Kansas City, who didn't have a chance to fire a single shot in self-defense.

Our present-day bandits, many of them, never knew a thing about killing until they were taught in France or learned from returning machine gunners of the A.E.F. We taught our present-day bandits how to kill. Our toymakers are teaching the babies of today in every

[28] *New York World Telegram,* April 14, 1934.

city, in every village, and at every crossroads how to strut with a gun, draw it quickly, aim surely.

Not less than a couple of million boys are playing bandit with toy weapons today. How many of them may possibly graduate into active crime within the next decade? It would be interesting to find out how many boys have killed parents, guardians, relatives, in the past few years; how many boys and girls have committed suicide; how much of this is due to careless familiarity permitted with weapons of murder and self-destruction.[29]

Chairman.—We shall be told later that the extent to which the carrying of toy pistols by youth is an incentive to crime and also to what extent it is an immunization against later temptation to engage in actual holdups depend upon many other factors in the personality make-up and environmental influences of different young people.

Movies and a Sensational Press

Two other influences that many people think are productive of almost a wholesale tendency to delinquency and crime are movies and a sensational press. I now call upon Eugene T. Lies, head of the National Recreation Association, who has observed and worked with youth in all parts of the country for at least twenty-five years, to begin our discussion of the influence of the press and the movies.

Mr. Lies.—Our people must be told how to spend their leisure time properly. The clinics, hospitals, courts, penal institutions, and reformatories of the country are crowded because we do not use correctly the time which is our own.

For everything except leisure, Americans depend upon school training; what we need is a school system which will give degrees in leisure craft.

This training is needed to offset the influence of money-grabbing purveyors of low-down leisure-time recreation. These people have flooded our newsstands, movie houses, and theaters with putrid matter which is taken up in our play time. We must prevent the success of these people who want to make play time whoopee time.[30]

[29] *New York Times,* November 5, 1933.
[30] *Philadelphia Record,* May 18, 1932.

Chairman.—Dr. Bernard Sachs discussed the influence of moving pictures on crime in 1934.

Dr. Sachs.—By showing in dramatic, succinct form the details of how crimes are committed, the gangster type of film actually teaches the young child how to go about community acts of violence.

The dramatic action of the film impresses the young mind many times more forcibly than would the same information printed in books or even shown in drawings or still photographs. A picture-minded public is an action-minded public, and will remember action when other images have completely faded from memory.[31]

Chairman.—Upon the occasion of the Twenty-fifth Anniversary Conference of the National Board of Review of Motion Pictures in 1934, a book by Henry James Forman, *Our Movie Made Children,* written after research by the Motion Picture Research Council, was quoted as holding moving pictures responsible for much juvenile crime. At the same meeting Dr. George H. Kirchwey, as Chairman of the National Board of Review, took exception to the opinion of the book and was supported therein by Dr. A. A. Brill, psychologist. We will hear the substance of the opinion of Dr. Kirchwey and Dr. Brill.

Dr. Kirchwey.—I take the position that moving pictures do not stimulate boys to run away from home. They merely satisfy the craving. When a boy actually takes to the road it is his home, and not the picture he has seen, that warrants close inspection. Dr. Brill says that pictures are an outlet for suppressed desire. The only way in which human beings get around the instinct to do something illicit is by reading or seeing something; the average citizen must have escape.[32]

Chairman.—A noted educator, Professor William H. Kilpatrick, in a conference at the Horace Mann School in New York, objected to the profit motive in the production of motion pictures. We shall hear the gist of his opinion.

Professor Kilpatrick.—So long as they are run privately, for the sake of private gain, so long they will continue to hurt and debase

[31] *New York Times,* May 6, 1934.
[32] *New York World Telegram,* February 10, 1934.

individuals. Until they are run coöperatively by and for society, any attempt to improve their standards will be at best palliative.

We cannot educate young people with any success so long as there are educative agencies controlled by warring interests fighting for profits.[33]

Chairman.—An opinion, with illustration, will now be given by Ernest K. Coulter who, as head of the New York Society for the Prevention of Cruelty to Children, was in daily contact with neglected and delinquent children in New York city for more than twenty years.

Mr. Coulter.—Many serious offenses committed by children, particularly by boys under sixteen, are inspired by the films shown in commercial motion pictures, with gunplay, holdups, and racketeering especially played up in a way to appeal to the youthful imagination. Boys of tender age have come into the custody of the society for holdups and have freely admitted that their ideas came fresh from the movies. For example, three boys went home from a movie, stole a father's pistol, and held up and shot a delicatessen dealer.

A close inspection of 102 moving-picture theaters during the summer vacation showed 41 with pictures of murder by shooting or stabbing, 33 with pictures of racketeering, gang terror, and gambling, 52 with "palpably sex" pictures, and only 16 with comedies suitable for children.[34]

Chairman.—For a more thorough study of the urgent problem of the influence of moving pictures upon youth I especially recommend two books in the Payne Fund series of studies of the influence of motion pictures upon the public.[35] From the first of these two books I took these items of testimony:

10% of the 368 male criminals believed motion pictures to have some effect upon their careers [p. 35].

49% of 110 inmates of a penal institution indicated that the motion pictures give one a desire to carry a gun [p. 36].

28% think the movies give a desire to practice stick-ups [p. 36].

[33] *Ibid.*, April 30, 1934.
[34] *New York Times*, January 11, 1933.
[35] Blumer and Hauser, *Movies, Delinquency, and Crime*, New York, Macmillan, 1933; W. W. Charters, *Motion Pictures and Youth*, New York, Macmillan, 1933.

20% thought that the movies taught them ways of stealing [p. 36].

21% ways to fool the police [p. 36].

12% that they were moved to plan a hold-up or to pull a job [p. 36].

Not all of the above yielded to the suggestions [pp. 36, 37].

The indirect influence is perhaps greater than the direct [p. 72].

What presents itself as a conscious connection to some, may exist as an unconscious connection in the experience of others [p. 72].

25% of 252 delinquent girls, mainly from 14–16 years, stated they had engaged in sexual relations with men following the arousing of sex impulses by a passionate love picture [p. 111].

41% to wild parties [p. 111].

38% to live a wild gay fast life [p. 111].

33% to run away from home [p. 111].

23% were led into sexual delinquencies [p. 111].

In recent years motion pictures seem to have become an important agency in transmitting patterns of thought and behavior, yet peculiarly the influence that they exert in this respect seems to be in inverse proportion to the strength of family and neighborhood, school, and church. Where these traditional institutions are highly organized, motion pictures are seemingly of lesser influence though nevertheless a factor in forming social attitudes and transmitting schemes of life [p. 161].

The child in the high-rate delinquency area tends to be *sensitized* and the child in the low-rate delinquency area *immunized* to delinquent and criminal attitudes and forms of behavior depicted on the screen [p. 202].

In the second of the series of books I have just mentioned, Mr. Charters writes a summary. I again urge the careful reading of these studies of motion pictures by writers in different states from Iowa to Connecticut.

This brief statement of the testimony of twenty superintendents of reformatories for girls was given at a conference in New York city, February, 1932: "Sensational magazines and newspapers, as well as movies, are influencing wrongly the minds of many young girls." [36] Just how large a part sensational publications and motion pictures are playing in juvenile delinquency none of the superintendents was willing to guess, but the consensus among the twenty women in charge of reformatories was that such influences present a major problem.

William Lewis Butcher passed on after a lifetime of work with

[36] *New York Times,* February 11, 1932.

boys on the Lower East Side in New York city. Like his predecessor Jacob Riis, Mr. Butcher knew from personal observation and experience "how the other half lives." He made the following statements in November, 1928, to the delegates at the New York State Conference of Social Work in Rochester, on "Spare Time and Community Causes of Crime."

Mr. Butcher.—The fact that leisure or spare time is the danger period in the life of boys and girls is no longer debatable. Anywhere from 70 to 80 percent of all juvenile delinquency takes place in spare time after school hours. The play life of the child of this and other congested urban areas is not spent in parks and playgrounds which have modern athletic equipment or trained leadership. However, the urchins here, without guidance, find an outlet for their surplus energy by using whatever is at hand.

Probably the chief difference between the child of the streets and the more sheltered, more supervised children of the better classes is the maneuvering to gain their pleasures. The word maneuver is used with particular intent.

The rich child is concerned with wheedling mother or dad into producing nickel or dime, a pair of skates, sled, suit with long trousers, a trip to an expensive summer camp, or a long automobile trip. The poor child has to figure out means of getting his pleasures directly or by appropriation. A wooden stick pointed at one end is a sword, a tin can is his target, stones are weapons, and the gutter is a rifle range. A ten-cent rubber ball is a football, the street is the gridiron, and manholes are goal lines. Frequently he tires of make-believe and wants something that works. An old soapbox on roller skates will satisfy him, but the problem is to find or steal a box, to sneak out the hammer and saw unnoticed, to buy nails, to barter other objects of work for the roller skates, and to do a good job mechanically. Therefore, he is versed early in life in working hard for his pleasures and in utilizing his ingenuity in his ceaseless search for materials with which to replenish his stock of playthings, but frequently he succumbs to temptation.

He discovers that money, if properly applied, provides a delightful short cut to pleasure and he turns his attention to getting money.

He sells things, he steals things, he sells stolen things, and he proudly sticks a grimy paw through the bars of the movie ticket booth.[37]

Chairman.—Mr. Butcher, as chairman of the Commission on Causes, a subcommission of the Crime Commission of New York State, issued a report on crime and the community. The following are notes on and excerpts from studies of four separate groups of delinquent or criminal individuals, as these studies are given in the *Report*.[38]

—The first study was of 145 males in prisons and reformatories. These males were all under thirty years of age and had been received by all but two of the state prisons and reformatories in New York state, during August and September, 1926. From this study the following abbreviated selections have been made:

There is no unit cause for crime. In every case studied there were many causative factors, such as bad or broken homes, poor neighborhoods, difficulties in school, drunkenness, feeble-mindedness, poverty, mental abnormalities, low moral standards, and other factors that might result in anti-social conduct [italics by H. W. T.].

The majority of these men committed to state prisons and to the state reformatory began their delinquent careers as children. They presented behavior problems in school and later became truant.

Community or neighborhood organizations such as settlements, community centers, spare time organizations for boys, clubs, and supervised recreations did not, except possibly in five instances, touch the lives of these offenders; but commercial amusements, prize fights, gambling, cheap musical and vaudeville shows, social clubs and night clubs, and cheap dances were the favorite recreational activities of the men studied.

Obtaining a gun to use in unlawful acts was apparently an easy matter, and in no instance in the cases studied was the person selling the gun discovered or prosecuted.

The second study was of 201 units in the New York city schools.

This preliminary study disclosed that truants disliked academic school subjects and liked shop subjects; were failures in academic subjects and successes in shop subjects; came from broken homes in 45 percent of the

---

[37] *Report of the New York State Conference of Social Work,* 1928, p. 212.
[38] *Crime and the Community: a Study of Trends in Crime Prevention,* by the Subcommittee on Causes and Effects of Crime (Harry M. Shulman, Director of Research), New York State Crime Commission, 1930, pp. 20–26, *passim.*

cases, a percentage higher than exists among delinquent boys known to the New York City children's courts; lived in poverty; were retarded at least several terms in school, and spent their hours while away from school on the streets and in moving picture theatres.

The third study was based on the careers of 251 truant boys from Manhattan, all of whom had been committed to the truant school. Among the findings were that 51 percent of the boys required the attention of police and courts during the period after release from truant school up to the time of the survey.

The survey covers their histories from the time of release from truant school to the date of survey, a period of six years to eight years, and reviews their remote childhoods.

Statistical study of 34 environmental and behavior factors in these cases indicated that only a limited number of these factors served to differentiate the truants who became adult offenders from those who, as a group, did not.

It is true that the conditions under which they lived were similar to those to which the underprivileged group in any community are subjected and that poverty and crime are associated in a general way. But in the group forming this study, as well as among the underprivileged group in general, the majority of the factors here studied threw no light on the reasons *why certain families fostered criminal behavior and others did not, nor why one child reared in the same family under the self-same general conditions became a criminal and his brothers did not* [italics by H. W. T.].

The fourth study was on problem boys and their brothers. Four years was the maximum difference in the age of brothers; the average difference was two years and five months.

The I.Q. of problem boys was on the average .75; of their brothers, .86. Problem boys were, on the average, inferior to their brothers in grasp of school subjects, their educational quotient being 81, compared with 92½ for nonproblem brothers.

The school retardation of problem boys was two and one-half times that of nonproblem brothers.

Problem boys were superior to nonproblem brothers in mechanical ability, and 60 percent of problem boys were superior to unselected New York schoolchildren.

In planfulness ability, both groups were below the average: problem, 83; others, 81½.

Delinquent behavior, involving property offenses, was in all instances associated with incorrigible behavior of other sorts. The young thief was socially ill in a variety of ways. Stealing was merely a symptom of graver and deeper social maladjustment.

As to the meaning of these four studies, we are told that:

The sociologist, in particular the criminologist, had to acknowledge that the findings relative to the influence of poverty, dependency, alcoholism, improper parental guardianship, and neglect, while illuminating in these descriptions of the portion of the population among whom crimes of violence and theft largely arise, do not explain the still more baffling problem of social and antisocial behavior, both within the same unfavorable setting—the phenomenon of law-abiding and law-defying families living side by side in the same slums, even in the same tenements, and the phenomenon of law-abiding and law-defying persons within the same family.

The present study shows that environment is selective. Members of the same family circle live in different environments as their varying intelligence, emotional stability, and other traits cause their acceptance by one social group and their rejection by others. The findings suggest the inadequacy of programs aimed at the presentation of a uniform environment with the hope of attaining uniform behavior.

Chairman.—The next voice that you will hear is that of Judge Frederick P. Cabot, who, as Judge of the Juvenile Court in Boston, formed a firsthand opinion of the basic causes of juvenile delinquency. Judge Cabot also served as chairman of the Committee on Delinquency for the Third White House Conference in 1930. Judge Cabot, will you now give us the gist of your opinion on the causes of juvenile delinquency?

Judge Cabot.—The committee recognizes delinquent conduct as one of the natural outcomes of those clashes of interest, prerogative, and need that are inherent in living as a social group. Finding fault, laying the blame, that most paralyzing and childish of all our human interests, has in the past invaded the philosophy of delinquency. The point in hand is not so much that delinquency is inevitable as that we appreciate the naturalness and ubiquity of those processes that lead up to it. This is fundamentally a matter of recognizing that the stresses which bend the delinquent are of precisely the same character as those that bend our own lives. The needs which have been pictured are those which exist in the lives of all of us.[39]

As a foundation for a satisfying life, every child needs to be wanted, loved, and understood. He needs to feel that he is accepted and belongs because of his own individual place and values in relation to the rest of the group.[40]

Juvenile Delinquents as Seen by the First Judge and the First Chief Probation Officer in Chicago in 1900

Chairman.—To compare with these relatively recent statements as to the complexity of causal factors in juvenile delinquency and as to the essential similarities between delinquent children and those who have not been so named, I would like the members of our forum to listen now to the opinions stated in 1900 by Richard S. Tuthill, the first judge, and Timothy D. Hurley, the first male probation officer, of the Chicago Juvenile Court. Judge Tuthill, will you now tell us what, after you had heard the cases of 1,939 delinquent boys and 111 delinquent girls, you said to the Illinois Conference of Charities in November, 1900?

Judge Tuthill.—My observation of delinquent children has convinced me that the percentage of these who are in any respect abnormal in their moral nature is not much larger than among children of well-to-do and honest parents. Their faults are not due to hereditary taint but to bad environment. A bad home, a bad father, more surely a bad mother, and want of parental care would make delinquents of any of us. Character is of slow growth. Like the body, it is built up imperceptibly. To the formation of a good character in any child kindly monition, wholesome example, constant watchfulness, and an infinite patience are absolute essentials.[41]

Chairman.—Mr. Hurley, will you tell us what you said at this same Illinois Conference of Charities?

Mr. Hurley.—The children coming before the Juvenile Court are

[39] *The Delinquent Child,* New York, Century, 1932, p. 51.
[40] *Ibid.,* p. 25.   [41] *Juvenile Court Record,* Chicago, December, 1900.

not what might be called deficient or demoralized; and they are not always children of the poorer classes. The facts are that they are the ordinary everyday children, boys and girls that you and I have met all our lives; and all we have to do is to look around us in our own homes or in the homes of our neighbors and we will find subjects whose counterparts have been at one time or another in the Juvenile Court.[42]

Causes of Delinquency as Seen by Workers in Two New York Reformatories of Today

Chairman.—In a personal effort to get opinions as to the conscious imitation of bad adult example [43] by boys now in some of our reformatories and also to get opinions as to other causes of juvenile delinquency, I recently wrote to several men now working with boys in reformatories, asking for such opinions. One of the men who gave me an answer bearing on both of these points was Dr. R. R. Williams, Psychiatrist at the Children's Village, Dobbs Ferry, New York.

Dr. Williams.—It is to be presumed that there are so many factors operating in the development of delinquent acts that a child or an adolescent could not definitely tie up a bad pattern and a delinquent act in a direct cause-and-effect relationship. There are always so many factors involved in conduct that one cannot say that *this* causative factor brought about *this* behavior. The ground must be prepared. The attitude of mind must be acquired through many preliminary procedures. There must be a certain absence of positive constructive training in order that a child may get into an attitude of mind whereby he will surrender to the temptation of a bad pattern by an adult or another child.

On the other hand, we know the potency of imitation. Probably one may be pretty well assured that if there were no bad patterns, or if there were so few bad patterns that children might not hear of them, or if bad patterns were not being frequently repeated, children would not develop an immunity of reaction to the good patterns. Probably sixty or seventy percent who become delinquent attempt to ration-

---

[42] *Ibid.*
[43] Again I refer members of our forum to Appendix B.

alize and self-excuse their delinquency upon the basis of "bad boys taught me to do these things." In a great many of these cases the parents put the words in their children's mouths. You know how one attempts to and does comfort one's conscience through the mechanism of self-justification. Other boys steal, and not infrequently children do point out that adults steal.

Chairman.—The second reply to my inquiry came from Mr. M. Winsor of the New York Training School for Boys, Warwick, New York.

Mr. Winsor.—A number of boys have told us that everybody, namely, the storekeepers in their neighborhood, big businessmen too, like bank presidents, policemen, probation officers, judges, lawyers, "all are in it for what they can get one way or another." Others have particularized and have stated that the people in their sections who are thought of as amounting to anything are those who have flashy clothes, have enough money for anything they want, ride around in cars, and get their money in an easy way. There are a few boys who indicate that their mothers or fathers, or both, knew that the boys were stealing and did not hesitate to accept money or stolen articles from the boys. There are more boys who were involved with adults in the offenses which brought them to the court. There are some who claim that adults in their community organized boys for stealing and provided the means for converting the stolen goods into cash. Although the above reasons, and others, are given for their delinquencies by youth, in the matter of etiology it seems to us that it has been accepted that we must look for complexity and an intertwining of factors, many of them not on a conscious level and most of them unknown to the offenders themselves.

An Opinion about Causes as Seen by the Children's Bureau in 1932

Chairman.—The United States Children's Bureau in "Facts about Juvenile Delinquency, Its Prevention and Treatment" gives the following statement about causes.

Children's Bureau.—There is no single cause for juvenile delinquency. The foundations of delinquent behavior are usually laid in very early childhood, the period which students of child life regard as the most significant in the development of personality and character. Many factors may contribute to produce delinquency but the central problem in any case is, after all, the delinquent himself. Why do children react in such different ways to the features of their environment? Why are some able to resist the influences of bad companions and the temptations provided by unlocked automobiles, easily entered windows, alluring display of finery, suggestions from newspapers and movies, or unhappiness or poverty at home, and countless other factors which contribute to make other children delinquent? Why are other children unaffected by the temptations to right doing which should serve to immunize them against possible stimuli to bad conduct? Clearly, it is only through scientific study of the delinquent himself that we can ever learn how to check delinquent trends as they may become known, or how delinquency in general is to be prevented.[44]

An Outline of Changes in Opinion as to Causes

Chairman.—From the many voices that we have already heard it is clear that there have been many different opinions as to the causes of juvenile delinquency, ranging from simple to complex. In order that we may have a connected outline of these changes in opinion, I call upon Dr. James S. Plant, Psychiatrist of the Essex County, New Jersey, Juvenile Clinic, who helped Judge Cabot prepare the 1930 White House Conference report on juvenile delinquency from which you have already heard Judge Cabot quote. Dr. Plant, how, during recent years, have our opinions about the causes of juvenile delinquency changed?

Dr. Plant.—First, the act itself was considered; then the act was integrated into the person (statistical studies of I.Q.'s and of types of delinquent); then the person was integrated into his whole life history (the psychiatrist and his guidance clinics); then the whole life history was integrated into the environment (the step that is just now, here and there, being taken).

Each of these efforts to study behavior problems began with the assumption of a philosophy as to life and then sought supporting data

[44] Children's Bureau, *Publication No. 215,* 1932, pp. 7–8.

for it. The resulting chaos has been in the clash of the basic assumptions rather than of data, yet a few principles have now gained rather general acceptance:

1. Delinquency is a way of living—an expected result of the ways chosen of adjusting oneself to the problems of life.

2. There is no single cause for delinquency, but rather as many and as varied causes as for successes.

3. Concepts of blame and punishment have been exchanged for psychological and sociological principles by means of which this way of living which the delinquent chooses may be understood.

In searching for the assumed causes of delinquency, attention was first directed to the possibility of there being criminal types. Lombroso's work was soon discredited as grotesque, because his school (living in the era of overt acts), naturally sought for typical characteristics in the physiognomy and in other superficialities.

Another group, about 1900, began searching for the criminal type in the degree of intelligence present. The earlier careful anthropometric studies were replaced by equally meticulous psychometric studies.

Admittedly, school progress depends largely upon what is customarily tested for as intelligence so that a high correlation is found between low intelligence and school problem-predelinquencies. Nevertheless, belief that intelligence tests will disclose a criminal type has now largely disappeared. Low intelligence, it is true, is disproportionately represented in what are known to be delinquent groups, but it must be remembered, first, that those apprehended in delinquency— the class usually studied—represent a selected group, and, second, that many devious social factors may operate to congregate those of low intelligence in areas that naturally tend to breed behavior problems.

The psychiatric group in general considers behavior problems as one of the natural outgrowths of the development of personality. Delinquency then becomes a way that anyone might live, instead of a way that a certain one must live. Criticized because of its frank inability to make objective measurement, this group's greatest contributions have been its emphasis upon the study of personality as a flowing continuous affair and its emphasis upon the importance of attitudes. The facts of handicap or privilege are seen as of slight importance in comparison with the individual's attitude about them.[45]

Chairman.—For testimony on the delinquent as an individual, I take pleasure in calling upon Dr. William Healy, of the Judge Baker Foundation in Boston, who began his special studies of juvenile delinquency in the Chicago Juvenile Court in 1909. He has kept at the job ever since, of late years with the assistance of Dr. Augusta F. Bronner.

Dr. Healy.—We have learned a great deal in the last twenty years of working with delinquents and studying them individually. We have a great deal more to learn. We know now, however, that delinquency very frequently is the beginning of a criminal career and crime is the continuance on into manhood of conduct tendencies which started in childhood or early youth.

We know also more of the tremendous differences in individuals who are delinquent; some we find victims of brain disease and brain injury, some are feeble-minded, some are pathological personalities, but the majority are normal young persons who are unfortunately influenced by their experiences and environmental conditions.

We know that the causation of delinquency is usually a thoroughly complex affair involving many elements and that logically it is very unfair to pick out any one quality in the make-up of the individual or in his circumstances and say that it is the sole cause of delinquency.[46]

New Light on Delinquency

Chairman.—Dr. Healy, I understand that, since you wrote the opinion you have just given, you and Dr. Bronner have made a study of the causes of delinquency in a group of 105 delinquents in comparison with an equal number of nondelinquent brothers and sisters, both of which groups you studied intensively for a period of three

---

[45] Dr. James S. Plant, "The Search for Causes," *Social Work Year Book,* New York, Russell Sage Foundation, 1933, pp. 35–40.

[46] *Year Book of the National Probation Association,* 1930, p. 31.

years. Will you give us a few rays from your *New Light on Delinquency?* We shall all try to gain illumination from this light for many days to come.

Dr. Healy.—The very essence of this reserve lies in the fact that no theoretical paths have been pursued either to causations or treatment. With the opportunity for deeper studies of factual material than have been hitherto possible the main aim always was to discover the forces creating delinquent trends which were actively at play within the individual or between him and his intimate environment. We naturally asked ourselves many questions.

But no line of inquiry concerning causations seemed likely to be more fruitful than the key questions: Why has a comparable sibling in the same family not been delinquent? Through comparison does the delinquent appear to be a deviate, or is he the more normal individual? Has he had different conditioning experiences? Has he in any way stood in a special relationship to his parents? Has he been in contrasting situations outside the family life? Has he had a different health history?

The challenge of these common-sense questions which can be answered only by a thoroughgoing scientific inquiry led to the attempt to make comparative studies of as many nondelinquents as possible. A sibling of the same sex, if available, and as near the same age as could be obtained was selected for study. We were finally able to accumulate adequate data for 105 pairs of twins (the compared nondelinquents we designate "controls"). The interpretation of data concerning these pairs of cases forms, as naturally would be expected, one of the most significant portions of the research.[47]

Chairman.—This study by Drs. Healy and Bronner was carried on for three years in full coöperation with the juvenile courts of New Haven, Boston, and Detroit. For an adequate understanding of its methods and results, all of us should read and study the whole report in detail, but I ask Dr. Healy to give our forum two further quotations

[47] Healy and Bronner, *New Light on Delinquency and Its Treatment,* New Haven, Yale University Press, 1936, pp. 22–24. This book presents the results of a research conducted for the Institute of Human Relations, Yale University, by William Healy, M.D., and Augusta F. Bronner, Ph.D. For a later statement, with a bibliography, see the article by Healy and Bronner in the *Social Work Year Book,* 1939, pp. 37–43.

from the report, emphasizing again the fact that no single cause for all delinquencies is possible. And I urge each one to ponder these two statements from his final chapter, "Practical Implications of This Report," and answer for himself this question: How can I make practical use of these implications as aids to my understanding of the causes of delinquency in each delinquent youth whom I personally know?

Dr. Healy.—First, it became evident from our data that there is practical value in a more penetrating interpretation of delinquency as a form of rational behavior just as dependent on definite causations as is any other form of behavior. In human beings there are urges, desires, and drives seeking satisfaction through various modes of self-expression, and delinquency is one mode of self-expression. But, we may ask, why and when is delinquency utilized as a means of gaining satisfaction? From our present study there is clear evidence that in the lives of delinquents the ever-flowing stream of urges and wishes, which in general follows the broader channels of socially acceptable behavior, has met obstructions or frustrations that cause part of the stream to be deflected into currents that sooner or later show the characteristics which we term delinquency. We are convinced that it is possible to discover in nearly every case the nature of these obstructions.[48]

Chairman.—Dr. Healy's next paragraph shows in substance that frustrations and obstructions, even for twins in the same neighborhood and the same home, may differ.

Dr. Healy.—It is through the lack of satisfying human relationship that feelings of inadequacy, deprivation, or thwarting are created. When these discomforts are powerfully experienced, the driving forces of wishes and desires naturally develop into urges for substitute satisfactions, and when the young individual does not then find satisfactions enough in socially acceptable behavior (or does not develop an inhibiting neurosis), he may find an alternative mode of self-expression through seizing upon the idea of delinquency. Thus delinquency really represents a portion of human activities which has a strong current behind it. Beginning with various types of dis-

[48] Healy and Bronner, *New Light on Delinquency and Its Treatment*, pp. 200–201.

contents at frustrations and continued as a drive for substitute satisfactions, the current has turbulently flowed along into the forms of self-expression that ideas of delinquency have suggested.[49]

Chairman.—Dr. Healy's words describing delinquency as a form of self-expression remind me of an article describing a gang of seven boys from seven to eleven years old who called themselves "the Robbers." [50] They met in an abandoned boathouse to plan burglaries in houses bearing signs "For Sale" or "For Rent." The leader had a big bunch of assorted keys and, when caught with a stolen article and asked by the police chief, "Why did you do it?" replied "We wanted something to do." This answer by a juvenile delinquent is a timely illustration of the need of youth for self-expression as one of the causal factors in delinquency. But, even so, we should clearly see that the problem of understanding the behavior of each delinquent youth is complex and unique. These individual characteristics of each delinquent youth are again emphasized by the judge of the juvenile court in Portland, Oregon.

Judge Long.—We cannot ever lose sight of the fact that the boys and girls with whom the court deals are not, merely because they have been reported as delinquents, any the less endowed with the individual traits and characteristics that differentiate human beings from each other. Their delinquency may be a "common denominator" so far as their having run afoul of the law, or having violated accepted standards of behavior, is concerned, but apart from that, each is as utterly different from the others as the rest of us are unlike our fellows. Individuals we were born, individuals we grew, and individuals we remain in spite of all attempts at classification.[51]

Chairman.—In short, the gist of the wisest testimony, to which we have listened during this forum discussion, is that each delinquent youth is "a total personality in a total situation." Therefore, only to the degree that we understand the *total personality in the total situation* of each delinquent youth can we hope intelligently to help him to give up his delinquent behavior and to begin to satisfy his need for

---

[49] *Ibid.,* p. 201.   [50] *New York Times,* January 10, 1939.

[51] Donald E. Long, Judge of the Court of Domestic Relations (the juvenile court), Multnomah County, Portland, Oregon, "Understanding Delinquency," *1940 Report,* p. 5.

self-expression in some legal way that will not be harmful to others.

The poet Browning offers inspiration to place an understanding friend beside every child who stands bewildered at his first "cross-road."

GUIDO'S DEFENSE

Oh, how I wish some cold wise man
Would dig beneath the surface which you scrape,
Deal with the depths, pronounce on my desert
Groundedly! I want simple sober sense,
That asks before it finishes with a dog,
Who taught the dog the trick you hung him for?
You both persist to call that act a crime,
Which sense would call—yes, I do assure you, Sirs,
A blunder! At the worst, I stood in doubt
On cross-road, took one path of many paths;
It leads to the red thing, we all see now,
But nobody saw at first; One primrose
In bank, one singing bird in bush, the less,
Had warned me from such wayfare, let me prove!
Put me back to the cross-road, start afresh!
Advise me when I take the first false step! [52]

Our task is not merely to help to find his way back to the right road each one of those who once took the wrong road at his crossroad. Our task also is to recognize each one who is for the first time approaching his crossroad, to understand him, and to help him to see and choose the right road and *to find satisfaction in walking therein.*

[52] Robert Browning, "Guido's Defense," in *The Ring and the Book*. See Appendix B for poems by amateurs.

Part Two: TREATMENT BY COURTS

Chapter III: TREATMENT
BEFORE 1840

IN CHAPTER I were given illustrations showing that some of our boys and girls—minor citizens—do many things which we adult citizens do not like, which we label crime or delinquency, and which range all the way from mischief to murder.

In Chapter II were presented opinions as to the cause, or causes, of juvenile delinquency of at least these varieties: physical defect, mental defect, emotional defect, and community defect. In short, champions have in turn emphasized as causal factors in delinquency the biological factor, the psychological factor, the psychiatric factor, the sociological factor, and an indefinite number of combinations and interactions among these factors.

Before I begin my discussion of the treatment of juvenile delinquency, I wish to remind the reader of the mention made at the beginning of Chapter I concerning punishment of juvenile delinquents by transportation, imprisonment, and death. To show the legal basis for such punishment, I quote this passage from the classical legal authority, Blackstone, relating to the punishment in England of youth of different ages for felonies:

By the law as it now stands, and has stood at least ever since the time of Edward the third, the capacity of doing ill, or contracting guilt, is not so much measured by years and days, as by the strength of the delinquent's understanding and judgment. For one lad of eleven years may have as much cunning as another of fourteen; and in these cases our maxim is, that "malitia supplet aetatum." Under seven years of age indeed an infant cannot be guilty of felony; for then a felonious discretion is almost an impossibility in nature; but at eight years old he may be guilty of felony. Also, under fourteen, though an infant shall be *prima facie* adjudged to be *doli incapax;* yet if it appear to the court and jury, that he was *doli capax,* and could discern between good and evil, he may be convicted and suffer death. Thus a girl of thirteen has been burnt for killing her mistress; and one boy of ten, and another of nine years old, who had killed their companions, have been sentenced to death, and he of ten actually hanged; because it appeared upon their trials, that the one had hid himself, and the other had hid the body he had killed, which hiding manifested a consciousness of guilt, and a discretion to discern between good and evil. And there was an instance in the last century, where a boy of eight years old was tried at Abington for firing two barns; and it appearing that he had malice, revenge and cunning, he was found guilty, condemned, and hanged accordingly.[1]

That death did not seem to everybody quite an appropriate penalty for a twelve-year-old boy even in England one hundred years ago, the following citation from a United States Children's Bureau publication gives testimony:

Somewhere in the neighborhood of 100 years ago, a 12-year-old boy was sentenced to death in London. Inexorable justice, as conceived in that day, took account of the law and the crime and ignored the age and circumstance of the offender. The sentiment of human pity was not wanting, however, and the reporter indulged in verse to describe the heart-rending scene—

> When he was sentenced at the bar,
> The court was drowned in tears,
> To see a child so soon cut off
> All in his tender years.[2]

Turning to the United States for comparison with England, I cite first, from a recent authoritative report, this general statement as to death penalties:

Until about a century ago there was very little distinction in the treatment accorded offenders against the rigorous criminal laws, whether these were children of tender years, youths, or adults. Mere children have been hanged for a variety of offenses. Under the general laws adopted by the Plymouth Colony, death was the penalty for *sixteen different offenses,*

---

[1] Grace Abbott, *The Child and the State,* Chicago, University of Chicago Press, 1938, II, 342. This is a book of great reference value. Part II of Volume II, "The State and the Child Offender," has 169 pages. After an introduction by Grace Abbott, it gives thirty-three original documents under these general headings: (a) Early Treatment of Child Offenders in the United States, (b) Massachusetts Provides a New System, (c) Early Institutions and Their Problems, (d) The Juvenile Court Movement; Juvenile Offenders against Federal Laws, (e) Existing Legal Status and Treatment in Great Britain.

[2] *Facts about Juvenile Delinquency,* Publication No. 215, U.S. Children's Bureau, 1932, p. 10.

some of them pertaining particularly to children. A child convicted of assaulting or cursing his parents or of persistent disobedience or stubbornness was to be hanged. . . . [Footnote] This provision was included in the criminal code of the Province of East Jersey adopted in 1688.[3]

The following specific illustrations of the treatment of juvenile delinquents by courts during the nineteenth century I cite from three cities, Chicago, New York, and Boston.

My first citation I copied while I was in the Chicago Juvenile Court, 1905–8, from a report made by a superintendent of a farm institution for delinquent boys in Wisconsin, which illustrated the language used just before 1900 by a Chicago criminal court in committing a boy to him for stealing. The superintendent said that the boy's commitment paper stated that he had "Burglariously, feloniously, and maliciously broken into his step-mother's pantry and stolen a jar of jam." Although the penalty in this Chicago case was not death or transportation for the boy, the reader cannot fail to note the similarity of judicial attitude toward juvenile stealing, and of language describing the offense, with the earlier attitudes and language of English courts in such offenses.

The following references to offenses by juvenile delinquents and of their treatment in New York city during the early nineteenth century I have taken from an unpublished thesis written by Miss Katherine Z. Wells in 1917 while she was a student in the New York School of Social Work. The descriptions given by Miss Wells were taken by her from issues of the New York *Evening Post*, 1810–24.

In 1815, the newspaper, after citing the case of a little girl of six who was frozen to death while sitting at a door on a city street, continues:

We have lamented until we are tired, for the want of a society to authorize and provide for the prevention of so many children being bred up to ignorance, vice and destruction by street begging, an evil which increases among us to the shame of every institution for religious, moral or charitable purposes in the city. Humane societies rescue persons from drowning—no society arrests the little troops of mendicants from moral and intellectual perdition. In Summer pilfering and in winter begging,

[3] *Justice and the Child in New Jersey* [report of the State of New Jersey Juvenile Delinquency Commission], Trenton, November, 1939, p. vi.

are trades to which great numbers of depraved parents devote their children, who ought to be in schools, manufactories and houses of industry. The streets are infested with the little vagabonds, and we drive them from our doors and take no more thought of them till we hear of them in Bridewell or the State Prison.

Quoted in the notes by Miss Wells are a report of a young thief who cuts the workbags from the arms of young ladies, a report of a gang of forty or fifty boy thieves who enter houses, and the complaint of a parent that gaming places are a menace to young boys. A more serious offense is described as the throwing of a stone by one boy which resulted in the death of another; the comment about this is the most interesting part: "The sentence will be pronounced Saturday the 13th instant at 12 o'clock. Parents and guardians ought to avail themselves of this circumstance to send their children to the City Hall on that day." Evidence of opinion against criminal law procedure is found in this record as follows:

The 1810 Grand Jury presentment mentions as an evil the necessity of presenting bills for high offenses against infants 10–14; who are usually found in the city prison as the receivers of stolen goods and are the tools of older rogues who pick them up on the streets. The Jury advises a "respectable, or work, house as in other populous cities" where such shall be supported and instructed.

Ten years later (1820) nearly ninety boys between the ages of fourteen and sixteen were reported to be in the penitentiary, and comment was made that contact with old offenders is no way to reform "Convicts." The next year, although boys were still kept in the city jail, an encouraging step ahead was reported: a school for boys had been started in the penitentiary.

The next year we are told that the Society for the Prevention of Pauperism, in a report on the penitentiary system in the United States, went a step further and recommended the establishment of a penitentiary for juvenile offenders. In December, 1823, the society resolves to establish a House of Refuge for Juvenile Delinquents, for which a considerable amount is subscribed, and, asking that more be given, says that the house will "combine together the advantages of a prison, manufactory, and school upon the Lancaster plan." By 1824, the arsenal at the junction of the Post and Bloomingdale roads had been leased from the Government and the house, for both boys and girls, was established, although it is stipulated that the power of the managers should not extend to females over eighteen.

Thus in New York was established the first reformatory for youth in the United States; called the House of Refuge, it was conceived by its founders, in the words just quoted, to "combine together the advantages of a prison, manufactory, and school." Similar institutions were established in Pennsylvania in 1828 and in Massachusetts in 1847. Many other states followed suit.[4]

Brief and inadequate as I admit the foregoing references to the treatment of juvenile delinquents in New York city over a century ago are, nevertheless they suggest that even then slow processes of change in perspective, in both theory and practice of treatment of juvenile delinquents, had begun in that city.

Although the House of Refuge was evidence of improvement in the treatment of certain types of juvenile delinquents in New York city in 1824, the word *slow* may well be emphasized in any study of further progress in that city. Evidence of this is found in 1853 in the words of Charles Loring Brace, the man who initiated another step forward in New York city. He cites [5] the report of the New York Chief of Police, 1848–49, stating that there were "nearly 10,000 vagrant children in the city; and that in eleven wards there were 2,955 children engaged in thieving, of whom *two-thirds* were girls between 8 and 16." Brace further cites a report of the Grand Jury of 1852 in these words: "Of the higher grades of felony, *four-fifths* of the complaints examined have been against minors and *two-thirds* of all the complaints acted on during the term have been against persons between the ages of 19–21." (Italics in original.)

And the warden of the city prison is quoted for the same year, 1852, in these words: "The astounding fact that more than one-fourth of the entire number committed to this prison, and that nearly one-half of these charged with petty offenses against persons and property had

---

[4] For details see Abbott, *op. cit.,* pp. 243–387.
[5] Charles Loring Brace, *First Annual Report of the New York Children's Aid Society,* 1853, pp. 4–5.

not attained the age of 21 years, calls loudly for the adoption of some measures which shall stay the progress of these cadets of crime."

Brace further states that the schedule for the city prison in 1852 shows that out of 16,000 criminals, 4,000 were under twenty-one years old and *800 were between nine and fifteen*. Of the 2,400 thieves, *1,100 were under twenty-one and 600 under fifteen*. In summary, Brace writes: "Crime among boys and girls has become organized, as it never was previously. The Police state that picking pockets is now a profession among a certain class of boys. They have their haunts, their 'flash' language, their 'decoys,' and 'coverers,' as they are called, or persons who will entice others where they can be plundered, and protect the thieves if they are caught."

Out of such conditions of juvenile delinquency came the impetus to found, not only the Children's Aid Society of New York for foster-home care of dependent and neglected and predelinquent children in 1853, but also, in 1851, the New York Juvenile Asylum for the younger delinquents who up to that time had been sent to the House of Refuge.

For comparison with the above glimpses of juvenile delinquency in New York city in the nineteenth century and also to find evidence of a growing awareness that something besides grand jury, criminal court, and promiscuous prison and penitentiary treatment was necessary for both youth and adults, I now introduce to you two Boston pioneers in probation.

Chapter IV: TWO BOSTON PIONEERS IN PROBATION

THE FIRST of these pioneers was John Augustus, a Boston shoe-maker born in 1785, who in 1841 began his volunteer and unpaid probation work with both adults and youth, work he kept up until his death in 1859.

Of his work John Augustus himself says:

In the month of August, 1841, I was in Court one morning, when the door communicating with the lock-room was opened and an officer entered, followed by a ragged and wretched looking man, who took his seat upon the bench allotted to prisoners. I imagined from the man's appearance, that his offence was that of yielding to his appetite for intoxicating drinks, and in a few moments I found that my suspicions were correct, for the clerk read the complaint, in which the man was charged with being a common drunkard. The case was clearly made out, but before sentence had been passed, I conversed with him a few moments and found that he was not past all hope of reformation, although his appearance and his looks precluded a belief in the minds of others that he would ever become a *man* again. He told me that if he could be saved from the House of Correction, he never again would taste intoxicating liquors; there was such an earnestness in that tone, and a look expressive of firm resolve that I determined to aid him; I bailed him, by permission of the Court. He was ordered to appear for sentence in some three weeks from that time. He signed the pledge and became a sober man; at the expiration of this period of probation, I accompanied him into the court room; his whole appearance was changed and no one, not even the scrutinizing officers, could have believed that he was the same person who less than a month before, had stood trembling on the prisoner's stand. The Judge expressed himself much pleased with the account we gave of the man, and instead of the usual penalty—imprisonment in the House of Correction, he fined him one *cent* and costs, amounting in all to $3.76, which was immediately paid. The man continued industrious and sober, and without doubt has been by this treatment saved from a drunkard's grave.

This was truly encouraging, and before January, 1842, I had bailed seventeen persons for a similar offence, and they had severally been sentenced in the same manner, which in all amounted to $60.87. Eleven of this number paid the fine, but the other six being too poor to raise the amount, I paid it for them.[1]

I had labored about a year when it became evident that much good had been and might be performed, by laboring in the field in which I had commenced operations, and to promote this object, several kind and philanthropic individuals placed in my hands donations of various sums, which enabled me to accomplish a much greater amount of good than I could have done from my own limited means alone.

In August, 1842, I found that I had bailed thirty persons. Scarcely an hour in the day elapsed, but some one would call at my house or my shop and tell their tale of sorrow.[2]

This summary statement is given by an anonymous writer in a "Letter Concerning the Labors of John Augustus, the well-known philanthropist, From One Who Knew Him": "Up to 1858 he had bailed out 1152 men and 794 women and girls." [3]

In addition to his work for and with men and women, John Augustus also gives us glimpses of his work with girls. He writes:

In the latter part of this year (1843), I bailed two little girls, *aged eight and ten years,* and one little boy *aged eleven* [italics by H. W. T.]. The girls were sisters. These children had been indicted at the October term and of course their cases were entered on the docket of the Municipal Court. The girls were charged with stealing five or six dollars from a grocery store on Washington Street. These girls sold apples, and entered the store daily to offer their fruit for sale, and at such times those employed would often tease them by playfully seizing their apples. This familiarity of course, caused the children to be pert and to act in a similar manner with the property of the grocer, and on one occasion one of them took a small sum of money from a drawer; they shared it equally, and were soon after arrested for larceny from a shop and confined in jail. The next day they were brought before the Police Court for examination. The father of the little ones was present and was allowed to speak for them if he desired, but he was evidently intoxicated; he spoke in a very

---

[1] *John Augustus: First Probation Officer* [reprint of the original report of John Augustus that was published in Boston in 1852, with an Introduction by Sheldon Glueck, Professor of Criminology, Harvard Law School], New York, National Probation Association, 1939, pp. 4–5. This book contains, in addition to the reprint (104 pages) and the Introduction (pp. xi–xxv), a Foreword by Charles L. Chute, Executive Director, National Probation Association.

[2] *Ibid.,* p. 7.   [3] *Ibid.,* p. vi.

unfeeling manner of the elder child, saying that "she was to blame, and might go to jail, it was good enough for her," but he spoke indifferently of the other. The justice ordered them both to find surety each in the sum of $100. and for default to be committed to jail. I offered myself as surety for the little one and was accepted. I took the child to my house, and placed her in charge of my wife: the other went to jail. The next day I went in quest of her mother, and after some difficulty found her, but in a state of intoxication, and of course unable to converse about her children. It was not a fit place for these little ones, neither were those whom nature intended as their guardians, at all competent to take proper care of them. A few days after I had witnessed this melancholy sight, a humane gentleman, Mr. H., called on me, and expressed his desire to take the little girl who was then in jail, into his own family. I offered to bail her, and immediately proceeded to the Police Court for that purpose and was at once accepted as her surety. We proceeded directly to the jail, where we found the little one crying bitterly. The iron door swung creaking on its hinges, to allow the egress of the little prisoner. I took her tiny hand in mine and led her from the place, while the child looked up into my face, and there beamed from her eyes an expression I can never forget. Who would know true joy, let him be a participant in a scene like this. I could fancy a language proceeding from that gaping cell which was not untenanted; it said in unmistakable language, "Take this infant under thy guardian care, for she has none to help her; be thou her father and her guide, then shall the blessings of those that are ready to perish come upon you. Say to her, remember this day in which you came from out the prison of bondage, for by strength of hand the Lord has brought thee out of this place."

My friend took the little one to the bosom of his own family, and the sequel is soon told:—They both became good girls and were brought up aright; the elder one is now married happily.[4]

As to work with boys he writes:

In 1847, I bailed nineteen boys, from seven to fifteen years of age, and in bailing them it was understood, and agreed upon by the court, that these cases should be continued from term to term for several months, as a season of probation; thus each month at the calling of the docket I would appear in court, make my report, and thus the case would pass on for five or six months.

. . . The sequel thus far shows, that not one of this number has proved false to the promises of reform, they made while on probation. This incident proved conclusively that this class of boys could be saved from crime

[4] *Ibid.*, pp. 13–14.

and punishment, by the plan which I had worked out, and this was admitted by the judges in both courts.

Great care was observed of course, to ascertain whether the prisoners were promising subjects for probation, and to this end it was necessary to take into consideration the previous character of the person, his age and the influences by which he would in future be likely to be surrounded, and although these points were not rigidly adhered to, still they were the circumstances which usually determined my action. In such cases of probation it was agreed on my part, that I would note their general conduct, see that they were sent to school or supplied with some honest employment, and that I should make an impartial report to the court, whenever they should desire it.[5]

And in further detail as to girls he writes:

That year I took seven young girls from houses of ill-fame; these girls were from ten to thirteen years of age. . . . For these children I was obliged to incur considerable expense, in providing them with a temporary home. Sometimes young girls were brought to my house by expressmen and cab-men who felt a kind interest in their welfare.[6]

He often had as many as fifteen of his protégés living in his house at one time. He drove about in a one-horse shay, and in fact wore out two or three shays in his visits to his probationers.[7]

Of the magnitude of Augustus's work a contemporary "One Who Knew Him" wrote as follows:

For the first several years he spent nearly his all on bails and fines for his "charges." Out of two thousand for whom he became responsible only ten proved ungrateful and absconded.

The unceasing calls upon his time destroyed his business as a shoemaker. He was not discouraged by lack of funds. Later a few friends helped him. . . .

In addition to those bailed, he had helped "over three thousand females, who, being neglected by the world, had no sympathy or protection but what he volunteered to furnish them."[8]

In recognition of the pioneer probation work of John Augustus, a few glimpses of which have been given, the National Probation Association held in Boston, May 29–31, 1941, a Centennial Anniversary Conference in his honor. Many persons of national reputation took

[5] *Ibid.*, pp. 34–35.　　[6] *Ibid.*, p. 35.　　[7] *Ibid.*, p. VII.　　[8] *Ibid.*, p. VI.

part in this conference.[9] At the time of the centennial a wreath was laid upon the tomb of John Augustus in the old cemetery near his house in Lexington. The conference members also dedicated a memorial tablet, now affixed to the outer wall of the City Hall Annex on the site of the Old Court House in which John Augustus met his first probationer and paid his bail. The June, 1941, issue of *Probation* has a full-page picture of this plaque. At the top of the tablet is a circle showing the face of John Augustus, with the date 1785 on its left and 1859 on its right. Below these dates are these words in capital letters:

JOHN AUGUSTUS

MOVED BY THE PLIGHT OF THE UNFORTUNATE IN THE JAILS AND PRISONS OF HIS DAY A HUMBLE BOSTON SHOEMAKER BEGAN A GREAT MOVEMENT IN THE REFORMATION OF OFFENDERS WHEN IN 1841 HE TOOK FROM THE COURT FOR A PERIOD OF PROBATION ONE WHO UNDER HIS CARE AND WITH HIS FRIENDSHIP BECAME A MAN AGAIN. THIS TABLET MARKING THE CENTENARY OF PROBATION IS INSCRIBED TO HIS MEMORY BY THOSE WHO FOLLOW IN HIS FOOTSTEPS. NATIONAL PROBATION ASSOCIATION MAY 30, 1941.

To what degree the work of John Augustus stimulated public interest in, and more understanding treatment of, juvenile delinquents in Boston cannot be definitely measured. Surely he sowed good seed during the last eighteen years of his life, while he was doing such work as we have been permitted to glimpse while reading the few words of description written by himself and others which we have quoted.

But we do know that, twenty-two years after John Augustus began his work, the sight of boys in Boston jails was the direct stimulus to Boston women to found in 1863 the Boston Children's Aid Society. In the 1864 *Report* of this society I find a description of this sight which led also to the first systematic probation work with juvenile delinquents in Boston by that second pioneer in probation, Rufus R. Cook, "Uncle Cook." Here is the description of children in Boston jails as the women saw them in 1863:

[9] *Probation*, the Augustus Centennial Issue, June, 1941, reports the conference. *Probation and Parole Progress Year Book*, 1941, National Probation Association, contains the speeches in full.

Some ladies interested in the Newsboy's School, having occasion to visit certain boys confined in Boston Jail for petty larceny, found that the jail always contained a number of children, from ten to fifteen years of age, who were left in solitary confinement. The cell in which the child is confined is large, clean, dry, well-lighted, and warmed and comfortable. His food is good, and ample provision is made for his bodily wants; but he is alone from morning till night, except when by accident he sees a passing face, or receives a visit. Little children, ten or twelve years old, accused of crime, but not convicted, unable to find bail, are here shut up by themselves, without society or occupation. They stand by their grated doors, clinging to its bars, as birds cling to the bars of a cage, watching hour after hour in hopes of seeing the face of a passing visitor or officer; or they sit on the bed, crying, refusing to sleep or eat.[10]

And now I quote two contemporary statements of the work done with delinquent boys by this second Boston pioneer probation officer. First, Boston ladies said:

The City Chaplain—Mr. Rufus R. Cook "Uncle Cook," who was also a paid agent of the Society was present at all sessions of the Police Court, and constantly on the watch for any cases that should come under our cognizance. His system of taking boys on probation by consent of the Court, instead of, as formerly, having them sent to jail to await trial, has worked most admirably. During the past year Mr. Cook has received at the Police Court 88 boys on probation for six weeks each; of these only four had to be returned to court as delinquents, and sent to the school ship at Westboro. At the Superior Court he has received 35 boys on probation for six months each, all for the crime of larceny; of these only three were surrendered to the Court. These probation boys are obliged to report to him, in person, every week at his house, or at the court, and so he is enabled to keep an eye on them. It proves a constant check upon them, and their evident desire, in many cases to improve is very gratifying.[11]

Second, the State Board of Charities of Massachusetts said:

It would perhaps be well if the State consistently provided for every minor, a defender, to whom it should be as much a matter of duty and of pride to acquit the accused, as it is of the State's attorney to convict him.

If this cannot be, then encouragement shall be given for some one to

[10] *Children's Aid Society: Its Origins and Objects*, 1864.
[11] *Report* of the Boston Children's Aid Society, 1866, pp. 7–8.

undertake, in every court, and before every magistrate to whom young offenders may be brought, the beneficent office which Mr. Cook so beautifully fills in the Police Court of Boston. He watches for the little ones as they are brought in by the officers; and whenever it seems advisable, he interposes the shield of mercy between the sword of justice and its victim. He becomes bondsman for the offender, and takes him tenderly in charge, until some fitting place is found for him. Out of nearly *four hundred children* whom he has so bailed, eighty percent are now doing well.[12]

[12] *Report* of the Massachusetts State Board of Charities, 1868, p. LXVIII. For further data about the treatment of juvenile delinquents in Massachusetts see Abbott, *The Child and the State,* II, 365–70.

Chapter V: ORIGIN OF THE ILLINOIS
JUVENILE COURT LAW OF 1899

WITH the work of John Augustus and "Uncle Cook" still in mind, I turn away from Boston to Chicago and Illinois. I shall give two glimpses of juvenile delinquents as treated by the law, by courts, and in the prisons of Chicago and Illinois during the last decade of the nineteenth century—over fifty years after the first probation work we have described started in Boston.

The first glimpse is given by a quotation from the words of Miss Julia C. Lathrop who, as a member of the State Board of Charities of Illinois, had visited practically every jail and prison in the state and so knew, at first hand, whereof she spoke. She says:

Until the opening of the Juvenile Court of Cook County, July 1, 1899, the offenses of Chicago children were dealt with under the same laws and in the same courts as were the offenses of adults. The police courts, 11 in number, scattered over the 190 square miles of the city, had jurisdiction over most of the offenses for which children were held. Children who were arrested and were unable to furnish bail, were placed in the cells of the police station, tried by the police justice, and if punished, were fined and imprisoned in the Bridewell, the City Prison. . . .

From the first of January, 1899, when the legislature met which enacted the measure popularly known as the Juvenile Court Law, until the first of July, 1899, when that law went into effect, 332 boys between the ages of nine and sixteen were sent to the city prison. Three hundred and twenty of them were sent up on the blanket charge of disorderly conduct, which covered offenses from burglary and assault with a deadly weapon to picking up coal on the railway tracks, building bonfires, playing ball on the street, or flipping trains, that is, jumping on and off moving cars. The fines imposed, varied from less than $5.00 to $500.00 and were "laid out" at the rate of 50¢ a day.

Nearly half of these boys were under fourteen and most served terms varying from a few days to nine months. One third of these boys had been committed before, some of them as many as six times. . . .

Out of the 332 cases sent to the Bridewell during the first half of 1899, nearly one-third were pardoned by the mayor. These pardons, usually an alderman's favor, depended upon "pull" at the City Hall rather than upon the merits of the case. But the significant fact which must not be overlooked is that, even if "let off" by the justice or the pardon by the mayor, no constructive work was done in the child's behalf. He was returned to the same surroundings that had promoted his delinquency, in all probability to be caught again and brought before another justice who, knowing nothing of the previous arrests, would discharge or fine him again, as seemed wise at the moment.

That is, whatever was done in the case was necessarily done with little or no relation to the child's history or surroundings. Not only in Cook County but throughout the State of Illinois these conditions existed. Boys were kept in "lockups" and jails in the company of adult prisoners, under circumstances which were a guarantee of ruined character, and were "let off" with a scolding by the justices because a jail sentence, however well deserved according to the law, was so manifestly bad for the boys.[1]

The second glimpse of the treatment of juvenile delinquents in Chicago previous to July 1, 1899, is given us by a Chicago lawyer who, as the first chief probation officer of the new juvenile court, also knew whereof he spoke. He says:

Until then, July 1, 1899, the law viewed mankind, its varied distinctions as to sex, age, environment and mental equipment notwithstanding, as a single class. Before the bar of a criminal court there was no difference, from the viewpoint of the law, between the adult and the infant. It is true that in the administration of the law, magistrates moved by feelings of humanity and oftentimes ignoring declared legal principles, leaned to the side of mercy and sympathy, and shaped their judgments in accordance with charity and common sense, and in defiance of the medieval rigor of the courts which were often influenced by the dictates of vengeance for so-called offenses against society, without taking into account the peculiar circumstances and mental condition affecting the accused, who was in truth, in too many instances, alas, more sinned against than sinning. But for such manifestations of humanity the law was not to be thanked. The judge followed the promptings of his heart and not of his head. Too often because of absolute absurdities which hampered the law, what kindness dictated was in fact prohibited by the cold, heartless, unrelenting canons of jurisprudence. To reconcile this contradiction, or rather to abolish it, was the task essayed by the projectors of the juvenile law. To obtain a closer view of the ludicrous procedure referred to, let us examine it in

[1] Breckinridge and Abbott, *The Delinquent Child and the Home,* New York, Russell Sage Foundation, 1912, pp. 1, 2, 4.

detail. When charged with a so-called criminal offense, it might be the stealing of an apple, which his childish appetite craved, or the picking up of a few lumps of coal to warm shivering brothers and sisters at home, no matter what it was, the child was arraigned at the same bar, under the same law, with circumstances similar, every one of them, to those which would attend the trial of the most hardened criminal charged with the most heinous offense. If a boy was arrested for something which the law books termed a felony, and he was over ten years of age, he was taken before a grand jury and indicted. Then he was tried before a petty jury, the theory being (oh, blessed reverence for precedent and Magna Charta!) that the little fellow should not be deprived of his liberty without being first convicted by a jury of his peers. Imagine the solemn farce of proceedings where the child rarely understood a scintilla of their nature or purpose.

But he was convicted, the LAW convicted him, and the LAW branded him with a brand as indelible as if it was seared into his forehead with a hot iron. Henceforward, among men, he was a CRIMINAL. No matter where he went, no matter how long he lived, foul taint of the convict remained with him. The LAW with all the solemnity of judge, jury, bailiffs and frenzy-consumed prosecutors, proclaimed him a CRIMINAL, that is, an enemy to organized society, and nothing short of a miracle prevented the child from growing up to verify this description in the fullest manner possible. Conviction for the diminutive prisoner meant ruin—ruin as certain and unerring as if the virus of crime could be injected into his childish blood. For society it meant an additional costly incubus, another enemy to be fought with police and prisons, another zealous missionary in the grand army of the devil.

And yet men marvelled that crime and criminals, lock-ups, jails, and reformatories and penitentiaries increased and multiplied. Schools and churches did not grow as fast as the gray, gloomy bastiles, the living hells of lost souls. More judges, more juries, more courts, more jails was ever the cry; more and more and more; but still the tide of crime outstripped them, and no wonder, for costly penal institutions were so many hatcheries for criminals. The youthful delinquents of the community were gathered into them, where they were shaped and fashioned after the models of degeneracy and vice.[2]

I have already told how, in New York and Boston, the plight of children in criminal courts and jails, similar to that described by Mr. Hurley and Miss Lathrop in Illinois, led to new efforts to rescue

---

[2] Timothy D. Hurley, *Origin of the Illinois Juvenile Court Law*, published by the Visitation and Aid Society, Chicago, 3d ed., 1907, pp. 10–11.

children from such a plight in those cities. I shall now describe, largely by quotation from the words of those who were then in the thick of the fight, how a growing awareness of the state of juvenile delinquents was the incentive that led to the drafting and passage of the first Illinois Juvenile Court Law in 1899. Again I quote Miss Lathrop:

For years a number of public spirited citizens in Chicago and throughout the state representing numerous organizations of men and women and various religious beliefs, had felt deep concern over these conditions. Finally, as the culmination of a long effort, there was enacted the law of 1899, drawn by Hon. Harvey B. Hurd. It was entitled a law for the Care of Dependent, Neglected and Delinquent Children.[3]

The following account by Hurley, who himself took part in the events he describes, gives us an intimate view of the actual process by which the persons who "felt deep concern over these conditions" set to work to better these conditions. Hurley says that Ephraim Banning, a Chicago lawyer and member of the Board of State Commissioners of Public Charities of Illinois during the year 1898 (which board made a report to Governor Tanner recommending certain changes in the law), wrote to Hurley after the Juvenile Court Law was passed, giving his recollections of the steps which led thereto, as follows:

My dear Mr. Hurley:—
    In answer to your inquiry in regard to the history of the Juvenile Court, as I recollect it, I became interested through the State Board of Charities. In our work as members of the State Board of Charities, Miss Lathrop and myself had to meet the delinquent and defective child question, and this led to the frequent consultations in our board meetings. As a result, I was asked to take the matter up with the Chicago Bar Association, and I did this by the introduction of a resolution providing for the appointment of a committee to take up the work of securing legislation.[4]

Hurley further reports that:

On October 22, 1898, Mr. Banning presented the matter to the Bar Association, Geo. A. Follensby Pres. in the chair. Resolutions of approval of the project were passed and President Follensby appointed as Commit-

---

[3] Breckinridge and Abbott, *op. cit.*, p. 4.
[4] Hurley, *op. cit.*, pp. 15, 16.

tee, Ephraim Banning, Harvey B. Hurd, Edwin Barrett Smith, John W. Ela and Merritt Starr.[5]

He also quotes Mrs. Lucy L. Flower, President of the Chicago Women's Clubs, on the history of the Juvenile Court Law, and states of her:

One of the most active and energetic workers for years in the children's cause has been Mrs. Lucy L. Flower. She had as much to do with drafting of the Juvenile Court Law, the Parental School Law, the St. Charles School for Boys and other laws as any other person in the State. She not only assisted in preparing the bills that were introduced in the legislature, but systematically and in a very business-like way kept in close touch with every movement relating to the bills from their inception until they became laws.[6]

Hurley further says:

Mrs. Flower, commenting on the history of the juvenile court, writes as follows:
"My dear Mr. Hurley:

"Governor Altgeld is entitled in a great measure for the adoption of the Juvenile Court Law by appointing a woman, Miss Julia C. Lathrop, on the State Board of Charities. Up to that time, visitation of state and county institutions had been largely perfunctory, done almost entirely by the secretary of the Board and limited in the main to State Institutions. Miss Lathrop determined to visit and see for herself and in the course of the work she went to every jail and poorhouse in the State, even in the most out of the way localities. She was shocked at the conditions she found, young children shut up with the most depraved adults and being trained in crime, instead of being kept away from it. She determined not to rest until some remedy for these conditions was found.

"Previous to this a bill had been drafted for the benefit of Chicago Children, including in its provisions a probation system and the trial of all children's cases in the city by a superior court judge and not by a police justice. This bill was submitted to Mr. S. S. Gregory, and the latter provision was pronounced unconstitutional. Miss Lathrop went to Judge Hurd to ask advice but he was disinclined to take up the matter, saying it would take too much time to study and that he was too busy. That he finally agreed to do it was, I think, entirely owing to the influence of Miss Lathrop and the interest she aroused in him by her statements of what she had seen in the jails throughout the state.

[5] *Ibid.*, pp. 16–17.   [6] *Ibid.*, p. 17.

*"At that time, Miss Lathrop said to me, 'this is a legal matter, it must
not go to the legislature as a woman's measure; we must get the Bar Association to handle it'* [italics by H. W. T.]. Through Mr. Banning, who
was her associate on the Board, and much interested, the matter was
brought before the Bar Association and a committee was appointed. But
before this was done the committee was selected with the advice of Judge
Hurd and Mr. Banning. Miss Lathrop saw everyone mentioned and secured promises of acceptance. It was the understanding that Judge Hurd
would draft the bill.

"During all the time that the form of the bill was under consideration
and while it was before the legislature, Miss Lathrop was unintermitting.
Hundreds of letters were written and visits made, to bring the influence
of county officials in the state and of friends she had made in her visits
to the counties to bear on members of the legislature. . . ."

A meeting was held in Judge Hurd's office, 94 Washington St., Chicago,
December 10, 1898. There were present: Hon. Harvey B. Hurd, Mrs.
Lucy L. Flower, Miss Julia C. Lathrop of the State Board of Charities,
Pres. T. D. Hurley of the Visitation and Aid Society, Hastings H. Hart,
L.L.D., Supt. Illinois Children's Home and Aid Society, State Represen-
tative John C. Newcomer, who had been selected to introduce the bill in
the House when completed; Supt. A. G. Lane of the Public Schools,
County Jailer John L. Whitman, Mr. Carl Kelsey from Dr. Hart's office,
and Frank G. Soule. The meeting was called to order by Mr. Hurley,
who nominated Judge Hurd as Chairman. Following his election, Dr.
Hart was elected Secretary.[7]

Hurley further states that Dr. Hart drew up the first draft of the
bill, in ten sections. Judge Hurd made suggestions, and Dr. Hart re-
drafted the bill in fourteen sections.

Then after three weeks of the most critical attention by Judge Hurd and
his assistant to every word and sentence the bill contained, after repeated
conferences with Mr. Hurly, representing the Catholic Church and societies, with Dr. Hart representing the non-Catholic societies; with Representative Newcomer and with officials of public and private institutions
interested, the bill was finally completed, with an addition of seven more
sections making twenty-one. It was then decided to announce it as the
Bar Association Bill and the committee from that body very willingly en-
dorsed it.

[7] *Ibid.*, pp. 17–18, 22.

A copy was then taken to County Judge Orrin N. Carter for his opinion upon its various provisions. He returned it with his hearty endorsement and congratulations.[8]

Passed April 14, 1899, the bill became operative July 1, 1899. I shall discuss the legal provisions of this epoch-making bill in more detail in the next chapter; but, as a prelude to this discussion, I now describe how the fact that some of the legal provisions in that bill were already written in the laws or used by the executives of other states and cities *was made known to Judge Hurd before he had finished drafting the Illinois bill.*

Hurley tells us that the man who gathered this information and gave it to Judge Hurd was Frank G. Soule. He was an insurance man who had been stirred to action in behalf of juvenile delinquents by what he had seen as foreman of a grand jury and by listening to a sermon by a Chicago rabbi, Emil G. Hirsch. In this sermon, Soule heard descriptions of how juvenile delinquents in the John Worthy School of the Bridewell were associating with adult inmates of this Chicago prison. He then had personal interviews with boys eleven to sixteen years of age who were, as related by Miss Lathrop, working out their fines in close companionship with adult prisoners.

What these interviews moved Soule to do are described in his own words, which Hurley quotes as follows:

"I was filled with a desire to find a better plan of correction to offer and thus if possible to start a campaign against the criminal treatment of these unfortunate children which would effect a prompt and radical change. I soon saw that this could be done only by new legislation.

"Ignorant of the repeated efforts, which had already been set forth upon this line, I began at the City Library, a nightly study of the child laws of other states. I secured from several states copies of these laws in which I found suggestions of value to our own state. I was attracted by the 'Probation Officer' idea as used in a limited manner in Massachusetts, and by the separate hearing of Juvenile cases as used in New York." [9]

After making the above quotation, Hurley goes on to state the following in his own words: "Mr. Soule met Judge Hurd on the street and introduced himself with the result that his studies of the laws of other

[8] *Ibid.,* pp. 22–23.   [9] *Ibid.,* p. 21.

states were made available to the Committee." [10] We hear nothing more about Soule in connection with the Illinois Juvenile Court Bill. But, as I read the above statements about what Rabbi Hirsch and Soule did before they dropped out of the picture, I could not dismiss from my mind the words of a rarely quoted parable (Mark 4:26-27): "And he said, So is the Kingdom of God, as if a man should cast seed into the ground; and should sleep and rise night and day, and the seed should spring and grow up, he knoweth not how." It is encouraging for each of us to remember that to sow good seed in good ground may bring great harvests—even without continuous cultivation by the sower.

I now go on to discuss, in the next chapter, what legal methods of service to juvenile delinquents were transplanted into the first Illinois Juvenile Court Bill from seed that had been sown, and that had already sprung up, elsewhere.

[10] *Ibid.*, p. 21.

Chapter VI: JUVENILE COURT LEGISLATION BEFORE 1925

THE PURPOSE of the Illinois juvenile court legislation is expressed in Section 21 of the law: "This act shall be liberally construed to the end that its purpose may be carried out, to wit; that the care, custody, and discipline of a child shall approximate as nearly as may be that which should be given by its parents."

First of all, then, in order to carry out the above purpose, the new juvenile court must be a chancery court, not a criminal court. Of this chancery power Julian W. Mack, once a judge of the Chicago juvenile court and now a Federal judge in New York city, while speaking before a New York state constitutional convention in 1919, said:

The underlying principle of the legislation which (as I have said), has been sustained as constitutional in every state in which the question has arisen, is this; that a child who has committed an offense, no matter what the nature of the offense may be, even what we call murder, should be dealt with by the state not, as an adult is, merely to punish but for the purpose of correction, for the purpose of training, for the purpose of education.[1]

For an outline of the long-ago beginning and the slow development of chancery court procedure in the treatment of juvenile delinquents by courts in France and in England, I shall now give a digest of, and a few quotations from, an unpublished study made by Dr. Philip Klein of the New York School of Social Work.[2]

The Roman criminal law, Dr. Klein states, provided treatment for children different from that for adults; punishments were graded for boys between seven and fourteen years and girls between seven

[1] Julian W. Mack, *Report of New York State Constitutional Convention June 29, 1919* [9th annual report of the New York State Probation Commission].
[2] See also Dr. Klein's article on the delinquent child in Volume III of the *Encyclopedia of the Social Sciences*, New York, Macmillan, 1935.

and twelve years (impuberes) and for young persons between these ages and twenty-five (minors).

Under the Code Penal of France (Articles 66–69) there was a differentiation between adults and delinquents up to the age of sixteen. Those under sixteen who acted without *discernement* were to be aquitted but might return to parents or be sent to a house of correction until twenty years of age. If the child acted with *discernement* he was sentenced to punishment, but to a less degree, according to a graduated scale, than an adult would have received for the same act.

In England and the United States under the criminal law seven years is the lowest limit of punishability. The statutes of different states in the United States vary from seven to twelve, the usual lowest limit being ten. In short, says Dr. Klein:

The law went half way toward treatment of the cause in acknowledging that lack of responsible, mature thinking is partly the cause of the offense, and in establishing the presumption of only partial responsibility in the case of juveniles. It failed to go the rest of the way, however, to find that youthfulness being the cause of the lowered responsibility, it was this youthfulness or immaturity that had to be dealt with, rather than the remaining amount of responsibility. . . .

The reduction of punishment is an unconscious argument for differentiation in treatment. The law is struggling for the concept, but it is like a man with the word he wants almost at the tip of his tongue, but he cannot say it. That *concept* is the *recognition that the child, though technically an offender against law, is really primarily a neglected child* . . . [italics by H. W. T.].

Within the last two generations, therefore, we find legislation concerning the delinquent [child] slides more and more from under the sway of criminal law, and tends to be assimilated with the provisions for the neglected child.

From Dr. Klein's study we see that the chancery power of the first Illinois juvenile court was but a climax to a trend in legislation. But, nevertheless, to make a complete substitution of chancery court law and procedure for criminal court law and procedure for youth charged with crime—juvenile delinquents—was a long new step.

The second essential of an adequate juvenile court law and procedure is that juvenile delinquents be kept separated from adult criminals. How this was done in the early days of the juvenile court of Chicago I shall describe in some detail in Chapter VIII.

The third essential was care and supervision of juvenile delinquents by probation officers. I shall discuss the early probation work of the Chicago court at considerable length in Chapter IX.

Recognition of the above two essentials was not original in the Illinois law of 1899. For a few glimpses of earlier legal provisions in some of our states and in other nations that tended toward a full recognition of Essentials Two and Three, I give here some quotations from a study made by a Chinese student:

In 1861 the mayor of Chicago was authorized by law to appoint a commissioner before whom boys between the ages of six and seventeen could be brought on charges of petty offenses. This commissioner was given authority to place boys under supervision and to send them to Reform Schools. In 1867 this work was transferred to the regular judge in the courts. Michigan, in 1873, established a state agency for the care of juvenile offenders, which in its powers and duties greatly resembled that of the probation officers. In that year the Governor was authorized to appoint in each County for the State Board of Charities and Corrections, an agent to have charge of delinquent boys and girls under seventeen paroled by the court.

A New York law of 1884 provided that when a person under the age of sixteen years was convicted of a crime he might, in the discretion of the court, instead of being sentenced to fine or imprisonment, be placed in charge of any suitable person or institution willing to receive him.

During the last decade of the nineteenth century in a number of states statutes were enacted which were the immediate precedents of the Illinois Juvenile Court legislation. For example, in 1892 New York added a new section to the Penal Code, allowing a separate trial, separate docket, and separate record for cases of children under sixteen. The Board of Children's Guardians Law of Indiana, passed in 1892 and amended in 1893, authorized the Board of Children's Guardians to file a petition in the circuit court if it should have probable cause to believe that any child under fifteen years of age was one whom we usually designate now as dependent, neglected, truant, incorrigible, and sometimes delinquent. If the findings of the court were true, the child should be committed to the custody and control of said Board of Children's Guardians until such child should become of age.

Rhode Island, following the general line of the Massachusetts acts, provided by law in 1898 for separate hearings of juvenile offenders, the presence of the state and private agencies at their trial, and separate detention before trial.[3]

And the separation from adult criminals was not new, as the beginnings of it in New York city dated at least from the time of the House of Refuge in 1824. Other laws and administrative procedure to secure some degree of such separation of juveniles from adults may be cited briefly as follows:

[In England] The first recognition was contained in The Juvenile Offenders' Act of 1847, amplified and amended by the summary Jurisdiction Act of 1879, which still governs the trial of children under fourteen and "young persons" between fourteen and sixteen and gives the justices power to try summarily such juvenile delinquents for all offenses other than homicide. . . .

In South Australia by a ministerial order in 1889, legalized by the State Children's Act of 1895 provided, among other things, for probation and separate hearing of charges against children under eighteen years of age in a room other than the public court rooms, to be approved by the Chief Secretary. . . .

In some parts of Canada, children were dealt with differently from adults since 1894. . . .

In Massachusetts by a law of 1870, separate hearings were required for the trial of a juvenile offender in courts in the county of Suffolk (mainly Boston). . . .

A law of 1877 not only authorized separate trial of children's cases but also used, perhaps for the first time, the term "session for juvenile offenders" of which session a separate record and docket should be kept.

[In New York a law of 1877] put forth by the Society for the Prevention of Cruelty to Children, in New York City, prohibited the placing of any child under the age of sixteen in any prison or place of confinement, or in any court room or in any vehicle in company with adults charged or convicted with crime, except in the presence of proper officers.[4]

Although the above quotations show that there were earlier beginnings of each of our three essentials of an adequate juvenile court law, is it not clear that to do what the first Illinois Juvenile Court Law did—namely, to tie up in one comprehensive law all three of

---

[3] H. H. Lou, *Juvenile Courts in the United States,* Chapel Hill, University of North Carolina Press, 1927, pp. 14–18. See also Grace Abbott, *The Child and the State,* Vol. II, Part II, "The State and the Child Offender," Sections a, b, c, and d.

[4] Lou, *op. cit.*

these essentials, chancery court laws and procedure, separation from adult misdemeanants and criminals, and the personal service of probation officers—was new, not only in the United States, but in the world? In short, as Miss Lathrop put the legal and social significance of the procedure set up by the new law: "For the first time in history, a court of law, the so-called juvenile court, reveals a great social situation, and thereby bestows the greatest aid toward social justice which this generation comprehends—the truth made public." [5]

For the spread of juvenile court legislation previous to 1925 in other states of the United States and in foreign countries, I cite two statements by Miss Grace Abbott.[6] By 1912, she tells us, "This law [the Illinois Law], since modified and improved, has been the model for similar legislation in twenty-two other states, Alabama, California, Georgia, Idaho, Indiana, Iowa, Kansas, Kentucky, Louisiana, Massachusetts, Michigan, Minnesota, Nebraska, Ohio, Oregon, Pennsylvania, Tennessee, Texas, Utah, Washington, Wisconsin and the District of Columbia." By 1925, when the twenty-fifth anniversary of the passage of the Illinois act was celebrated in Chicago, Miss Abbott further tells us, "every state except two has enacted juvenile court laws and these two exceptions have laws which make possible to a considerable degree the kind of care and protection which is the object of juvenile court legislation."

Regarding the adoption of similar juvenile court legislation in foreign countries by 1925, Miss Abbott listed national laws as follows: Austria, 1912; Belgium, 1912; Netherlands, 1921; Croatia, 1918; France, 1912; Germany, 1923 (courts existed in a number of German cities for some years before 1923); Great Britain, Act of 1908; Hungary, 1913 (courts existed in Budapest in 1911); Spain, Act of 1918; Switzerland, determined by the cantons, not all of which have such laws, Geneva having enacted the first in 1910.

Other countries and territorial units in which there had been legislation or activity in the direction of legislation were: the Scandinavian countries, Portugal, Italy, Czechoslovakia, Poland, Canada, Mexico,

---

[5] Breckinridge and Abbott, *op. cit.,* p. 10.

[6] Grace Abbott, "History of the Juvenile Court Movement throughout the United States," in *The Child, the Clinic and the Court,* New York, New Republic, 1925.

Argentina, Brazil, Egypt, Madagascar, the Union of South Africa, Australia, New Zealand, British India, and Japan. With such a start during the first twenty-five years, may we not hope to make the twentieth century increasingly a "Century of the Child"?

In Chapter VII we will visit the early juvenile courts of Chicago and New York, to see how juvenile delinquents were treated by the judges.

Chapter VII: JUVENILE DELIN-
QUENTS IN COURT

FOR THE following contemporary descriptions by visitors to the first juvenile courts of Chicago, New York, and Denver, we are indebted to the first chief probation officer of Chicago, Timothy D. Hurley, whom I quoted in Chapter V about the drafting of the first Illinois Juvenile Court Law. For several years after 1900, Hurley edited and published a monthly, *The Juvenile Court Record*. The eight bound volumes of this monthly, from which I shall now quote, are filed in the Library of the New York School of Social Work. In 1909 Hurley gave these books to his fellow worker in Chicago, Dr. Hastings H. Hart. After the death of Dr. Hart, they were given to the New York School. I know of no other available record of so many contemporary statements about the spread of juvenile court legislation, 1900 to 1909; of such vivid description of active procedure, not only in the courts of Chicago, New York, and Denver, but in several other courts; and of information about the community and institutional services available to children in different states and cities.

Inside the Chicago Juvenile Court

The first account gives the impression that the first judge, Richard S. Tuthill, made upon a visitor who signs himself "Communicated." Three other accounts by another visitor to the Chicago court will also be quoted. These accounts give, as no later accounts can give, both a basis for understanding how the court sessions were actually carried on in Chicago during the first years and also vivid glimpses of the impression made upon citizens of those days by the court treatment of actual boys and girls and their parents.

The first account reads in part thus:

The casual visitor to the court is struck, first of all, by the strained expression on the faces of parents. The number of children sitting about the court would stamp it at once as the Juvenile Court, and when all these little ones are taken into account, it is realized that the court is well named, "The Children's Court." Here, "some in rags, and some in tags, and some in velvet gowns," sit little waifs and strays, derelicts on the stream of life, neglected, homeless, hungry, frightened, wondering in their own little way where the current will carry them next. Looking into their little faces, and watching them as they are taken away from their old unwholesome surroundings to be placed among environments that will lift them up and make them noble men and women instead of burdens upon society, one wonders how much these little ones really feel, and how deep their suffering really is when they are snatched away from home and parents.

Speaking of impressions, the first impression gained from a casual study of the Juvenile Court by the casual visitor is, that it is cruel to separate children from their parents, and to break up families. Then when the real facts are looked into, and it is remembered that it is not the welfare of the parents that must be studied, nor, for the matter of that, the welfare of the children as they are, but that the question must be studied in the relation to the welfare of the child in the future and its influence upon the great public at large, all doubt as to the value of such separation disappears and one wonders how [he] could have doubted. It is cheaper, from a monetary point of view, to save a child in the first place from becoming a criminal, by taking it when it is young away from its vicious surroundings, and placing it where it will grow up to be a benefit to the community, than to leave it alone, and after it has grown up among its criminal surroundings to be a menace to the public welfare, build prisons in which to incarcerate it, and pay people to watch it. As a matter of public good, as a matter of accomplishing the best in all things for the child, it is a proper thing to snatch it away from the degradation that surrounds it and save its soul at the same time you save its body. . . .

When court has adjourned and it comes time for the final separation of the parents and children, brothers and sisters, it is sometimes heartrending in the extreme. The weeping and wailing and gnashing of teeth spoken of in the Good Book are discounted daily in the Juvenile Court. But out of the chaos comes order. Almost to a child a great deal of sniveling and crying is done more because of the strangeness of it all than because of any real feeling on account of leaving home. As soon as the first fright is passed, the child brightens up and curiously watches the proceedings. Out of the confusion and distress hope rises as a star, and after hearing fifty-four cases on Monday, Sept. 24, 1900, when it was realized that the children had, that day, been started on a path that is bound to lead them to something higher, when the full force of the work that is being done dawned on the visitor, one went away with a prayer in their heart, "God Bless the Juvenile Court and the work it is accomplishing."

The country might have been searched over in quest of one to administer the Juvenile Law, and no one so perfectly fitted in every respect as Judge Tuthill could have been found. He is ideal in his position, and assumes towards the (for the most part) terror-stricken little ones, a way that is fatherly, motherly, brotherly, anything rather than the demeanor of the ordinary judicial officer. When Judge Tuthill talks with the little defendants or delinquents, he is not avenging justice, with the scales on one hand and the sword in the other. He calls the youngster up beside him, pats him on the head, and in quite the ordinary tone of voice, asks "Why did you do this, son?" The child usually melts into tears, and by the time the Judge gets through talking with him he knows more about the case than the people who brought it before him know. He grasps intuitively all the points, both for and against, and so perfectly do all of the officers trust in his judgment that there is never a question as to the proper disposition of a case.[1]

How far does the reader of today share the optimism of the above visitor that the procedures he described were adequate to put those young delinquents back upon the road to good citizenship from which they had strayed?

The same writer, after visiting the court a second time and after mentioning his former feelings in the court as he saw the separations and sorrows, describes the law and different functions of the court for dependents, for neglected children, and for delinquents and concludes:

Judge Tuthill has a heart as large as a house. In case a child brought before him in the Juvenile Court as a delinquent has committed a first offense, it seems to be almost impossible for the Judge to bring himself to the point of separating the child from his parents, if there is a possible excuse for not doing so. He acts at all times on the theory that "the quality of mercy is not strained." A great deal of weeping on the part of the child, and a few tears thrown in by older relatives, are almost sure to touch Judge Tuthill's heart and cause him to exercise every bit of clemency that is consistent with the case in hand. Perhaps some people, after a first experience with the judge, form the idea that on any occasion tears will form a poultice that is sure to draw Judge Tuthill's heart out in pity towards the little culprit. Just let the same people try the crying and sobbing act upon a second appearance before him and see how frigid he may become.

[1] "One Day in the Juvenile Court," *Juvenile Court Record,* Vol. II (new series), No. 1, November, 1900, pp. 7–8.

Judge Tuthill knows his business, and he is seldom misled in reading character and deciding upon the cases that come before him. In every case he impresses the child culprits with the idea that, while he has the great right arm of the law behind him, he still stands in the light of a father, and his kind fatherly advice to the child to always be good from that time on and not get into trouble again, is invariably followed by a description of the terrible things that will happen if he ever does do wrong again.

The fact of the matter is, that the attitude of the Juvenile Court towards the child is such that, perhaps for the first time in its life, the child realizes its responsibility towards the public around about it.

For the first time it realizes its responsibility, as an individuality, and the trouble terminating in the Juvenile Court is really the turning point in its life—the *cross roads branching toward useful, manly, law-abiding citizenship* [italics by H. W. T.]. In many instances talents are brought out by a short visit to the John Worthy School [a school on the same grounds as the city prison] or to other institutions, that would, perhaps, have lain dormant during the entire life of the boy, had he been left to run at large. This was proved, when the other day a spice cabinet was exhibited in court with the explanation that it was the work of a boy who had been confined in the John Worthy School for several months. Although the boy had no previous knowledge of cabinet work, the little cabinet shown the court was as perfect in detail and outline as if it had been designed by one old in the business. Judge Tuthill, in paroling the boy from school, told him kindly that a boy who could do such work as that ought never to allow himself to do anything but honest work. He endeavored to impress upon the boy's mind that a brain that could accomplish such a piece of work, if directed in the right channels, could make more money honestly and enjoy more peace of mind than if dishonesty was indulged in. This illustrates the pivot upon which the entire work of the court turns. It is endeavoring at all times and in every case to study the child and develop the natural powers and latent talents so it will not be necessary, when maturity is reached for it to be dishonest because it does not know how to do honest work.

And the foundation idea of the Juvenile Court in caring for the delinquent child is not to punish it as a criminal, but to find out why it went wrong in the first place and remove the cause of the fall from grace.[2]

The same writer visited the court a third time. He says that on the first day his attention was focused upon the treatment of dependent

[2] "Second Day in the Juvenile Court," *Juvenile Court Record*, Vol. II (new series), No. 2, December, 1900, pp. 18–19.

and neglected children and on the second day upon the treatment of
delinquent children. On this third day he will concentrate upon the
parents and friends of the child. He says:

The parents of children appearing in the Juvenile Court may be divided
into three classes, the dull kind . . . gazing about them with wide-open
dumb-animal eyes, not realizing, in their stupidity, what is taking place
until their child is led off by a probation officer in an opposite direction
from the one they are taking; then after making a feeble protest, submit-
ting with the stolidity born of ignorance.

The second class is composed of people of a higher order of intelligence,
who realize they are unable to cope with the problem of properly rearing
their children, and who are anxious for the Court to take them in hand.
The third class cannot be made to understand their inability to care for
their own children. They are defiant, openly rebellious, and breathe out
all sorts of vengeance against the court and the laws of the land for dar-
ing to interfere with what they consider one of the inalienable rights
granted them by the Constitution of the United States. The people designated in the last class are, in their hearts, ever afterwards anarchists, for
almost invariably the one who fights against the enforcement of a law
and loses the fight, becomes an anarchist.

Sometimes they hire a lawyer to fight for them. Frequently they place
themselves in most direct and flagrant contempt of Court, but Judge
Tuthill is such a deep student of human nature, he does not stand on his
dignity in administering the affairs of the Juvenile Court, and on such
occasions, out of the kindness of his heart, he overlooks the contempt or
dismisses it with a single sharp cutting word. These defiant ones usually
bring a younger sister of the young defendant into court with them. This
young lady has been schooled as to the proper time to break forth into
tears, and she usually carries out her share of the performance to the
entire satisfaction of every one else concerned except the Judge. She weeps
and begs clemency just this once for the small culprit, and when clemency is denied not infrequently breaks out into a flood of reproaches that
cannot be checked until it has spent itself.

On the whole the separation of child and parent is usually accomplished
under protest. It is one of the most difficult things in the world to overcome Mother love, even when the love is not in evidence outside the court
room. Her child is her own, after all, and the tug at the heart strings when
enforced separation occurs, is bound to be severe even with the most cal-
loused. Even when parents are willing for the child to be taken from them,
it still hurts. For no matter how willing a parent may be for an arm or
a leg to be cut off, no matter how much they may realize the necessity

and benefit that will arise from it, still the actual surgical operation causes pain. So it is in the forced separation of parent and child.

But it is not the wish or the intention of the framers of the Juvenile Court Law to break up families except in the most flagrant cases of dependency and delinquency. The worst thing that can happen to a child is to allow it to be institutionalized. When a child lives a number of years in an institution it becomes so used to living according to rule and obeying someone over it that it is almost impossible for it to become the master of its own destiny when it leaves the protecting walls of the institution. Realizing this, and realizing also the absolute hopelessness of being able to provide family homes for all the cases coming before it, it is the constant effort of the court to leave the child in its own home, with its own parents, wherever it is at all possible to do so. In order that this may be done, the law provided for the appointment by the Court of a number of Probation Officers, whose duty it shall be to "make such investigations as may be required by the Court; to be present in Court in order to represent the interest of the child when the case is heard; to furnish to the Court such information and assistance as the Judge may require, and to take charge of any child before and after trial as may be directed by the Court."

The probation system is the cord upon which all the pearls of the Juvenile Court are strung. It is the key-note of a beautiful harmony, without it the Juvenile Court could not exist. Upon the intelligent work of the probation officers depends the successful operation of the Court. Enough institutions do not exist in the State of Illinois to care for all the children coming before the Court. The probation system makes it possible to leave the child in the home environment, and provides proper guardianship for the child whose parents are not fitted to care for it. The work of the probation officer is ideal work for one who wishes to be of real benefit to his fellow-beings and to help build up a better citizenship; with the force of the law of the state of Illinois at his back, the probation officer can go into the home of a dependent child and demand to know the cause of the dependency. Having discovered the cause he still has the power to remove it. He becomes practically a member of the family, and by lessons in cleanliness, and decency, of truth and integrity, by threats of what will happen if his demands are not complied with, if threats become necessary, he can transform the entire family into something the state need not be ashamed to own as citizens. One child in a family attending school has an influence upon the entire family. One home cleaned and beautified and uplifted has an influence for good upon the entire community. The more deeply the subject is delved into, the more clear it becomes that the probation system, because of its effect upon the entire family is the most important thing comprehended in the Juvenile Court law.[3]

Another visitor thus gives his first impressions of the Juvenile Court:

The force of the trite old saying, "One half the world does not know how the other half lives" is brought strongly to one's mind on a first visit to the Juvenile Court. Thousands pass, day by day, along the busy streets that border the City Hall, unmindful of the fact that, within the grim old structure (in one of the regular court rooms) they pass so heedlessly, the fate of helpless fellow mortals is being decided:—Children of the indigent, and unfortunate, and to the credit of humanity, be it said, children who claim no earthly parent's care, and the assurance for whose well-being rests with the All-Merciful Father of all, who has said that without Him not even a sparrow shall fall, and who, by His promise that whatever was done unto the least of these little ones was done even unto Him, has given to man a constant incentive to the most noble, self-sacrificing charity.

For those who would know life as it is, with all its stern realities, its pitiful weaknesses, a visit to the Juvenile Court is of undoubted interest. If the proper Study of Mankind be Man, then one cannot afford to miss such an opportunity. One comes away with a deeper insight into human nature, a truer, broader humanity, and a sense of being more in touch with one's kind.

The visitor, here for the first time, sees and hears, apparently as every day affairs, things appalling to all his previous ideas. The picture is of sadness for the most part; but always one is conscious of a pride and gladness that in the busy whirl of this great city there are clever, kindly, capable men and women striving unceasingly for the good and upliftment of neglected little ones, rescuing them from scenes of want and degradation and putting them in the way of a proper start in life, that they may be able to fight its battles with equal chances with their fellow men.

The work is beyond all praise. It needs only to be known to be appreciated, arousing, as it must, the sympathies of all who have the welfare of Humanity at heart.[4]

A third visitor records, in part, his visit to the court, in which on that day a substitute judge was sitting:

[3] "Third Day in the Juvenile Court," *Juvenile Court Record,* Vol. II (new series), No. 3, February, 1901, pp. 15–17.

[4] A. E. Bradley, "First Impression of the Juvenile Court," *Juvenile Court Record,* Vol II (new series), December, 1900, pp. 15–16.

Fifty-eight children, abandoned, neglected, or with parents too poor to care for them, were in the Juvenile Court on the morning of September 9, 1901, waiting a hearing by the judge. Poverty or crime and immorality of their parents were the causes which placed the names of most of these children, many of them were less than a year old, on the docket of a court. Long before court was called the room was crowded with those interested in the disposal of the children. Parents, neighbors, and friends whispered together in awed groups, the murmur of suppressed conversation arose in half a dozen different languages. On some faces were expressions of anxiety, many hardened there by years of suffering. Others showed only stolid indifference. Several of the children were crying, their noise adding to the confusion in the room.

Judge Richard W. Clifford (not the usual judge) conducted the court. The cases were disposed of in the *average time of two minutes to each child* [italics by H. W. T.]. Even to him, with his years of experience on the bench, the Juvenile Court presents problems which he is reluctant to decide in such summary manner. "I would be broken down with worry if I was obliged to pass through this experience every week," he said, while waiting for a case to be called. "There is so much sorrow and misery shown, and the little children are so deserving of pity that even a judge cannot fail to be affected. I do not believe there is another court like this with its human interest characters and situations in any other city in the world. If it makes such an impression upon one accustomed to courts and their working, a visit to it must make a much stronger one on the layman or person interested in charity work." . . .

The afternoon session when the cases of the delinquent children were heard is as characteristic of the Juvenile Court as the morning session, but to one accustomed to the appearance of the court at the two periods, the difference can be distinguished at a glance. The afternoon crowd shows less suffering. Sorrow for the children thrown into such vice producing surroundings is more liable to be awakened in the heart of the spectator than the pity which was felt for the suffering of the children brought to the court in the morning.[5]

Illustrations of delinquent children noted by the above writer on the occasion of his afternoon in the court follow. The reader will note that some were being released from the John Worthy School with, or without, parole, and that some were being committed or recommitted to that school or to some other institution. The reader

---

[5] [Anonymous], "A Day in the Juvenile Court," *Juvenile Court Record,* Vol. II (new series), No. 9, September, 1901, pp. 11–13.

will also not fail to note the particular offenses, acts of bad citizenship, which these youngsters had committed.

There are some happy children in the Juvenile Court in the afternoon. They are the ones released from the John Worthy School.

1. Louis, aged 13 years, had lacked a father's control and been sent to the school for throwing knives and chairs at his mother. He was paroled to Miss Minnie E. Low of the Hebrew charities.

2. Roy, 15 years old, also was fatherless, and though he came from a home of refinement had been in the John Worthy School three times. He was paroled to Miss Collson and allowed another trial at respectability.

3. Arthur, aged 13 years, had stolen a copper lightning-rod from a roof and gone to the John Worthy School. For six years he has had no mother. He was paroled to Miss Collson.

4. Not only was the father dead, but the mother of 13-year-old Alexander is an invalid. He had struck her, been at the Illinois Manual Training School farm for three years and at the John Worthy School several months. He was paroled to Miss Low as it is believed that he has learned to respect his mother.

5. Tony, aged 14 years, had no father. He had run away, stole and gone to the bad generally. It was his second release from the school and as twice before he had been paroled to a man he was given in charge of a woman to see if she could influence him for the better.

6. Milo and Elie, two Arabians, aged 14 and 11 years, probably enjoyed the shortest sentence of any boys in the school. They were in the institution less than a week. Their misery touched Miss Olive L. Phelps, teacher at the school, who wrote the letter to Judge Tuthill which secured their release. They had been sent to the school for stealing kindling wood from freight cars, having been caught by a railroad detective. Miss Phelps believed that the boys were entirely strange and ignorant of our customs, and according to Arabian nature thought it right to steal for their father and mother. "The older boy says he is the sole support of his parents," she wrote. "He bursts into tears, crying, 'Oh, I can no stay here; what will my poor father do without me?' They admit the school is as good as home but grieve constantly over their condition." Mrs. Sara Franklin was appointed as probation officer as a precaution that their ignorance of American customs does not again involve them with the law.

7. John, aged 14 years, it was said by his mother, was being ruined by his father's coarse language and inebriety. The boy also feared his father and ran away to his grandmother. He had been arrested by the police, charged with stealing a dozen oil barrels. As it was his first offense,

he was paroled to Probation Officer Sherlock, who was to keep him at the grandmother's home, away from the evil influence of the father.

8. Kitty, a 15-year-old girl, had been arrested for assaulting and attempting to rob a man at midnight. She did not appear wholly bad, and the judge, believing that she could be reformed outside of an institution, paroled her to Mrs. Peavey.

9. Ray, 16 years old, had no father. He had been arrested for disorderly conduct and for being in company with a thief. He had previously been in the John Worthy School, but was this time sent to the Cook County hospital, as he was suffering from sickness.

10. Four boys were brought in by a railroad detective for stealing from a grain car. They were all sent to the John Worthy School. Edward, 15 years old, had a stepfather. He had never been in court before, but trouble with the police. Guy, 15 years old, was motherless and had been arrested previously for robbing freight cars. Harry, 14 years old, also was motherless. He had steadily refused to attend public school and had served one term in the John Worthy School. Joseph was only 9 years old and had a distaste for school and had assisted in the burglary of a grocery store on a previous occasion.

11. Florence has no Father. She was 17 years old and had been frequenting saloons and gambling houses. She proudly told in court her aptitude for shooting craps. Her face showed that she had a stubborn nature, and neither education nor refinement. She was sent to the State Home for Female Juvenile Offenders at Geneva.

12. Three boys were brought by Officer O'Meara for stealing a horse and carriage. All were sent to the John Worthy School. Each had both parents living. Dorcy, aged 10 years, was a colored boy who had never been in any serious trouble before. William, also aged 10 years, was a Catholic and brought a letter from Rev. J. E. McGavick stating that he had attended school regularly and that the priest was willing to forgive and take him back. Robert, aged 9 years, had German Protestant parents. He brought an unfavorable letter from the principal of his school saying that since its opening he had been present only one-half the time.

13. William, aged 14 years, had no mother. He had once been arrested in the basement of a store for burglary, had twice been found sleeping at night in the streets and was now before the Juvenile Court for stealing from a cash drawer. He was sent to the John Worthy School.

14. George and Andrew, aged 13 and 11 years, were arrested for sleeping in alleys. Both were sent to the John Worthy School. Both had steady, church-going parents and no occasion to stay away from home. George had been to the school once before and paroled to two different probation officers.

15. Susie, aged 15 years, persisted in remaining away from home. She associated with bad men and women, and her parents asked that she be sent to an institution. She was sent to Geneva.[6]

Inside the New York Juvenile Court

Comparison with the foregoing accounts of the Chicago Juvenile Court is provided by the first session of the New York Children's Court in 1902. This was the first children's court in the United States to have a separate building, but it still operated without the advantage of a law giving it the chancery jurisdiction. Yet there was an effort to utilize, so far as the criminal law permitted, something of the attitude and procedure of the juvenile courts that had full chancery jurisdiction.

In silken robes of solemn black Justice Willard Hall Olmsted, of the Court of Special Sessions, inaugurated the New Children's Court of New York City in the old building of the Department of Charities, Third Avenue and Eleventh St., on the morning of September 2nd. Altogether sixty-three cases were brought before Judge Olmsted before the court closed for the day. Complaint Clerk Le Mon drew up 40 complaints and only one child, Mamie Norris, was committed. Children who have sinned themselves or suffered innocently for the sins of parents, a pitiful throng gathered up in the highways and byways of the city, were the defendants in the court when it opened for the first time at half past ten o'clock. Some of the little ones, all of whom were under sixteen, were sad and others were merry, apparently caring little for what became of them. There were children in rags and others in expensive clothes, but in each case there was a tale of wrong or of cruelty that would soften the heart of any person with human feelings. . . .

One of the most interesting of the cases and one of the saddest was that of Mamie Norris, 13 years old. She confessed to taking $5.00 from the cash drawer of a grocer near her home. Mamie went to the store one night and while the grocer had his back turned took $20.00 from a cash drawer according to the story of the grocer. Though she knew she had done wrong, the child went a long way toward righting it by a touching piece of unselfishness. She went straight home and gave the money to her father, who was out of work, out of money and despondent. The girl declared to him that she had found the money. It was like a small fortune to the father, and he soon exchanged most of the money for clothes

[6] *Ibid.*

for her and her mother. The father, a gas fitter who never works, and her mother, a dish washer in a restaurant, failed to appear. But Mrs. Lillie Gillen was in court declaring that the Norrises were drunkards. They were janitors of her home earlier in the year when the innocent looking Mamie stole $35.00 from her bureau in her absence. Norris was arrested but was discharged, as it was apparent he had no guilty knowledge of the theft. Mamie wore a neat blue gingham frock bought with a part of the money stolen from the grocer. She owned up to the theft and was committed to the Female Guardian's Society where she will have a good home. . . .

"You are charged with the serious offense of playing ball in the streets of New York on a holiday," said the judge sternly. "Are you guilty, or not guilty? The City isn't for boys, it's for business; boys must give way to business, and they can't play ball in the streets." Frank McQuade, Jacob Swain and Hugh Kelly, sturdy lads in knickerbockers, said through their tears that they were not guilty. Policeman Schauhoff testified that he caught them, balls, bats in hand, in Twelfth St. The court found them all guilty, in the severest voice he could summon and then he told them to go to some park next time and discharged them all in a tone as gentle as a mother's. The three boys dried their eyes, put on their caps and ran home. . . .

Luigi Reda, nine years old, was arrested for stealing four loaves of bread from a wagon. When arraigned in the court, he had to stand on a chair in order that Magistrate Olmsted might see him. He was so dirty and so worn were his clothes that Magistrate said if they were not replaced by new ones they would fall off.

Luigi held on tightly to the bread. The policeman who took him to court had forgotten to take it away. Now and again he would take a bite of one loaf and then of another. Then he would rub his eyes with his dirty little fist. "You are charged with stealing bread!" said the justice. "I took the bread," murmured the child through a mouthful of crust. "What have you to say about this awful crime?" "Me fader's a rag picker, me mudder's dead, me fader didn't turn up dis mornin wit der breakfast. Gee, I was hungry! I went in der street and walk't and walk't, and I didn't find nothin. I walk't to Park Row and Broadway, I seen er waggon full of breads. Gee, but I was hungry. Der bloke wat owns it wasn't in sight, and I just had a feast till der cop came along and pinched me." The little fellow, still hugging the remnants of three loaves, burst into tears and said, "I wus sorry for the bloke what owns der bread, but I was hungry, an'—an' I wus—"

"Guilty," said the magistrate.

"Guilty," echoed the youngster.

"You are," said the judge.

"Well, if I is, I is, I can't pay der bloke, and I spose I must cry fer er mont."

"To be sentenced Thursday," said the magistrate. "In the meantime give him a bath, and above all a good meal." . . .

Before the Court opened, several patrol wagons filled with boys and girls, who had been cared for at the rooms of the Society for the Prevention of Cruelty to Children (then at 23rd and Fourth Ave.), rolled up to the door, and their passengers were hurried up the stairs to the waiting rooms, on opposite sides of the corridor above the court room. There are two of these, one for boys and one for girls. . . . In the boys' room there were toys and books galore, and when the offenders were turned loose in this haven of play, each made a rush for the kind of toy he liked best, and all enjoyed "a bully good time" as one of them said. The girls' room had not yet received its equipment. There was only one little doll. It was pink-cheeked, blue-eyed, flaxen-haired, like every other French doll, but some of the little girls had never had a dollie of their own, and they stood around and gazed with tearful admiration at the pretty creature. . . .

E. Fellows Jenkins, Supt. of the Society for the Prevention of Cruelty to Children [sometimes called the Gerry Society] was present to see that everything went smoothly and it did. . . .

Waifs whose parents had starved or beaten them; children of poverty whose mothers had sent them to the market to collect garbage and half-spoiled food to take the place of wholesome bread and vegetables, homeless children of the streets, picked up at random, and almost unwilling that the city should find a comfortable home for them, poor little human rats who thought poverty with liberty was better than comfort with metes and bounds—this was the grist which came to the mill. It was a sad grist, yet not all sad.

There were touches of humor here and there in the incongruous picture. The children looked with awe upon the Justice in his silken robes of office. But they soon found they had little to fear from Justice Olmsted, whose heart is a gentle one. Magistrate Olmsted is considered the tenderest-hearted judge on the bench, and his fondness for children was one of the reasons he was chosen by his fellow-judges to be the permanent incumbent at this court. Several times during the recital of the circumstances leading to the arraignment, the magistrate's eyes glistened, and he used his handkerchief to conceal his emotion. . . .

In the past, two days in the week have been set aside in the Court of Special Sessions for the hearing of children's cases, but this is the first court of the city where those who have just started in the wrong way are arraigned exclusively.[7]

Two months later another visitor to the New York city Children's Court wrote the following account:

New York Juvenile Court Sketches

"Benny," says Justice Mayer, "step up here where I can take a look at you."

Benny runs his hands through his red hair and steps forward. He begins to shift his feet uneasily as the judge looks at him. "Benny," continues the judge, "have you ever seen me before?"

For the first time the defiant eyes drop.

"Yessir," says Benny.

"I am glad," says the justice, "that you are telling the truth. We do not like boys that lie here. Now didn't you see me before, because you were arrested for stealing?"

"Yessir," whispers Benny.

"And didn't I let you go because you said you would never do anything of the sort again? Didn't I tell you that if you would go to the officer of the court here once a week and tell him everything you had been doing, you could go free after six months without any punishment at all? Do you think you acted very well, Benny, stealing bananas from this poor Italian after that?"

"Didn't steal no bananas," muttered Benny, "me and Mulhearn was wid de gang goin to de Dewey, cause a cigar store man give us free tickets for havin pictures hung in his winder, and two of the fellows jumped the dago and pinched the bananas. They ain't never told us they was goin to do it. We run cause they did. The cop had orter got the other fellows, it wasn't us."

"Ah!" said the judge, "Mulhearn, what did you do with the bananas you got?"

"I hadn't got mine yet," said Bobby frankly, "the cop grabbed me before I got mine."

Justice Mayer shook his head in grief. He called for Benny's mother. She was a poorly dressed, worn-looking German woman. She started right off with a torrent of thanks to the good judge for having let her boy off before and for having made him behave so well for so long. She hoped he would do well this time. She was a poor washerwoman and she couldn't get along without Benny to carry her bundles for her. She would

---

[7] [Anonymous], "New York Inaugurates a Juvenile Court," *Juvenile Court Record,* Vol. III, No. 8, September, 1902, pp. 4–5.

like to keep him off the streets by sending him to school, but there was no room for him in the schools.

Mrs. Mulhearn was a ponderous Irishwoman of fifty years or more. She leaned over the judge's desk, and assured him that Bobby was as good as any boy that ever lived, except that the good God made all men creatures—devils. She had five and he was the youngest, and God knows she would rather have all four taken away from her than Bobby. He was the only one who made any money for his poor old mother.

The Justice's mind was made up. He motioned the parents away and called the two culprits before him.

"You boys," he said, "are bad, your mothers have to work hard to pay for things for you to eat and for clothes for you to wear. You know how hard it is, because your mothers say you help them.

"You are not altogether bad, because you tell the truth, or almost the truth. You would be better if you would tell it all. But when you know how poor your mothers are and how hard they have to work you ought to be ashamed to steal 30¢ worth of bananas from this poor Italian. You know how hard he has to work. He is just as poor as your mothers are. He has little boys too, they need all they can make, yet you steal 30¢ from him; it is just as bad to steal bananas as it is to steal money, and I don't believe either one of you would steal money. But 30¢ is a whole lot. Now you must both go to the Gerry Society office every Sunday for two months and answer all the questions the gentleman there will ask you, and you must tell him the truth. Then next month you will come to me, and if I find you have both been good boys and have told the truth, I will be as easy on you as I can. But be good to your mothers and behave yourselves."

The listener cannot but feel, after hearing such a case, that this isn't much like most criminal courts. It is a pretty comforting sort of court in these days when some people think the world is going to the devil.[8]

And a month later we have the following account of another visit to the New York court:

The Crime of Shinny in a Large City

Go up to the squat little court building at Eleventh Street and Third Avenue in the morning. A crowd of court idlers, witnesses, gossipers, is gathered behind the rail. In front of it are a lot of policemen and lawyers, and Gerry agents.

A side door opens. Enter the clerk, bland, bald and smiling. "Stand up,

[8] Trevanian G. Cook, "New York Juvenile Court Sketches," *Juvenile Court Record,* Vol. III, No. 10, November, 1902, pp. 4–5.

stand up," orders the Sergeant, for this is a silk-gowned ceremony.
Enter the Judge.

It is Mayer, cool, alert, dignified, his searching blue eyes scanning the room through his gold-rimmed glasses.

There is a "Hear Ye!" in resonant tones from Clerk Coulter, a rustling of papers and the Children's Court is opened.

"Walter Smith."

A half-grown frightened boy is thrust in through a side door and jerked not unkindly up on the prisoner's block. A big policeman takes the witness stand. One of the court officers gives his elbow a friendly prod, up goes his right hand to the oath that the facts he sets forth in the affidavit are true.

Justice Mayer reads from the affidavit, "Having violated section 675 of the Penal Code in having played shinny in a public street."

Shinny a misdemeanor!

Shades of the shinny sticks with which we played in our boyhood days, has it come to this in New York? Is it for this that a fun-loving boy is seized by the strong arm of the law, is hurled for one night into that dread place of mystery, "the Gerry"? But listen! the judge is speaking:

"My boy," his tone is not unkindly, "there is nothing wrong about shinny, it is a good game. I used to like to play it myself. It was manly of you to admit that you had been playing it. The trouble is, Walter, it doesn't do to play shinny everywhere. It's a dangerous game to play on a narrow sheet, where there are a lot of children. You might break some windows. Now, Walter, if I let you go, will you promise not to play shinny in the street any more?" Of course Walter promises.

This Children's Court is a peculiar court. The justices seek to teach responsibility, to explain why things are wrong, to put the fear of punishment in the place of punishment itself. . . .

Three boys are charged with stealing lumber. A portly wood merchant is their accuser. He tells of the many petty thefts that have become unendurable. "Where are the parents?" the judge asks sternly.

Three women of the tenement come forward. He lectures them severely. He tells them it is their fault. They sent the boys out to gather wood. They knew it was stolen. They are the ones that should be punished.

They listen in shamed silence. Would they have their boys become burglars? asks the judge, would they encourage them in theft?

The boys brighten up, they expect to go free. They don't, the judge holds them until the next day. Probably then he will release them, but he reasons that a night of worry will impress the wrong doing better on both the boys and their parents." . . .

A brazen little girl of fourteen takes the stand. "Where are her parents?" asks the judge. A worried tearful woman sinks into the witness chair. The child looks at her mother, but doesn't even smile. The judge begins speaking, she turns her face to him boldly. There is sorrow and sternness in his tones.

"You have been bad. You have stayed away from school, and out late at night." Briefly he rehearses the history of her misdoings. He dwells on the worry she has caused her mother; a tear wells up unbidden in the child's eyes, the mother is sobbing quietly. "I could send you away where you would not have your freedom until you are twenty-one. But I think you are going to be a good girl. If you will go home with your mother, if you will do what your mother tells you, if you will promise to come here," he consults a calendar, "on December 17, if you will promise to do this, I will suspend sentence until that time."

"I promise," the girl faltered, turning to her mother.

"Now understand," the judge continued, "if you have to be sent away in December, it will not be my fault, nor the law's fault, it will be your own fault. It all depends on you."

"I understand, Sir," the girl said simply; and when she left the Court room, it was with her hand clasped within her mother's. . . .

And so the grist goes on. To this mill of justice comes the messenger boy who tore up the cable-gram and kept the money, the boy who stopped to shoot craps, the girls that run away, the boys that threw stones, the boys that fight, the boys that steal.[9]

Inside the Juvenile Court in Denver

A glimpse of Judge Ben B. Lindsey's treatment of a delinquent boy in Denver in 1905 follows. The account is from a statement by Dr. Lilburn W. Merrill, who at the time was employed by the Denver court.

The Judge [Lindsey] had left the bench at five o'clock and gone into Chambers to hear half a dozen children's cases that had been carried over from the Juvenile session last Saturday. After an hour and a half the last of these cases was called, and as the lad entered the room the judge arose and took him by the hand and invited him to sit down at the end of a table by his side. The police had placed the boy under arrest on the charge of robbing a saloon. He was fifteen years old, physically well developed

[9] [Anonymous], "New York Juenvile Court Graphically Described," *Juvenile Court Record,* Vol. III, No. 11, December, 1902, pp. 4–5.

but morally of no value in the eyes of a large number of complaining witnesses. He had inveigled four younger boys in the robbery. A past record of numerous offenses stood against him, and after frankly talking over the seriousness of his wrong conduct and of the importance of placing him under good influence and protection, the lad was sentenced to the State Industrial School.

The Superintendent of the Detention School was instructed to take charge of him for the night and to secure commitment papers the following morning and start him to the Industrial School alone. The boy dropped his head on the table and sobbed; "My boy," said the judge, as he arose and laid a friendly hand on his shoulder, "You may not get away from the Industrial School for several years. It would be better if you were able to live as a citizen here at home, but you have shown that you were too weak to do this; therefore I feel that I am doing you the very best kindness in my power in sending you to a place where you will be well cared for and trained. It is not necessary for me to send an officer with you, even though I am told that you will never go alone; I know you will. Good-bye."

The boy and the superintendent left the office and the night's work was ended.

Dr. Merrill then described his own doubt that the boy would go, and how he called up the school the next day to find out. At the end of the day he told Judge Lindsey who was visibly pleased, for this lad had completed an unmarred record of two years of unviolated trust. "I am proud of the record," said Judge Lindsey, "for despite the fact that many of the boys have had criminal records, some of them entirely out of proportion to their ages, every single lad whom I have committed under normal conditions has kept his word with me. In many cases the police have warned me against permitting certain offenders to have the chance of slipping and have entered an emphatic protest against my plan of allowing these boys to go to school alone, but I have never been thrown down in any instance. It proves there is always some good in every boy, no matter what his previous surroundings or his life may have been, if you only go about it in the right way to find that good." And I guess the Judge was right.[10]

From the foregoing detailed stories written by contemporary visitors to the first juvenile courts of Chicago, New York, and Denver we can get a fairly clear perspective on the attitudes toward juvenile de-

[10] Dr. Lilburn Merrill, "Denver, Colorado," *Juvenile Court Record*, Vol. VI, No. 7, August, 1905, p. 5.

linquents taken by judges in these courts under their new chancery jurisdiction in such cases. In other words, we get a perspective on the early use made of the first essential of an adequate juvenile court law. The second essential—separation of juvenile delinquents from adult criminals—is discussed in the next chapter.

Chapter VIII: CHILDREN IN JUVENILE DETENTION HOMES AND IN JAILS

THE FIRST Illinois Juvenile Court Law (as amended in 1907, Section 11) said:

No court or magistrate shall commit a child under twelve years of age to a jail or police station, but if such child is unable to give bail it may be committed to the care of the sheriff, police officer or probation officer, who shall keep such child in some suitable place provided by the city or county outside of the enclosure of any jail or police station. When any child shall be sentenced to confinement in any institution to which adult convicts are sentenced, it shall be unlawful to confine such child in the same building with such adults, or to confine such child in the same yard or enclosure with such adult convicts, or to bring such child into any yard or building in which adult convicts may be present.

Mrs. Joseph T. Bowen of Chicago, who was the second president of a juvenile court committee which was formed by a group of women in 1899, describes the new provision made by this committee for the separate detention of children awaiting hearing in the Juvenile Court and for the care of children who, after hearing, had been committed to some institution which could not for some reason accept them at once. In Mrs. Bowen's own words:

We had no place to confine children pending their hearing. They could not be kept in the jails at the police stations, so we took an old house on West Adams Street. . . .

[Until 1907] the girls and dependent children were kept in the house, which was a very simple homelike place. Behind it was a large two-story building which had been used as a stable. We fitted this up, using the first floor as a kitchen and sitting room and the second floor as sleeping quarters. It contained fifty beds for the boys who were confined there. We maintained this house for seven years in cooperation with city and county, from twenty-six to twenty-eight hundred children passing through it yearly. The city allowed us eleven cents a day for food for each child and the county gave us certain things, among others the services of the county physician, transportation to and from court, etc. During these seven years the institution was never quarantined on account of contagious diseases. When a child was ill the county physician was immediately called and if the child had a contagious disease, he was at once removed to what, I think, was the contagious ward in the county hospital.

This Detention Home was under the charge of one of the members of our committee, now Mrs. Harry Hart. She was at the home every day and looked after every detail, using the greatest economy in purchasing. It was owing to her good management that we were able to maintain the home for so long a period.

Our Superintendent was a little old woman, I should say over seventy years of age, but there was nothing she did not know. On one occasion when I was at the Home, she came in from the stable quite irate at the boys, as they had been acting badly, she said. I asked her what they were doing and she said, "Oh, I thought something was wrong and went out there and found they had their guard on the floor and they were all sitting on him jabbing his head with his own revolver." When I asked her if she called the police, she said, "No indeed, why should I call the police? I told them to get up and unbind the guard and apologize at once." "Did they do it?" I asked, and she replied, "Why of course." [1]

The foregoing description of the two-story barn, with fifty beds on the second floor, and of the incident of an armed guard overpowered by the delinquent boys gives the reader the basis for a judgment of his own about the influence such a congregate life in idleness would have upon the Chicago delinquent boys who were kept there for a few hours, a few days, and sometimes weeks while they were awaiting admission to the institutions to which they had been committed.

This detention home provided separation from adult criminals; but what were the influences of these juvenile delinquents, with nothing to do, upon each other? Again it was Miss Lathrop who saw a possibility to better this situation. Soon after I was appointed to be the chief probation officer in 1905, she invited me to go with her to see E. G. Cooley, who was then the superintendent of Chicago schools. She asked him what the law was, regarding school facilities for children. He said that children under a certain age had a right to go to

---

[1] Jane Addams and others, *The Child, the Clinic and the Court*, pp. 300 *et seq.*

school. She then asked if the Board of Education was excused by law from providing teaching for children like those in the detention home. He said, "No. Where can I get the right teacher?" This led to the placing of Miss Florence Scully in the home as a teacher. Miss Scully had had experience in teaching boys in the John Worthy School of Chicago. She improved the atmosphere of the detention home by the hanging of curtains, the use of a piano, individualized teaching of each boy in numbers, reading, and writing, and the introduction of handwork, including clay modeling. She also made reports to the judge concerning particular bents or abilities that she found different boys to have, so that he might be guided in his decisions on the boys' treatment.

As to the transportation of children between the home and the court, Mrs. Bowen says, "The county had given us an old omnibus, drawn by a very small horse, which struggled painfully to drag the omnibus between the Court and the Home. The old vehicle grew older and older and became very rickety, and one day the driver came to say that some of the boards had fallen out of the bottom and he had nearly dropped the children on the street."

The disagreeable personal experiences that Mrs. Bowen and Miss Lathrop were willing to undergo to help provide better service for the dependent, neglected, and delinquent children of Chicago is vividly illustrated by the next paragraph in Mrs. Bowen's narration: "The omnibus could not be repaired, so I went to the County for relief and was told that this was a City matter and I must go to the Chief of Police. I went to his office and stood up against the wall all day. The office was full of expectorating gentlemen who occupied chairs and were rather amused at a woman wanting to see the Chief of Police. When I went to luncheon, Miss Lathrop took my place in holding up the wall and we spun out the day until the Chief left by the back door when it was dark. Next day I was in my place again and this time I saw him. He said he had nothing to do with the matter, and referred me to the repair department." Mrs. Bowen then details the further efforts of the committee, over more than six weeks of time, to get a new omnibus and horses from the city and county authorities. She says that at last in desperation "the Committee bought its own omnibus, its own horses, rented its own stable and furnished its own horse feed."

Meanwhile the sessions of the Juvenile Court were at first held in one of the regular courtrooms in the County Building; then for a period in rented rooms on the second floor of a business building on crowded Clark Street where the din of traffic noises was constantly heard; then in 1907 in a new building on Ewing Street near Hull House for which the city furnished the site and the county appropriated the money for the building. In this building both the court and the detention home were housed and the children were provided with teachers. In 1923 the court and detention home moved farther west, as the court is a county court and it is claimed that the present site is more accessible to parents and friends from all parts of the county than the site farther east on Ewing Street.

This home, as was true of the first Chicago detention home, previously described, and also of the second home, receives dependent and neglected children, as well as delinquent children, pending hearing in court, and others after one hearing, but pending other hearings or acceptance by the institution or agency to which they have been committed.

Of this last Chicago detention home we are told in a recent study initiated and financed by the National Probation Association,[2] that:

The Juvenile Detention Home of Chicago, which is located in the turmoil of a noisy business district, is a massive building with windows well-guarded by efficient looking bars and by heavy doors which are always kept carefully locked. In the rear of the building is a cindered playground of three and one half acres, surrounded by a stone wall fifteen feet high. The playground is also the site of portable school rooms, which are presided over by teachers employed by the City Board of Education. . . .

The long detention home periods of a large number of the 86 girls and the 120 boys whose records were studied stand out as the most arresting factor in the findings. Sixty-five percent of these children were kept four weeks or longer. Twelve percent of the group remained in detention fourteen weeks or longer, and almost four percent were held for twenty-two weeks or more. The average length of detention for the group was

---

[2] Florence Warner, *Juvenile Detention Homes in the United States* [report of a field survey of the National Probation Association], Chicago, University of Chicago Press, 1933.

about forty-eight days. The present use of the detention home can hardly be described as temporary, measured in such periods as these.[3]

The study from which the above quotation was made was not confined to Chicago. We are told that it included a study of:

The methods of detaining children awaiting court action carried on in 1930 and 1931 in one hundred and forty-one selected areas in all parts of the United States. [In this study] are presented the findings of the first thorough-going, nation-wide study of Juvenile court detention. From the data here submitted it becomes evident that children in 1930–31 were still commonly kept in jails, all over the country; that there was an absence of adequate facilities in many jurisdictions; that detention homes were little better than jails; that all too commonly policies of intake and discharge were inadequate; that the wrong kind of children were detained; that children were confined for long periods; in short, that what is technically known among social workers as "good case-work standards" were too often lacking in the treatment of these children. On the other hand, here were described the best and most successful detention homes and other plans for meeting the problem, which is by no means insoluble if intelligent ingenuity is applied to it, together with a reasonable investment of public funds. How this can be done is here set forth.[4]

In Chapter XIII, the summary and conclusion of this study, we find in more detail what varieties of detention treatment of juveniles were found in connection with some of the juvenile courts of our various states. Miss Warner says:

In the preceding chapters an attempt has been made to present the statistical returns of this study of 17,045 children, and a brief summary is here presented.

Detention is usually presumed to be the care of children pending disposition by the court. It is the method of caring for children which was inaugurated when children were taken out from under the criminal law and given into the jurisdiction of the juvenile court with chancery proceedings. Under the *parens patriae* philosophy of the juvenile court, children in detention would be cared for as a wise father would care for his children. Accordingly it would be evident that a wise father would not place his children in jails where they would be exposed to adult offenders.

---

[3] Phyllis Osborn in Appendix B, "A Cross Sectional Study of Population in the Chicago Detention Home," *ibid*.

[4] Foreword (p. VIII) by Charles L. Chute, Executive Director of the National Probation Association, *ibid*.

But the practice has not followed the ideals of the Juvenile Court, for a considerable number of children, even children under twelve years of age, are held in jail. Furthermore, a wise father would not place his children in an almshouse or county infirmary, yet too many dependent children were found in almshouses, where they associated with the aged, the crippled, the venereally infected, the feeble-minded, and the "queer" people who drift to this institution which is under the control of the poor-law authorities. Again, a wise father would not place his children in a children's home where they could hear the good times of the other children and yet be segregated from them with little or no attention or supervision. A wise father would not place his dependent or younger children in a congregate institution where they would mingle with older, delinquent children who might contaminate them morally or injure them physically. A wise father would not lock his children in a room and keep them in solitary confinement, which is considered severe punishment even for adults. A wise father would protect his children from many places where children are detained in the various communities.

While detention is presumed to be a method of caring for children for the court, yet it appears that many children held in detention never have formal court hearings. In some communities the detention home has degenerated into a sort of parking station for children, and almost any person can bring a child to the detention home and leave him until called for.[5]

Jails as Places of Detention

Of the use of jails for the detention of juveniles, we have this testimony by Margaret Steele Moss, Assistant Director of the Bureau of Children for the State of Pennsylvania in 1929: "Thirty counties have reported the use of the local jail for detaining children—usually with a pathetic tribute to womanhood in the added comment—'But we always put them in the women's section.' Some of these counties were small and had little need of detention but others were large." [6]

To give some idea of what life for juvenile delinquents in a jail may still be I quote a description by Joseph Fishman, former Inspector of Prisons, who has seen jails in all parts of the United States. He says:

Jails are unbelievably filthy institutions in which are confined men and women serving sentence for misdemeanors and crimes and men and

[5] *Ibid.*, pp. 146–47.   [6] *Bulletin of the Department of Welfare,* 1929.

women who are simply awaiting trial, with few exceptions, having no segregation of the unconvicted from the convicted, the well from the diseased, the *youngest* and most *impressionable* from the most degraded and hardened. Usually swarming with bedbugs, roaches, lice and other vermin; has an odor of disinfectant and filth, which is appalling; supports in complete idleness countless thousands of able-bodied men and women, and generally affords ample time and opportunity to assure inmates a course in every kind of viciousness and crime; a melting-pot in which the worst elements of the raw material in the criminal world are brought forth blended and turned out in absolute perfection.[7]

This book also gives many descriptions of jails in California, Kansas, Georgia, Indiana, Florida, North Dakota, Wisconsin, and North Carolina.

From the reports already cited it is clear that more than thirty years after the establishment of the first juvenile court, one of whose essential principles was separation of juvenile delinquents from the corrupting influences of adult offenders, many children in many states were still kept in jails. It is also clear that merely to make a law is not enough to guarantee that juvenile delinquents in detention will actually be treated so as to promote recovery from past delinquencies and to prevent further, and possibly more serious, bad citizenship. It is discouraging—but also stimulating to each of us to try to do something about it—to find that the same conditions which Miss Lathrop found in the 1890s in the counties of Illinois, which Boston women found in 1863 in the jails of Boston, and which led Charles Loring Brace in New York city in the 1850s to found the New York Children's Aid Society still prevail to some degree in many parts of the United States. Having personally received a nudge that even a good law is not enough, would not the next step be for each of us in his own community to make personal and group studies of what the facts about detention of juvenile delinquents in his own community actually are? We have seen from the few illustrations given that, in the past, in Chicago, New York, and Boston the motive power in the process of taking the next step toward better treatment of juvenile delinquents has come from persons who have seen with their own

[7] J. F. Fishman and Lee Perlman, *Crucibles of Crime: the Shocking Story of the American Jail*, New York, Cosmopolis Press, 1923, pp. 13–14.

eyes unsatisfactory treatment of children. As Miss Lathrop said about the first Chicago juvenile court, "The truth made public is the greatest aid toward social justice."

Worthy of note is the fact that in New York detention home care has been supplied from the beginning of the juvenile court in 1902 until the present time by the Society for the Prevention of Cruelty to Children, which began its work in Manhattan in 1875—the first branch of such work to be organized in the United States.

In the next chapter I shall quote what the 1899 Illinois Juvenile Court Law said about the third essential of such courts, namely, probation for juvenile delinquents, tell how such service was first established in Chicago, and then report in some detail my own personal relations to the Chicago court and to probation.

Chapter IX: PERSPECTIVES OF
A PROBATION OFFICER

THE ILLINOIS law of 1899 provided that "one or more discreet persons of good character" could be appointed or designated by the judge but could "receive no compensation from the public treasury." The law as amended and in force July 1, 1905, made provision for the public pay of probation officers "in counties having over five hundred population." This amendment applied only to Cook County, in which Chicago is located. In the other counties the judge could designate or appoint persons to serve as probation officers if they could be paid by private agencies. The duties of the probation officers were defined in the new Illinois law, Section 6, as follows:

In case a probation officer shall be appointed by any court it shall be the duty of the clerk of the court, if practicable, to notify the said probation officer in advance when any child is to be brought before the court; it shall be the duty of the said probation officer to make such investigation as may be required by the court; to be present in court in order to represent the interest of the child when the case is heard; to furnish to the court such information and assistance as the judge may require; and to take charge of any child before and after trial, as may be directed by the court.[1]

The clerk was to notify the probation officer that a certain child was to come into the court on a certain day, since the law provided that "any reputable citizen resident of the county" could file with the clerk a petition to the judge asking that a child should be brought before him for hearing. It should therefore be noted that the probation officer himself, as a discreet citizen, was also in fact able to file such a petition. In practice, it soon worked out that probation officers filed most of the petitions or coöperated with parents, guardians, custodians, or others when they filed petitions.

As there was at first no pay for probation officers from the public

[1] Hurley, *Origin of the Illinois Juvenile Court Law*, pp. 124 ff.

treasury, and as the objects of the new court in the care and treatment of children could not be carried out without probation officers,
the latter were provided in the following ways. Hull House provided
one of the first probation officers, Mrs. Alzina Stevens. Other private
agencies assigned members of their staffs to be probation officers,
notably the Visitation and Aid Society, of which the first chief probation officer, Timothy D. Hurley, was the head; and the Children's
Home and Aid Society, of which Dr. Hastings H. Hart was the
head. There was also a police probation officer designated from each
of the police court districts of the city and paid by the city.

We are further told by Mrs. Bowen, whose story of the setting up
of the first Chicago juvenile detention home has already been cited,
that the Juvenile Court Committee also:

. . . raised the money for the salaries of other probation officers, beginning with five and ending, July 1, 1905, with twenty-two. It called an
educator, Mr. Henry W. Thurston, to be chief probation officer. . . .
It also paid an assistant chief probation officer and the salaries of one or
two clerks in the court. During this time the probation officers were most
carefully selected by the Juvenile Court Committee. They met frequently
at Hull House and we talked to them on their duties. We really knew
absolutely nothing about such duties. There was no literature on Juvenile
courts at that time, nor on probation officers, and those of us who had
the training of these officers had to fall back on our knowledge of human
nature and on our best thought as to their duties.[2]

What the best thought of the Juvenile Court Committee at that
time was, as to the duties of probation officers, Mrs. Bowen states as
follows:

Mrs. Alzina Stevens was perhaps the best example of what a probation
officer should be. Her great desire was to be of use to her fellow men. Her
love of children was great; her singleness of purpose and strength of
character so remarkable that she exerted a great influence over the children
committed to her charge. . . . I find among some old papers the follow-

[2] Jane Addams and others, *The Child, the Clinic and the Court*, p. 299. There had
been two chief probation officers previous to my appointment in March, 1905. Timothy
D. Hurley, the first, was followed by J. J. McManaman; both were lawyers. In July,
1905, all of the probation officers that had been paid by the Juvenile Court Committee, including myself, so far as they were reappointed after civil service examination, came under the pay of Cook County.

ing concerning the duties of probation officers: "They must be men and women of many sides, endowed with the strength of a Samson and the delicacy of an Ariel. They must be tactful, skillful, firm and patient. They must know how to proceed with wisdom and intelligence and must be endowed with that rare virtue, common sense.

"These qualities would seem to be needed just as much today as they were twenty-five years ago." [3]

The reader who has followed our story carefully up to this point may well pause and ask this question, which I myself, since 1905, have often asked: How many of these policemen, social settlement workers, workers in child-protective and foster-care agencies, and teachers were equal to the jobs they faced more than thirty years ago? Would the reader of these words, if he, with all he knows today, stood in the shoes of one of these probation officers, be equal to that officer's job? In 1905, no one of us had more than an inkling of the complex causes of delinquency that were mentioned in Chapter II. The job was at least suggested in the words of the law (Section 1 and Section 6):

The words delinquent child shall mean any male child who, while under the age of seventeen years, or any female child, who, while under the age of eighteen years, violates any law of this state, or is incorrigible, or knowingly associates with thieves, vicious or immoral persons; or without just cause and without the consent of his parents, guardian or custodian absents himself from its home or place of abode, or is growing up in idleness or crime, or knowingly frequents any saloon or dram shop where intoxicating liquors are sold; or patronizes or visits any public pool room or bucket shop; or wanders about the streets in the night time without being on any lawful business or lawful occupations; or habitually wanders about any railroad yards or jumps or attempts to jump onto any moving train; or enters any car or engine without lawful authority; or uses vile, obscene, vulgar, or indecent language in any public place or about any school house; or is guilty of indecent or lascivious conduct; any child committing any of these acts herein mentioned shall be deemed a delinquent child and shall be cared for as such in the manner hereinafter provided . . . at any time after the filing of the petition and pending the final disposition of the case, the court may continue the hearing from time to time and allow such a child to remain in the possession of its custodian or in its own home subject to the friendly visitation of a probation officer;

[3] *Ibid.*, p. 300.

or it may order such a child to be placed in the custody of a probation officer of the court, or of any other suitable person appointed by the court, or to be kept in some suitable place provided by the City or County authorities [italics by H. W. T.].[4]

Incidentally, an interesting query for each of us is how many girls under eighteen and boys under seventeen do we personally know who could not have been haled into the first juvenile court under one or more of the above counts? How many of the readers, when young, if detected, could have escaped?

Section 6 of the law, quoted at the beginning of this chapter, defines the duty of a probation officer; with the authority of the court behind him, he was given the job of influencing the delinquent boy or girl, by means of "friendly visitation" or otherwise, not to repeat the delinquent act which brought him or her into court or to commit other delinquent acts named in the law.

To aid us in judging the probable competence of the reader and the early Chicago probation officers in this job of reform of juvenile delinquents, let us look at the cases of twenty-two boys and girls involved in the fifteen hearings described by the third visitor to the Chicago court in the fall of 1901, whose report for the afternoon session was quoted in Chapter VII. Some of these children had never been sent to an institution and were put on probation; some were being released from the John Worthy School and were put on parole; some were being sent to other institutions but might later be paroled. Each probation officer, as a rule, had in care some delinquent youths who were technically on probation and some who were technically on parole after experience in an institution. In both cases the powers and duties of the probation officer in respect to the child were practically the same.

After he has read the impressionistic report of the visitor on each case, many such questions as the following might occur to the reader if the youth mentioned were to be put on probation or parole to him:

Cases 1 and 4.—Have I *all* of the *same causal factors* in delinquency to deal with during my "friendly visitations" to Louis that I have

---

[4] Hurley, *op. cit.*

with Alexander, merely because I know that the father of each is dead and that each boy has struck at his mother? If not, why not? If I had been a probation officer in 1901 how much would I have known about social case work? About mental hygiene?

Case 2.—What characteristics other than that of "refinement" and father dead has Roy's home? What reasons are there for thinking that Roy will behave better after his third stay in the John Worthy Home than after his second? In what ways will my "friendly visitation" of Roy be more than a social call?

Case 3.—Is Arthur a young Benjamin Franklin or an embryo junkman? What difference does the answer to this question make to Arthur and to me?

Case 5.—Why does the judge think that a woman can do more for Tony than a man? What do I think about it? How shall I proceed?

Case 6.—Is the supposed ignorance of American laws and customs of Arabian immigrants the only problem I have to deal with in my probationary care of Milo and Elie? If not, what other problems are suggested and what means of solution are in my power? For example, if the family is desperately poor, what can I do about it?

Case 7.—What connection is there in John's mind and feeling between his fear of his father and his stealing and between both and his running to the home of his grandmother? What relations between John and his father, John and his mother, John and his grandmother, and what relations between father, mother, and grandmother shall I try to bring about in the course of my "friendly visitations"?

Case 8.—Why did the judge think Kitty not wholly bad? Do I agree with the judge? What difference does one belief or the other make in my probationary responsibility for Kitty?

Case 9.—What kind of sickness? How well equipped is the hospital to deal with this sickness? Is that any of my business? What was done with the thief? By whom? Is that any of my business? Why?

Case 10.—Should the judge and I treat these four boys alike? Why? Or why not? What other experiences besides stealing grain have these four boys had together? What difference to my work does a knowledge of this fact make? What were they planning to do with the grain? What difference does this fact make to me? Are the schools which Harry and Joseph disliked interested in these boys? How? What should be their attitude? What can I do about it?

Case 11.—What other recreations were available to Florence besides visiting saloons and gambling houses? What difference does the fact make to me as a probation officer in this district? What ought I and can I do about it? What laws and police control are in operation as to admission of juveniles to saloons and gambling houses? How much can a judge and a probation officer know about a girl's nature, education, and refinement by a few glances at her face in a courtroom?

Case 12.—Why did these boys steal the horse and carriage? What substitutes for satisfying this urge does the community furnish? Should these three boys all be treated alike while on parole? Why? How are the churches and schools with which these boys had some connection concerned over their future? Of what concern are their attitudes to me?

Case 13.—What connection is there in William's mind among his experiences—in a home without a mother, sleeping in the streets, burglary, and stealing from a cash drawer? What help is the John Worthy School in making a good citizen of William?

Case 14.—How do the steady churchgoing parents account for the fact that their boys slept in alleys? Of what service had two probation officers and the John Worthy School been to George in the direction of helping him to be a good citizen? Why or why not?

Case 15.—Why do the parents ask that Susie be sent to an institution? What does Susie think of her parents? What else could Susie do in her neighborhood except associate with men and women who were "bad"? Can the parents and the probation officer help to change conditions in the neighborhood? How?

One chance visitor to the early Chicago juvenile court for one afternoon has thus, in one report, given vivid glimpses of the fact that the court and its probation officers faced the most fundamental causal problems of human behavior as this behavior is determined by the personality of each individual. Each individual is shaped by his heredity and prenatal environment and is modified for years by the postnatal environment of home, industrial order, school, church, and all other personal and community influences.

In brief, to the seeing eye, these twenty-two children, even as described by the reporter, gave vivid illustration of the fact that those early probation officers could only be equal to their job of making good citizens out of bad juvenile citizens if they were capable of understanding each child as a "total personality in a total situation," and not only capable of such understanding, but, having understood, in such command of personal and other environmental resources that they could change the interactions between an individual and his environment. That the reader may clearly realize some of the other handicaps of these probation officers of more than thirty years ago, I shall describe some of my own experiences and give some quotations from my probation reports as printed in the Cook County Charity Reports. Such descriptions and quotations will also give the reader a basis for comparison of work in the Chicago Juvenile Court during its first decade with what had gone before, what has gone on since, and what the reader thinks should go on in his community in the future, both to treat and to prevent juvenile delinquency.

For example, when I first entered the Chicago court as chief probation officer appointed by Judge Julian W. Mack, March, 1905, nearly six years after the court began to function, I doubt if any of our probation-officer staff knew anything about social case work. Miss Mary E. Richmond's two books, *Social Diagnosis* (1917) and *What Is Social Case Work* (1922), were still more than a decade ahead. The Binet-Simon mental tests were not available in the United States until they were translated by E. S. Kite at Vineland, New Jersey, in 1916. Dr. William Healy's Juvenile Psychopathic Clinic, the first such clinic in any juvenile court in the United States, was not set up in the Chicago court until 1909; and, in general, the judges, the probation officers themselves, and the public looked upon probation officers, not as we now look upon social workers, but as officers of a court having authority, however kindly and civil or chancery this authority and procedure might be, in contrast to criminal court authority and procedure.

In fact, one of the greatest difficulties of probation officers in my time in Chicago (1905–8) came from one of the practices of the Chicago Bureau of Charities, as the Family Welfare Society of that period was called. This practice was to have a petition filed in the Juvenile Court charging neglect of a child or children whose parent or parents had not proven responsive to their suggestions. When such cases were heard in the Juvenile Court the decision often was that the children be allowed still to live at home but that they be on probation to a probation officer. The Bureau of Charities record was marked "Closed—taken to—or transferred to—the Juvenile Court." The purpose of all this was to get authority over the parents and the child. The result, in actual practice, often was to transfer the care and responsibility for many a family situation that had proven too difficult for the Bureau of Charities officers to the shoulders of probation officers who at that time were much less skillful "case workers" than those who had up to that time failed on these cases. My suggestion to Ernest P. Bicknell, then Superintendent of the Bureau of Charities, was that some of his family workers be commissioned as probation officers and that the neglected children of the difficult families be put on probation to his own officers, who already knew the situation in detail, thus giving them the authority they thought necessary. Needless to say, this suggestion, made in good humor and in good faith by a neophyte in social work, was not accepted by Bicknell. Accordingly, the early probation officers of the Chicago court, in addition to their delinquent children, also had in fact many very difficult parents, brought to them on the shoulders of so-called dependent and neglected children.

If the reader is to visualize the kind of job these early probation officers faced, two other aspects of their work should be considered: the large number of neglected and delinquent boys and girls that were committed to the officer's care; and the demands of their work as investigators of new complaints about children in their district.

First, as to number of cases: at the close of the year 1905 the average number of children on probation to each of the twenty-two officers paid by Cook County (since July, 1905) was one hundred. Earlier in the year, before a systematic clearing of records had been made, the number was much greater. One officer, Joe Riddle, who lived at Hull House, carried on his list three hundred children. Up to 1905, children were put on probation or parole for an indefinite period.

This period was ended only by a repeated offense, which resulted in a new petition, a new hearing, and often a commitment to an institution; or else, in the midst of more pressing duties, the "friendly visitations" of the officer gradually ceased and the child was practically off the probation officer's mind.

In addition to these officers who were paid by the county, there were fifteen others who, gratuitously or paid by private funds, gave part of their time to probation work. Also in the fifteen police districts of the city there were twenty-three police officers who were commissioned as Juvenile Court probation officers. Altogether, in addition to the 2,213 children on probation to the twenty-two regular officers, 1,012 other children were on probation to police and to the fifteen part-time officers.

The lowering of the average number to one hundred children per officer at the close of 1905 was a result of a request by the chief probation officer that each officer scan his list carefully and retain only those for whom he was in fact still actively at work. The others were made subject to a court order "Dismissed from Probation" and duly so recorded by the clerk of the court. Thereafter each officer's list of children was kept cleared by court order made on the officer's recommendation, and the children were either dismissed from probation or committed to some institution. The number of children left in his care was still too large, on the average, for the officer to bring about those magical changes in personality and environment which the bad behavior of the children indicated were desirable.

Second, as to investigation of new complaints against children or their parents. Of this work my report of 1905 as chief probation officer has this to say:

A third task, fully as important and sometimes of greater magnitude than either of the other two [probationary care of delinquent children and authoritative supervision of incapable and neglectful parents], is thrown upon the shoulders of the probation officer. Hundreds of complaints about dependent or delinquent children come into the office of the Chief Probation Officer every year. From July 1, 1905, to December 31, 1905, 700 such complaints were filed. Each was referred to the officer of the district for investigation and report. Many more such cases come directly to the attention of the officers in their own districts, especially to the police probation officers. In these cases many were brought informally before the police judges who gave their advice and influence in informal hearings, and were supposed to order petitions filed to bring only the more serious cases to the Juvenile Court. There was a great variety of practice and attitude toward children among the police probation officers and police judges. The more efficient these officers and judges were, the greater the percentage of such cases settled to the best interest of the child, without bringing him into the Juvenile Court.[5]

For further facts regarding the actual work being done by the probation officers at that time, other extracts from my Chicago Juvenile Court reports are now quoted. Some opinions of later dates, even up to the present, will later be given for comparison.

During 1905, 4088 new cases have been filed. This means a small army of children equal to the total membership of four great public schools, each of twenty rooms, fifty children to a room; in other words, the equivalent of the pupils of eighty public school teachers, have for the first time filed before the judge of the Juvenile Court.

To this number must be added truant cases, those who have had their cases continued, for a second and third hearing, and those "repeaters" who have been before the judge at a later date on a new petition.

These truant and rehearing cases, added to the number of cases cited above, make the total number of hearings in which an order was given 5051 for the year.

As each child is accompanied, on the average, by at least two relatives or acquaintances, in addition to the officers, the number of persons in the County who have got impressions of the Juvenile Court procedure cannot be estimated at less than fifteen thousand. To so conduct the Court that a maximum effect in the direction of good citizenship shall be produced, not only upon the children, but upon their parents and guardians, is a task worthy the best thought and effort of all responsible officials.

To this end, the fundamental question for the Judge and Probation Officers must, in the light of all the facts in the case, always be "What is best for this child?" No consideration of any sort that cannot abide the test of this question should be urged or treated with respect in the Juvenile Court.[6]

The life of each paroled child (and child on probation) is in some sort of tangle. It is the delicate and difficult task of the Probation Officer to

[5] Henry W. Thurston, "Report of the Chief Probation Officer," *Cook County Charity Report,* 1905, p. 96.

[6] *Ibid.,* p. 95.

become such a friend to the child that he is able to see the cause of the tangle. Then the Probation Officer must, in person, or with the aid of others, strive to remove these causes of evil and misfortune and surround him with helpful people and uplifting conditions. In some cases, if the child is to be saved to his better self, this watchful care must be kept up for years.

Only the highest type of men and women can make ideal officers. Among other characteristics that should be thought of as essential in such officers are: good health, sound common sense, love for children, sufficient education for accuracy and rapidity in making out papers and reports, such an idea of the importance of the work that conscience will not permit him to neglect anything within his power for the good of the child, and such a broad gauge view of social classes, nationalities, politics, religion, etc. that he can get into sympathy and harmonious working relations with every person and institution in his district that can possibly be of service in upbuilding the life of any child.[7]

The following extract refers to the inchoate beginnings in Chicago of a work that was more definitely organized in New York by Ernest Coulter, clerk of the Children's Court and named by him the "Big Brother Movement," which was followed by the "Big Sisters."

In harmony with the parents, the school, and the rabbi, minister or priest of the special parish in which each paroled child (or child on probation) lives, there should be a group of the best men and women upon whom the Probation Officers could call for special help in the form of employment, material aid or personal friendship for the children under parole. These volunteer helpers should at all times work under the legal Probation Officers and in no case enter a family as a dictator, a meddler or for curiosity. Unless they can bring some new help into the life of the child with such delicate tact that he and his guardians do not resent it, they will not succeed. There are about seventy-five such helpers already working. Each helper, as a rule, has only one or two cases.[8]

Of the relation of the Juvenile Court to the schools, factory inspectors, county court, and other groups, this 1905 report made the following statements:

Truancy, dependency and delinquency of children are closely related. The Compulsory Education Department of the Board of Education looks after truancy, and the Probation Officers have jurisdiction over dependents and

[7] *Ibid.*, p. 96.   [8] *Ibid.*, p. 98.

delinquents. Sometimes a child is a truant, dependent and delinquent at the same time. For the sake of the child the closest cooperation is necessary.

Often the teacher is the strongest ally of the Probation Officer. Unless each can work in such a way as to strengthen the influence of the other, the child suffers. [In that day, schools had no visiting teachers.]

The Factory Inspectors run across many cases of dependent and delinquent children, which they report to the Juvenile Court. Probation Officers likewise find many labor conditions for which they invite the aid of the Factory Inspector.

As the County Attorney prosecutes fathers for the non-support of their children and the County Court takes affidavits as to the age of children who desire to get a work certificate, there is also frequent interchange of cases between Probation Officers and these two branches of the County service.[9]

As if in anticipation of Clifford Shaw's studies of delinquency areas about twenty-five years later, and in recognition of the need for small parks and playgrounds that would be easily accessible to children in every section of the city, this brief word was spoken:

The congested centers of population furnish more than their share of court wards. As the positive opportunities for activity, play and education in a neighborhood increase, the percentage of delinquent boys and girls decreases. The Juvenile Court therefore urges the extention of small parks and playgrounds to every section of the city.[10]

Queries for the reader: To what extent are the above suggested cooperations between juvenile courts and other community agencies now adequate to the needs of all children in your community? Why? Or why not? What business of yours are such matters?

Alas, that the following statement should ever have seemed to an officer of the Chicago court a step ahead:

In addition to the Court files and records required by law which are kept by the Clerks of the Court, I have begun two forms of record for each child for the use of Probation Officers. 1. A card catalogue which gives the present address and brief summary of the case to date for every child. 2. A folder for each child which, containing reports from Probation Officers, is filed in such a way as to show at any time all the children in the care of an officer or institution.

[9] *Ibid.*, pp. 98–99.   [10] *Ibid.*, p. 99.

Beginning with November, 1905, a monthly meeting of Probation Officers for the study and discussion both of the internal work of the Court and its relation to other important phases of work for the children was started.[11]

But again, alas, the probation officer's record was little more than a mechanical device for record by check, in an appropriate column and line, of such activities as "visited child at home," "child reported," "visited school," and "visited employer." Almost nothing was recorded to show that the probation officer understood the causes of the child's delinquency, what he and others had tried to do for the good of the child, or the occasions of these recorded contacts and interviews. As was said before, we knew nothing of social case work as it is understood today. We might well have studied with more care and discussed more earnestly in our probation officers' monthly meetings the meanings of such statistics as those of Table 2.[12]

TABLE 2. DELINQUENTS AND DEPENDENTS IN COURT 1904–6

Appearance in Court	*1904*	*1905*	*1906*
		DELINQUENT BOYS	
First	885	1927	1300
Second	324	381	433
Third	180	194	201
Fourth	97	84	106
Fifth	59	41	49
Sixth	0	15	21
Seventh	0	6	11
Eighth	0	0	8
Ninth	0	0	2
		DELINQUENT GIRLS	
First	275	345	348
Second	79	81	91
Third	0	20	15
Fourth	0	8	7
Fifth	0	1	0
Sixth	0	0	1
Seventh	0	0	2

[11] *Ibid.*, p. 99.
[12] *Report of the Clerk of the Juvenile Court of Cook County, Illinois, 1906*, p. 17. Reprinted by the Juvenile Court Committee.

Appearance in Court	1904	1905	1906
		DEPENDENT BOYS	
First	773	953	881
Second	125	221	249
Third	0	35	78
Fourth	0	3	29
		DEPENDENT GIRLS	
First	659	859	692
Second	71	189	201
Third	0	35	63
Fourth	0	5	11

In most of the cases filed as "Dependents" there was really some form of parental incompetency or neglect. Note that the number of dependent girls nearly equals that of dependent boys, while delinquent girls are far less numerous than delinquent boys.

How optimistic we were is indicated by this entry:

To one who sees only dependent and delinquent children, unworthy parents and the pathos of the family separations, a session of the Juvenile Court seems a continual tragedy. But to him who likewise sees the institutions and agencies through which the parental love of society stretches out the helping hand to every kind of juvenile misfortune and mistakes, the Juvenile Court seems to be in a truer sense an open door of hope.[13]

Two questions for the reader are: (1) What, in your opinion, do their experiences in court, as they today file through, do to the juveniles and adults in your own community, as regards citizenship? (2) In what ways in your community can the parental love of society stretch out its helping hand in the more efficient prevention of juvenile misfortune and mistake?

The Juvenile Court Not a Cure-All but a Challenge to Existing Institutions and Agencies

As evidence of at least the beginning of a reaction against the community feeling that the new Juvenile Court, with its chancery procedure, its effort to segregate youth from habitual delinquents and

---

[13] Thurston, "Report . . . ," 1905, p. 95.

criminals, and its earnest but largely untrained corps of probation officers was to be a cure-all for the woes and sins of youth, the following citations are given from a paper which I wrote after I had been chief probation officer of the Chicago Juvenile Court for a year and a half. After my comparatively quiet and safe experiences in country schools, small-town and city high schools, and a city normal school, my entrance into the work of the Juvenile Court was like a sudden plunge into a maelstrom of hitherto unknown human activities, failures, successes, fears, hopes, frustrations, aspirations. Some of my own current reactions to the situations were stated as follows:

One who has worked for even a little time in the Juvenile Court becomes more and more strengthened in the opinion that, while institutional care of children must always be kept up, and while the probationary care of the child with all the supplementary forms of service must be developed to the highest degree of efficiency, after all, both forms of care of children are to a very great degree only palliative and unsatisfactory. Such a worker feels more and more keenly the force of the Biblical injunction, "These things ought ye to have done, and not to leave the other undone." In short, *the Juvenile Court is a challenge to existing institutions* [italics in the original].

Inquiry must be directed toward all forms of preventive and constructive work in behalf of the child, to the end that a smaller percentage of children shall become dependent and delinquent. *During every Court day the failure of every institution of society with reference to some particular child is revealed to the Judge and probation officers of the Juvenile Court.* [Italics not in the original.] It is, therefore, inevitable that the same social spirit which created the Juvenile Court law and the probation system will not be satisfied by palliative measures. The mere act of massing juvenile misfortune and delinquency of a great city or town in one room is a great social object lesson, and will of itself lead to the inquiry, "How can this be stopped?"

The phenomena of child misfortune are for the first time being brought, by the machinery of the Juvenile Court, forcibly to the attention of all intelligent and philanthropic members of society. The next steps in the Juvenile Court movement may, therefore, confidently be expected in the direction, not only of perfecting the institutional and probationary care of children, but in preventive measures. Illustrations of this are being manifested in several directions. For the last two or three years Judge Lindsey of Denver, the high priest of the Juvenile Court movement, has been developing the Juvenile Improvement Association, which is devoted to the protection of the children of Denver against every destructive tendency, and toward furnishing to them the best possible positive means of development.

During the month of April, 1906, there has also been organized in Chicago a similar incorporated organization, known as the Juvenile Protective League.

Three of the objects of this League, as stated in its by-laws, are as follows:—

1. To suppress and prevent conditions and to prosecute persons contributing to the dependency and delinquency of children.

2. To cooperate with the Juvenile Court, compulsory education department, State factory inspector, and all other child-helping agencies.

3. To promote the study of child-problems and by systematic agitation, through the press and otherwise, to create a permanent public sentiment for the establishment of wholesome, uplifting agencies, such as parks, playgrounds, gymnasiums, free baths, vacation schools, communal social centers, and the like.

The directors of this League have been chosen from the strongest and most efficient workers in behalf of childhood in the City of Chicago.

Some of the concrete ways in which such movements will doubtless find expression are as follows:

a. The concentration of the attention of all classes of social workers upon the improvement of the home in all possible ways. A fit home for every child is a social necessity.

b. A re-examination of the function of the school, to the end that a smaller and smaller percentage of the children shall become truant and delinquent. Society cannot long tolerate the suspension of troublesome children from the public schools.[14]

c. A more careful study of the relation of the church to the problems of childhood, especially as related to the Sunday School and other religious exercises and activities of the Church.

d. A stimulation of the movement for an adequate play opportunity for every child.

e. A similar stimulus toward such municipal sanitation, inspection of food supply, and control of diseases as will permit a normal percentage of children to survive.

f. A more efficient charitable organization, especially in relation to the responsibility of adults for the dependency of children.

[14] This had been a frequent practice in the Chicago schools, with the result that many such suspended children got into some kind of trouble and were brought into the Juvenile Court and unloaded upon that new community agency.

g. Criticism and control of the industrial order, so far as it tends to destroy children.

h. A frank and full discussion of the sex question as related to birth control and education of children.

In short the chief social significance of the Juvenile Court movement in connection with the child-labor movement and the compulsory education movement, is to be found in the inevitable educational effect upon the intelligence and conscience of society. Because of the juvenile court we shall the sooner become convinced that the proper genesis and education of children is the biggest job ahead.[15]

As I read these words, penned by me more than thirty years ago, several mental comments occur to me that I venture to share with the reader:

1. How much of the above was written by a poor "George" with an inferiority complex as a sort of defense reaction against the community that had in the spirit of the saying "Oh, let George do it" expected the Juvenile Court to do impossible things?

2. Was not the writer himself just about as blind as the public had been in respect to the Juvenile Court, when he in turn implied that a new "George" in the form of the Juvenile Protective League could and would make rapid progress in the solution of the problems that both the community and the Juvenile Court had thus far failed to solve?

3. Was it not true, is it not now true, and will it not in the future always be true, that, only as the writer, the reader, and other individuals, as the home, school, church, and other social, industrial, and civic groups—in fact, all organized groups of individuals—stop saying, "Let George do it," and all of us do our utmost for the welfare of children—only then will the welfare of all children in fact be assured?

4. What are some of the evidences that some progress in this job has been made in the last thirty years?

5. Where and how does the reader think that he personally can "get into the game" most effectively?

The view that the work of the juvenile court was, and can be, but

[15] Thurston, "The Social Significance of the Juvenile Court," *Illinois School Review*, Vol. XIV, No. 6, June, 1906.

one step in the right direction in the care of neglected and delinquent children was confirmed by an intensive study of the methods and results of the work done by the Chicago Juvenile Court during its first ten years. In the Introduction to this study Miss Julia C. Lathrop says:

While the study gives reason for going forward in the direction already taken it shows no cure-all. It makes the question of youthful delinquency very searching and subtle, not to be solved by any court or system of institutions, or probation, or otherwise contrivances, attempted or substituted for wholesome, orderly, decent family life. These contrivances wholly restore some children, partly restore others, and sometimes fail; but they never seal up the sources of delinquency.[16]

After the brief account I have given of the treatment of bad young citizens preceding the juvenile court era, of some steps toward ushering in this era, of the essential principles of the Juvenile Court Law, of some early observations and comment on the actual work of this court, and, finally, of some opinions as to the necessarily limited place of the juvenile court in the whole program of securing adequate welfare for every dependent, neglected, and delinquent child, I continue this chapter with some evidence both of progress and of failure during the last thirty years. Here, in my 1907 "Report," are some further early expressions of my own opinions:

When we succeed . . . it is partly by social contact, inhibitions, prohibitions, but more frequently and more surely by leading the way and making possible other forms of self-expression and activity than had been possible before, until the abnormal, unbalanced tendency to some form of delinquency loses its dominant hold upon the boy or girl. As preventive measures—the school, home, neighborhood, church, and municipality (business?) have as yet great unfulfilled possibilities to furnish a sufficiently varied and genuine opportunity for life to young people so as to reduce to a minimum the number of those who unwittingly run toward death in search of life.

As Tennyson says:
> " 'Tis life whereof our nerves are scant
> More life and fuller that we want."

If the decrease in the number of new cases filed as recorded on page

[16] Breckinridge and Abbott, *The Delinquent Child and the Home,* New York, Russell Sage Foundation, 1912, p. 9.

125 means that probation officers, police and citizens generally are failing to do their full duty, and as a consequence, the children of Cook County are increasingly neglected, this decrease is a sign of failure and should stimulate all concerned to a more faithful performance of duty. If, on the other hand, the decrease, instead of being accompanied by increasing neglect of the welfare of children, is in fact attended by better and more discriminating care of dependent and neglected children, the decrease in numbers is a sign of genuine progress. It is perhaps too early to say with authority which interpretation is the true one. In either case, the needs of the children are far greater than the services of officers and citizens combined, and there should be no cessation of effort in their behalf. Three thousand, two hundred and sixty-six new cases of dependent and delinquent children in one year in any twentieth century city are just 3,266 too many. Every one of them is the product of one or more imperfect institutions.

Every one of them is a challenge to us to build such homes, schools, business organizations, political administrations and churches that no child shall be thrown out as a waste by-product of our imperfect social machinery. It is up to this community to prove during the coming years, that we can continue to reduce the percentage of new cases in the Juvenile Court and at the same time raise the standard of welfare for the average child.[17]

The foregoing quotations from my written statements give the perspectives I formed during the first decade of this century. I close this chapter with the perspective of one of my students twenty-four years after the above report was written.[18]

"If" for a Probation Officer

If you can use your heart when all about you
Have silenced theirs and think you sentimental too;
If you can trust your boy when all men doubt him
And let him see you really trust him too;
If you can know large victory comes by small ones
Yet always keep the larger one in view:
If you can wait results with endless patience
Yet never feel that waiting's all to do;
If you can praise the lad when praise is needed
Yet never let him feel that victory's easily won;

[17] "Report of the Chief Probation Officer," *Cook County Charity Report,* 1907.

[18] While the students in some of my classes were, in times past, discussing with me the problem of juvenile delinquency, I asked them to write parodies on Kipling's poem "If." This poem by Miss Bland Morrow is typical of the scores that I received.

If you can let him blunder when so doing
He'll know himself the stronger once the task is done;
If you can see him fail and then repeat his failures
Yet keep your courage and sustain his courage too;
If you can see beneath his awkward strivings
The same impulse that motivates you too;
If you can get him thrills that hurt not him or others
And help him fill his days with zestful things to do;
If you can represent for him adulthood
Possessing poise and vigor and an appetite for fun;
If you can help him see himself becoming
The victorious person he really would become;
You'll then discharge in part your duty
And help to make a social being out of him!

Chapter X: THE JUVENILE COURT
AT THE BAR

D R. WILLIAM HEALY gave some of the first authoritative
evidence of the failure of the Chicago Juvenile Court to treat
many individual juvenile delinquents so as to prevent further delinquencies by them. Mention of Dr. Healy's entrance to the court
is made by Dr. James A. Britton, house physician for the Juvenile
Detention Home, as follows: "The Chicago Psychopathic Institute
has through its physician, Dr. William Healy, started and is now
carrying on a remarkable piece of work in connection with the
Juvenile Court. Dr. Healy is making an exhaustive study of habitual
offenders, both as to their physical and mental conditions. No effort
or time is spared in an attempt to determine the cause of delinquency
in each case." [1]

As I left the court during 1908, some of the cases of habitual delinquency that Dr. Healy began to study were boys and girls that
my fellow probation officers and I had failed to help during my years in
the court. Data for Dr. Healy's first book, *The Individual Delinquent,*
were therefore to some degree furnished him by our inefficiency.
Furthermore, Dr. Healy went to Boston in 1917 and in *Delinquents
and Criminals: Their Making and Unmaking* (1926) compared the
later careers of Chicago delinquent children, whom he began to
study in 1909, with the careers of Boston delinquent children, so that
the probation work of my day in Chicago was somewhat under
scrutiny in this book also. Dr. Healy's diagrams of the number of
experiences of juvenile "repeaters" in Chicago courts and Illinois
institutions and his findings of far less effective work in Chicago than
in Boston were such as to cause cold chills to run up and down the
backs of Chicago probation officers and officials in charge of disciplinary institutions for youth in Illinois. For example, in his diagrams

[1] *Cook County Charity Report,* 1909, p. 89.

of failures in Chicago [2] he makes a pyramid on each page by noting on each line the initials of the successive probation and institutional experiences a boy or girl had had, those having had only one experience, or the fewest such experiences, on the top line and those having the largest number of such experiences on the bottom line. I give

MALES IN PENITENTIARY [3]

PRO-PEN

PRO-PLA-PEN

PRO-JWS-PEN

DEP-SC-PEN

PS-SC-JWS-PEN

SC-PLA-PEN-PEN

PRO-CT-SER-PEN

PRO-JWS-HC-PEN

DEP-JWS-HC-PEN-CT

PRO-PRO-JWS-PLA-PEN

PRO-PRO-HC-CT-PEN

PRO-SC-CT-HC-CT-PEN

fm-PRO-FM-FM-FM-CT-PEN

DEP-JWS-PRO-JWS-CT-PEN

PTL-PTL-PRO-PLA-REF-PEN-REF-PEN

PRO-PTL-SC-JWS-JWS-SC-PEN

DEP-PTL-JWS-DEP-PLA-HC-PEN-PEN

pS-PTL-PTL-JWS-PRO-SC-PEN

pp-DEP-PTL-JWS-PLA-SC-SC-SER-HC-REF-PEN-REF

PRO-PRO-PRO-PRO-PRO-JWS-JWS-REF-PEN

PRO-SC-PRO-SC-JWS-PLA-PRO-PRO-PRO-PRO-PRO-JWS-REF-PEN

DEP-DEP-PTL-PTL-JWS-JWS-JL-REF-REF-JL-REF-JL-HC-PEN

---

[2] Healy and Bronner, *Delinquents and Criminals: Their Making and Unmaking*, New York, Macmillan, 1926, pp. 284–311.

[3] Key to Abbreviations (*ibid.*, pp. 284–85).

PRO—Probation, as enumerated always meaning a new offense
PLA—Placing in foster home
DEP—Commitment to institution for dependents
JWS—Commitment to John Worthy School
SC —Commitment to St. Charles School for Boys
HC —Commitment to House of Correction

PTL—Parental school
REF—Reformatory
CT —Adult Court
FM —Institution for feeble-minded
JL —Adult county jail
SER —Army or navy service
ps —An individual showing signs of mental disease
pp —An individual of psychopathic personality
fm —A feeble-minded individual

herewith a sample page [4] of the successive court and other experiences of twenty-two Chicago boys all of whom were finally sent to the penitentiary. Each line gives in succession the court orders for a different boy and each order meant a new offense, the number of orders ranging from two to fourteen per boy.

As a one-time probation officer, I find myself looking again and again at the line next to the last in the above table; *this boy was placed on probation seven times.*

In another table in the same book I find this record for one boy: "Parental school, parental school, parental school, parental school, probation, probation, probation, probation, probation, St. Charles School for Boys, adult court, St. Charles, adult court." [5] Here the parental school and the St. Charles School for Boys share responsibility with the probation officers.

In short, these pyramids of experiences of the delinquent boys of Chicago whom Dr. Healy began to study in 1909 flash to the eye on every page the challenging question "Why such experiences?" I try to get comfort, though cold comfort it is, through reminding myself that only the most difficult cases known to the Chicago probation officers were brought to Dr. Healy's attention during those first years of his clinic in the Chicago court.

The comfort for early Chicago probation officers grows still colder when we read another table [6] by Dr. Healy. In this table, the facts of

TABLE 3. COMPARATIVE PAST JUVENILE RECORDS 1909–14

	Total Committed	Total Recommitted	To House of Correction	To State Reformatory	To State Prison	To County Jail
Chicago	420	157 (37%)	72	73	22	45
Boston	400	25 (6%)	14	10	0	6

which I present as Table 3, the later records of 420 Chicago boys who were in Dr. Healy's clinic 1909–14 are compared with the later records of 400 Boston boys "who constitute all the more serious repeated offenders who appeared in the Boston Juvenile Court from 1909–1914." [7]

[4] *Ibid.*, p. 300.   [5] *Ibid.*, p. 291.   [6] *Ibid.*, p. 67.   [7] *Ibid.*, p. 59.

Later in his report, Dr. Healy implies that the differences between Chicago and Boston in the treatment of delinquent and predelinquent youth were, in 1909–14 and later, not confined to differences in probation efficiency alone but included also differences in community resources and agencies for giving youth a more abundant life. This paragraph reads as follows:

From our analysis of comparative community backgrounds it is evident that social resources and agencies as they exist for recreational, educational, foster-home placing and other child welfare resources have very vital relationship to prevention, causation, and treatment of delinquency and crime. The much greater proportionate development of such resources for child welfare in the one community as correlated with the much better state of affairs in regard to delinquency and crime betokens a relationship of cause and effect.[8]

Boston should not become too smug because of its superiority over Chicago in its early success with juvenile delinquents; there is an intensive study, by the Gluecks in 1934, of the later Boston work of Dr. Healy's own clinic, of the Boston Juvenile Court, and of other agencies correlated therewith. Two extracts will here be quoted from this book, which, as well as the book by Dr. Healy previously cited, should be studied in detail by the reader. These extracts are especially pertinent to our discussion of treatment, since the juvenile court was founded for youth who are bad citizens, and since they reëcho our questions: Why such youth? And what further responsibility rests not only upon the juvenile court, but upon all citizens in all our communities, to help find the answer?

What was the conduct of our boys in the five-year post-treatment period? *Eighty-eight percent of them continued their delinquencies during this period.* They were arrested on the average of 3.6 times each, nor were the arrests of our youths essentially for petty offenses; two thirds of the entire group of 905 boys whose post-treatment conduct was determinable committed serious offenses, largely felonies. The major conclusion is inescapable then, *that the treatment carried out by clinic, court and associated community facilities had very little effect in preventing recidivism.* [Italics in the original.] [9]

[8] *Ibid.*, p. 211.

[9] Sheldon and Eleanor T. Glueck, *One Thousand Juvenile Delinquents: Their Treatment by Court and Clinic,* Cambridge, Harvard University Press, 1934, p. 233.

And second, for all of us who think the problem of making good citizens out of bad young citizens and of preventing the development of bad citizenship in youth is a simple one, comes this statement:

In brief, the success of the juvenile court does not depend exclusively, or even primarily, on the kindly and understanding interview that a wise and humanitarian judge has with a juvenile delinquent and his parents. It depends on the day-to-day treatment carried out by various officers and agencies after the judge has had his talk. Re-orientation of a personality, substitution of wholesome for morbid attitudes and habits, cannot be brought about in a half-hour or one-hour contact which a judge has with a child and his parents. It is a long and delicate process, requiring frequent adaptation of means to ends, ingenious changes of approach, the mutual cooperation and unflagging interest of probation officers, social workers, school teachers, parents and companions of the delinquent, and, in a certain proportion of cases, psychiatric therapy. Rehabilitation does not occur in the court-room; it occurs, if at all, in the home, the school, the playground or boy's club, the place of work. Hence it is futile to look for single nostrums that will "cure" delinquency. We are dealing with a complex problem; the stage on which the drama of personality distortion and unwholesome behavior is enacted is as broad as society and as deep as human nature.[10]

As to a division of responsibility, in the future, for the more successful treatment of juvenile delinquents, the Gluecks make this statement, which indicates once more the environmental circumstances which remain practically unchanged:

It is convenient to classify the forces and agencies responsible for the poor post-treatment results under the following general heads, always remembering that in each category we are dealing with a complex of interacting institutions and personalities:
1. Practices largely within the control of the court.
2. Practices largely within the control of the clinic.
3. Practices largely within the control of other social agencies, or of society in general.
4. Limitations in knowledge of human nature.[11]

In short, this study, by its iteration and reiteration of the complexity of the problem of making over youthful citizens who have been delinquent, shows that the juvenile court alone cannot do the

[10] *Ibid.*, pp. 260–61. [11] *Ibid.*, p. 243.

job. All of this also points unerringly to the great job of the future: to prevent delinquency and to educate in the positive activities of good citizenship.[12]

For comparison with the above-quoted opinions of the Gluecks, I cite a few words by a probation officer, who is himself up against the job, as to the complexity of the work of a really competent juvenile court probation officer:

Probation officers are not experts in law, education, medicine, psychiatry, economics, sociology, recreation or religion.

Practically all our clients need the guidance and assistance which only those who are thoroughly trained in the above sciences can offer.

It follows that one of the first duties of a probation officer is to acquaint himself fully with all community resources and policies, and to associate actively with other workers who are engaged in the general program of community improvement and human amelioration. . . . We must be the community links between the courts we serve and the social agencies in the interest of our clients and for the general welfare of our community.[13]

That a juvenile court judge does not need all the above qualifications if he is physically strong enough to use a strap on a boy was apparently the opinion of a New Jersey judge in 1932. What this judge did in court was reported in a newspaper, in substance as follows:

Three boys, twelve, fourteen, and fifteen years old, were in court for breaking the lock on a motion-picture theater exit door to see the

---

[12] The reader who is deeply interested in knowing the facts as to the weaknesses of our juvenile court procedure should read not only this study by the Gluecks but also some later comments by noted writers both for and against its findings. These include Richard Cabot, M.D., in the *Survey*, Feb., 1934, and June, 1934; Judge Henry L. Eastman, Cuyahoga County Juvenile Court, Cleveland, Ohio, in the *Survey*, June, 1934; David Dressler, Senior Parole Officer, New York State Division of Parole, in the *Survey*, June, 1934; George S. Stevenson, Director, Division on the Community Clinics, National Committee of Mental Hygiene, in the *Survey*, June, 1934; and Charles L. Chute, Executive Director, National Probation Association, in the *Survey*, April, 1934. A later study by Sheldon and Eleanor Glueck is *Juvenile Delinquents Grown Up*, Commonwealth Fund, 1940.

[13] William J. Harper, Director of Probation, Westchester County, N.Y., "The Criminal and Society," *Proceedings* of Gov. Herbert Lehman's Four-Day Conference on Crime, Albany, 1935, p. 1032. See also the suggestions for the training of probation officers put forth by a commission of which Mr. Harper was a member. This commission's report, *Sub-Committee on Content of the Committee on Training of Workers; Appointed by the New York State Conference on Social Work, 1936* (Albany, 1938), contains a valuable bibliography.

movie in a New Jersey town. The judge asked the mothers who were present if they thought the boys should be spanked. Upon their assent and promise to do it, the judge said he wanted to make sure and would do it himself. Having asked the police sergeant to give him his Sam Browne belt, the judge doubled the belt in his hand and directed the boys to take off their coats. Then he had the sergeant, a burly man, hold each of the boys during the whippings. With their distressed mothers looking on, the three hapless boys did not flinch as the judge wielded the belt ten times on each without attempting to lighten his stroke. The youngest boy of the trio gasped audibly as the strap fell on his back, but he held back his tears. The sentence meted out, the judge returned to his bench and the boys, with their mothers, left the courtroom, accompanied by more than a score of their schoolmates, some cheering and others jeering and hooting them.[14]

And now, having paused for the above interlude, I ask: How far toward an adequate performance of their complex tasks had our juvenile courts gone during the first third of the present century? An answer to this question was given in 1930 by Dr. Sophonisba P. Breckinridge. She describes their complexity and lack of coördination as follows:

While the court is, as has been said, a nation-wide expression of this determination to rescue the child from the criminal law and from the power of the irresponsible parent, it is not national. It is, on the contrary, a highly local institution—the judicial organization. There are forty-nine or fifty systems of courts and of law, if one counts in the District of Columbia, for by the appellate procedure, unity and uniformity of law within each of the several states may be secured, and the statute prescribes rules of procedure and practice, but juvenile courts, in other matters besides these, are more than courts of law. They are agencies of social practice. Lower courts are highly local, each a law unto itself. They have, therefore, the strength and the weakness of all local public authorities— namely a certain reality in expressing the will and thought of the locality —and a consequent wealth or poverty of ideal and achievement in accordance with the experience and resources of the community. There will be some courts expressive at points of the best and most forward looking thought, some which represent the poverty of the more remote past. . . .

The judges may organize to scrutinize themselves, but it is on the

[14] *New York Times,* February 17, 1932.

whole hardly possible to set up a supervisory authority over the judges and in the case of the probation staff there are less than half the states in which such an authority as a commission, as in Massachusetts or New York, or a state probation officer, as in Illinois or in California, has been provided. The lack of these central agencies means, as has been said, the greatest diversity in organization, personnel, professional attainments, and social resources, within the same state as well as divergencies between and among states.

The court, then is not only local; it is like all courts complicated. In order to understand the work of any court (this has been evident in the recent surveys of criminal justice or of civil practice), it is necessary to examine: first, the channels through which the parties came before the court, which means in the case of the juvenile court, the police who bring in the delinquent children, the relief or protective agencies which call attention to the dependent or neglected children; the organization of the detention places through which the children pass en route as it were, the officers of the court who receive complaints or petitions and make the initial investigation; second, the facilities offered to supplement or replace the lacking parental care or the substitutes in treatment for the punishment of the criminal law; third, the children in whose behalf the machinery is set in motion. This is the question of what the social workers when speaking of the ordinary agency or institution call the intake. With the children must be studied the neglectful or unfortunate parents who are said not to be giving the "proper parental care" and the injured persons who say that the children have broken the law. Fourth, how the court, which is deciding issues so momentous in the life of the child and of the community, is equipped to make the decision. What nature of evidence—social, mental, physical, domestic, legal—is laid before him or her as the case may be.

For every court one should know each of these features, and in every case the court is exactly as strong as its weakest link. From an analysis of the statutes it looks as though jurisdiction could be exercised by something like fifty-one different classes of courts. To say how many this means actually, it would be necessary to ask how many of each kind there are in a state. For example, there may be in Illinois, 101 county courts, 18 circuit courts, and as many city courts as happen to be created under a recent statute. There are in Arkansas 75, Colorado 63, Connecticut 8, and Kentucky 120 counties, and each may have a juvenile court. Thus one could go through the list.

It is, in fact, impossible without an examination in each state to know what the court actually is. In Alabama, for example, or Connecticut,

Delaware, Florida, Georgia, Indiana, Louisiana, Maryland, New Hampshire, New Jersey, New York, North Carolina, Ohio, Tennessee, Texas, Wisconsin, any one of several courts may exercise the jurisdiction.[15]

From the evidence I have submitted in this chapter it seems clear to me that the heading chosen for the chapter was a pertinent one. For this heading I am indebted to J. Prentice Murphy who, in 1929, wrote an article on "The Juvenile Court at the Bar." This article is encyclopedic, based on fifty-three different authorities and reports, from all of which he quotes. At the end, the author challenges us all to supplement the work of the juvenile courts and to surround the child with such home, community, and economic conditions as will make possible the rearing, not only of children who will be, negatively, nondelinquent—not-bad—citizens but who will be, positively, good citizens. Mr. Murphy says:

We need to be reminded of the fact that the quantity and quality of work in the Juvenile Courts are closely related to living conditions throughout these United States. When more people receive higher wages and are thus enabled to secure for themselves higher standards of living in terms of health, good housing, education, leisure, thus allowing the spiritual forces within them to develop, the work of the courts will be reduced to its limited and rightful place in the scheme of things.[16]

For another challenge to us to supplement the work, not only of juvenile courts but also of criminal courts for adults, with such constructive community agencies and conditions as Murphy suggested, I now cite from an address given in 1935 by the then New York State Commissioner of Correction, Austin H. MacCormick. His address on "Revenge or Reform" was given before the 65th Annual Congress of the American Prison Association in Atlanta, Georgia.

The criminal comes predominantly from the underprivileged groups; from those people who live on the economic fringe; from the unskilled and poorly educated laboring group; from the poorer parts of town, no matter what town or how big the town may be; from the families whose homes

---

[15] Sophonisba P. Breckinridge, "A Reëxamination of the Work of the Children's Courts," *Year Book of the National Probation Association,* 1930, pp. 52–65.

[16] J. Prentice Murphy, "The Juvenile Court at the Bar," *Annals of the American Academy of Political and Social Science,* Vol. CXLV, September, 1929, pp. 95–96.

are crowded, unattractive, and poverty-stricken; from the street corners, pool rooms, dance halls, and gin mills; from those social and economic conditions which would make criminals of you and me unless, by the grace of God, there were something within us strong enough to combat the constant downward pull. Poverty may not breed criminals, but the things bred by poverty breed them.

I am not trying to draw a sentimental picture of the criminal. I can be as hard-boiled with him as anyone else, when the occasion demands. But, after twenty years in the business, my desire is increasingly to understand the criminal, partly that we may protect ourselves more competently against him, and partly because I would want to be understood by my keeper if I were Prisoner Number 32,971.

It is because of the factors just cited that I am so interested in crime prevention and believe it is to be the only answer to our problem in the long run. We shall have to shoot down or throw into iron cages all the criminals that we can for the time being. Unless we attack the criminal at the same time in his sources and in his development, society will be as impotent as King Canute commanding the sea to recede.

Crime prevention involves better homes, schools, and churches, better cities and towns, more decent working and living conditions, a closer approach to a square deal for the poor and ignorant, development of more agencies such as child guidance clinics for the diagnosis and direction of human behavior, recognition of the fact that the roots of crime are found in our social and economic order, and sincere determination to do something about modifying society so that juvenile delinquency and crime will not be so natural a growth or grow so rapidly. We shall not have very much less crime until we have a better Atlanta, a better New York, a better America. The criminal has his beginning in the alleys, and on the Main Streets, and metropolitan avenues of America and develops with little effective restraint. We do not begin to worry seriously about him until he appears as an adult before the bar of justice. Then it is usually too late. The attack on crime must be an attack on its roots and on its growth processes. It must be an attack on the whole social order.[17]

With the evidence cited in Chapter X in mind, both as to the inadequacy of the juvenile court alone to cope with the whole problem of juvenile delinquency and as to the great variety of other community agencies whose services must be enlisted to treat and prevent such

[17] Austin H. McCormick, "Revenge or Reform," *News Bulletin* of the Osborne Association, December 1, 1935. See also the American Law Institute, *Official Draft, Youth Correction Authority,* Philadelphia, June 20, 1940.

delinquency, I now go on to describe briefly in Chapter XI how some of these necessary community agencies and services started and what some of their approaches to the problems of juvenile delinquency have been.

Part Three: TREATMENT IN THE
COMMUNITY

Chapter XI: AGENCIES OTHER THAN THE COURT

THIS CHAPTER, a discussion of some of the agencies connected with the juvenile court, will serve to connect the preceding discussion of the limitations of the juvenile court with the succeeding discussion of the problem of coördinating or orchestrating the work of this court with the work of all other community agencies that are needed in order to render a symphony of service to juvenile delinquents.

Societies for the Prevention of Cruelty to Children

In these later years some of the societies for the prevention of cruelty to children, the first of which, commonly known in the early days as the Gerry Society, was founded in New York city in 1874, have changed their emphasis somewhat from drastic legal and court procedure to various forms of preventive work. The extent to which the first New York society relied upon the use of fear is illustrated by the common use of this expression among the people, "The Gerrys'll get ye if ye don't watch out!" In order to state in the words of their own officers the original primary purpose of the work of the New York society, I give here two quotations. The first is from Elbridge T. Gerry's 1898 report of the society:

Our societies are the hand of the law, attached to the arm of the law, plucking unfortunate children from atmospheres of poverty and crime and placing them where they will be properly cared for, and preventing the depraved and brutal from wreaking their vengeance on these who but for our action and efforts would be helpless and at their mercy.[1]

The second quotation is from the words of President John D. Lindsey in the 1907 report, as follows:

[1] *Report of the New York Society for Prevention of Cruelty to Children*, 1898, p. 9.

We are, as the Court of Appeals has said, engaged in the stern task of making war upon crime and vice in peculiar forms. We are not engaged in missionary work among children. It is our province and duty to rescue the unfortunate little ones whose destiny might otherwise depend upon chance or circumstance to save them from moral destruction, and to ruthlessly pursue the wretches who make our intervention necessary.[2]

In another report these "wretches" were called "cruellists"—those who were cruel. Some societies, as the ones in Boston, Buffalo, Brooklyn, and Newark, have of late years taken a view different from the above.

I have already referred to the notable fact that it was this New York society which first performed such probation service as was available to the Children's Court in New York city and that to the present day it has maintained a juvenile detention home service.

The Big Brother Movement

Furthermore, it was a former head of the New York Society for Prevention of Cruelty to Children, Ernest K. Coulter, who, while he was a clerk in the New York City Children's Court, started the Big Brother Movement. Coulter also wrote a book entitled *Children in the Shadow* (McBride, Nast and Co., 1913).

Of the development of the Big Brother work up to 1935, Douglas Falconer, in an article on "Child and Youth Protection," states that:

There are at present 55 Big Brother or Big Sister Organizations united in a national federation, each with a paid secretary and a group of volunteer leaders. In 267 other cities the organizations are composed of volunteers. Each volunteer takes a brief course of training and then assumes responsibility for one child. Many of the children thus befriended, about 23 per cent of the total, are referred by juvenile courts and for them the service is an informal probation service. The Big Brothers and Big Sisters attempt to keep boys and girls who have begun to show behavior problems from becoming delinquent, *to improve their environment,* and to help them with their various personal and family problems [italics by H. W. T.]. The problems presented by these children are so complex, and require so much time, understanding and patience that the turnover

[2] *Ibid.,* 1907, p. 11. The quotation from the Court of Appeals refers to a decision earlier made by this court which exempted the S.P.C.C. from supervision by the State Board of Charities on the ground that the S.P.C.C. was not a charitable agency.

among boy leaders has been large. While a few of these associations have shown a great vitality and have made a genuine contribution, their number is limited and they play only a minor role in the general field of child protection.[3]

Attendance (Truant) Officers

The first compulsory school law was passed by Massachusetts in 1852, and sixty-six years afterward, in 1918, the last state, Mississippi, passed such a law.[4] Changes in the aims of truant officers are thus described by another writer in 1935:

When the task of teacher was not inaccurately described as drilling pupils in reading, writing, and arithmetic, it was the business of the truant officer to see to it that pupils were in school to be drilled and so far as parents were concerned that they were suitably punished by fine or imprisonment if they failed to require the attendance of their children. In well organized schools today, however, the aim is not primarily to impart information, it is to prepare children for life. To that end teachers endeavor to understand the pupils in their charge and the individual needs of each. Such understanding is not possible unless the teacher has some way of knowing both the advantages and the limitations of each child's home and community life, for these contribute largely toward making him what he is. To fill this need the truant officers of earlier days have been succeeded by attendance officers, increasingly trained to see the social possibilities of their work.[5]

In 1941 these statements were made by another writer:

In 45 states, legislation requires the employment of local attendance officers. Requirements for appointment vary greatly among the states and localities, comparatively few prescribing educational qualifications. One State (Wyoming) authorizes the sheriff to investigate truancy. Eight states, however, have set up some kind of standard and require that the attendance officer be certified according to state regulations. . . .

In most states there is little or no state supervision of attendance work and much of the work in rural and smaller communities is poorly done. Many cities have set up their own requirements, some of which are very high. . . .

[3] Douglas Falconer, "Child and Youth Protection," *Social Work Year Book*, New York, Russell Sage Foundation, 1935, p. 64.
[4] Henry J. Gideon, "Compulsory Education," *Social Work Year Book*, 1933, p. 101.
[5] Charles L. Mosher, "Compulsory School Attendance," *Social Work Year Book*, 1935, pp. 89–92.

School systems having well-organized attendance departments find it necessary to resort infrequently to court and compulsion. In many cities special classes and institutions for truant children have been abolished.[6]

From the foregoing statements about the work of attendance officers, it is clear that, while real progress has been made both in ideal and in practice in some schools, the task ahead is still one of great magnitude and complexity. All of us may well ask ourselves these questions: For the help of children handicapped by broken homes, homes of poverty, life in slum houses, life in neighborhoods without wholesome recreation, association with lawbreakers, and familiarity with spoils politicians, what new resources have the newly awakened teachers and the most efficient attendance officers? How can teachers and attendance officers cure the injuries caused by broken and inadequate parentage, improve slum housing, provide an economic system that will give every worker wage enough for decent and healthful living, provide wholesome recreation for all children, protect them from vicious and debased adult example, and banish the evils of spoils politics? These were the foes that the juvenile court and probation officers did not at first clearly recognize and against which they, so far as these evils have even yet been recognized, have thus far been unable to make much headway. But are we, as our eyes gradually open to the magnitude of the job to cure and prevent juvenile delinquency, content to throw up our hands and exclaim, "What's the use? We can't do anything! Let's give it up as a bad job!"

Surely it is no permanent solution of even so concrete a problem as that of food for school children, however generous and definite in its proof of opened eyes among school teachers, for teachers to furnish children food paid for out of their own pockets. During 1932–33 the teachers in New York city contributed for this purpose over $4,000,000. Much less is the teacher alone able to provide an adequate remedy for faulty home, community, industrial order, politics, and religion.

[6] Wilma Walker, "Social and Health Work in the Schools," *Social Work Year Book*, 1941, p. 514.

Visiting Teachers

Starting at about the same time as the mental hygiene clinics, the service of visiting teachers has slowly become available to a small number of schools. The first visiting teachers started work in New York, Boston, and Hartford in 1906–7. Of their work Miss Jane F. Culbert, author of *The Visiting Teacher at Work*, says: "The visiting teacher is a member of the school staff who brings to this task the two-fold equipment of social worker and teacher. She uses the social case work method, and through her knowledge of school conditions and procedure works out constructive plans with the school for its treatment of the individual child." [7] The limited extent to which this constructive work had developed up to 1940 may be seen from this statement:

In 1940 there were 209 members in the American Association of Visiting Teachers, some few of whom were associate members not engaged in active work. The members were located in 62 cities in 29 states. There are a good many persons, engaged in visiting teachers work in the public schools systems, many of them no doubt well-qualified social workers, who are not qualified for membership in the professional association or who have not affiliated themselves with it. Considerable development of the work has taken place in California, Connecticut, Massachusetts, New Jersey, New York, and Ohio. No school system employs the number of visiting teachers which has been recommended by the 1930 White House Conference as adequate, namely, one visiting teacher for every 500 pupils.[8]

Special credit is given by the writer of the above statement to the work in Rochester, New York, Minneapolis, and San Diego. Although visiting teachers, wherever available, are of unquestioned help toward the prevention of delinquency in children who show behavior problems in school, the above numbers of themselves show how pitifully inadequate to meet the needs of all our school children these few visiting teachers are.

[7] Jane F. Culbert, "Visiting Teachers," *Social Work Year Book*, 1929, p. 467.
[8] Wilma Walker, "Social and Health Work in the Schools," *Social Work Year Book*, 1941, p. 514.

Psychiatric Clinics for Children

Mention has already been made of the first such clinic under Dr. William Healy, in 1909 in Chicago, and of Dr. Healy's later work under the Judge Baker Foundation in connection with the juvenile court in Boston. Although challenging evidence has been quoted of the limitations of success achieved by these clinics, under the conditions that obtained in the juvenile courts in both Chicago and Boston, still, no one at all familiar with the job of trying to cure or to prevent juvenile delinquency doubts for a moment that these clinics have already been a great help and progressively will become of still greater help as we learn more and more about the conditions that are essential to their development and effective use and as we learn to make them available in every community. The status of these clinics in the United States in 1934 was thus stated by George S. Stevenson, Director of the Division on Community Clinics, National Committee for Mental Hygiene:

Approximately thirty-five states have mental clinics in some form, and probably half the service set up for children only is tax-supported. Clinics are chiefly urban. Twenty-eight of the largest 50 cities are so equipped and include a very large proportion of the existing service in the United States. The clinic is usually community-wide in scope, but at times it is limited to the range of one agency, of which it may be a part. While rural travelling units are more numerous than urban units, the aggregate time they give to the community service is relatively small. These travelling clinics, connected usually with public institutions or agencies, especially mental hospitals, are increasing in rural districts and small cities.[9]

In 1941 Dr. Stevenson makes this further statement about the work of these clinics:

It is highly improbable that psychiatric clinics will ever be available for all children with problems of behavior or even for those that are dependent on psychopathological causes. *It would not be desirable, even if possible, to divorce the handling of these problems completely from child care, probation, pediatrics, and public health nursing.* It is therefore necessary to clarify a narrower scope for psychiatric clinics and to develop further the resources of these other agencies for dealing with the less

[9] Dr. George S. Stevenson, "Psychiatric Clinics for Children," *Social Work Year Book*, 1935, pp. 350–52.

·complex problems. *The clinic has a responsibility for contributing to this progress.* [Italics by H. W. T.] [10]

For emphasis upon the responsibility of other community facilities, as well as the clinic and the court, for the successful treatment of juvenile delinquents, this statement of January 12, 1942, by a doctor who works in the New York city Domestic Relations Court Clinic is pertinent here. He says:

There has recently been published a series of articles condemning the Domestic Relations Court of New York. As a physician in the treatment clinic of that court I am in a position to know at first hand many of the problems met by these courts and many of the limitations under which they must operate. . . .

The emphasis should be, not upon how the Domestic Relations Courts are failing in their duties, *but upon how much society in general is failing in its duty to come to the aid of an institution which serves such an important function in the community. Until we have the correct concept of treatment and where responsibility for it lies, our problems of juvenile delinquency will continue unabated.* [Italics by H. W. T.] [11]

From these statements the reader can see that only a limited number of communities yet have psychiatric clinics, and he can also imagine the serious failure to achieve continuous teamwork by the clinic and all the persons and agencies concerned with a particular child, even in communities that have clinics. The studies of Dr. Healy in Chicago and in Boston and the studies of the Gluecks in Boston, both previously quoted, also showed that without inclusive and continuous teamwork, success has hitherto been discouragingly infrequent in changing bad young citizens into citizens who no longer get into trouble with the law.

Men and Women Police

Mention has already been made of the large place assigned to special policemen who, at least one from each police court district, were at first appointed as juvenile probation officers in Chicago. Of the long-ago service of these police officers to children, I here make this comment based on my associations with them in the Juvenile Court of

[10] *Ibid.,* 1941, p. 356.
[11] Henry H. Drewry, M.D., letter to the *New York Times,* January 12, 1942.

Chicago, 1905–8. Police, like all the rest of us—teachers, judges, ministers, social workers, and parents—are likely to see the individual delinquent youth in the light of their personal and professional experiences and philosophies. There was then, therefore, and doubtless is now, a tendency for many policemen to use authority, threats, and fear as methods of dealing with the individual delinquent. But there were also in Chicago several outstanding policemen on the Juvenile Court staff who often opened the eyes of the judge and the probation staff to the possibilities of a more considerate and understanding treatment of children. For example, one of the two police probation officers who worked from the central police district of the city protested against more punishment of some boys who had driven a horse and buggy into the country. His words to me were "Don't be too hard on these boys. They didn't know any other way to express themselves." This was before any of us had even heard of mental hygiene. Another officer, who was ordered by the judge to go at once and bring into court a boy who had neglected to report to the judge as he had previously been ordered to do at a certain time, said "Your Honor, if I go now to the place where this boy is working I may cause him to lose his job. May I wait until tonight and go to see him at his home and arrange with him a definite time to come to see you?" "Yes," said the judge.

If we are to succeed in the cure and prevention of juvenile delinquency to any great degree, we must have to the utmost the understanding coöperation of the police in all our congested urban communities. Signs begin to appear that such help is possible. Two such signs shown by the police of New York city are here cited.

In the New York *Times* of May 2, 1932, is an account of a meeting of 4,000 Brooklyn and Queens policemen at the Annual Commission Breakfast of the Police Department Holy Name Society of the two boroughs, held at the Brooklyn Elks Club. Police Commissioner Mulrooney is quoted as saying to these officers:

As you understand, far more clearly than the average citizen, we are now in difficult times. There is a great deal of unemployment and much of that unemployment is found in the ranks of the boys and young men. The boy who left school as soon as possible under the law in order to work has suffered greatly in these times of depression. He requires careful handling if he is to become the type of citizen we want him to be. The boy in the city has never had the proper breaks. It is within your power to help him and see that he gets some of the breaks.

Don't drive the boy from the empty lot, but on the contrary do all in your power to make his life easier. The boy who has a place to play and something to play with does not turn to crime later on. The Crime Prevention Bureau has done wonderful work; do your part to help them carry on.

It was under Commissioner Mulrooney that the Crime Prevention Bureau was set up in New York city in 1930. Henrietta Additon, the woman who, as Deputy Commissioner, 1931–34, was the head of this bureau, describes its work and also that of policewomen in New York and other cities. She says that in 1935 there were some 850 policewomen in about 290 communities in the United States. The Crime Prevention Bureau of New York city was thus at the outset a special development of the policewoman movement, although it had policemen on its staff. In 1935:

. . . there were 24 women crime prevention investigators, 42 patrol women, and 16 policewomen. Units similarly named have also been established in Berkeley, Chicago, Dayton, Detroit, Los Angeles, Newark, Philadelphia and Richmond. These vary greatly as to personnel and methods of procedure but they all deal chiefly with children and youth and usually have both men and women on their staffs. In the latter particulars they differ from the women's bureaus and other policewomen units. [Policewomen are often without uniforms, which former Chief Police Vollmer of Berkeley, California, says "The right kind of woman does not need any more than *other social workers* do" (italics by H. W. T.).] . . . In the main policewomen are not employed for the purpose of detecting crime. They are regarded as social workers with police powers, undertaking a program for the prevention of crime and for the protection of women and girls.[12]

In New York city the first name of the Crime Prevention Bureau was changed to the Juvenile Aid Bureau of the police department. In a radio broadcast, the director emphasized his belief that recreation is an important factor in preventing crime and outlined his plans to coöperate with and to supplement all existing agencies in an attempt to achieve a normal and natural activity for that great neglected

[12] Henrietta Additon, "Police Women," *Social Work Year Book*, 1935, pp. 330–32.

majority of one and one-half million youth, out of a total of two
and one-half million, who are not now "reached by any social program
whatever." I shall mention this work again later in connection with
other community efforts.

In thus placing the emphasis upon the *prevention of juvenile
delinquency,* the Crime Prevention Bureau of New York city and
other cities and the policewomen of many cities may thus both be
regarded as an extension of the work undertaken by the first Juvenile
Protective Association of Chicago. The reader will remember that
it was to this association that the women of Chicago, who had hitherto
supported the Juvenile Detention Home and probation officers of
the Juvenile Court, shifted the use of their money and some of their
personal support after the county took over the expense of the work
they had previously supported.

Widow's Pension or Mother's Aid

Following the declaration of the first White House Conference on
Dependent Children in 1909 that "No child should be removed from
his own home for poverty alone," the first mother's pension law was
enacted in Missouri in 1911; it applied only to Jackson County. The
first state-wide law, in part stimulated by the Chicago Juvenile Court,
was enacted in Illinois in the same year. We are told by Miss Grace
Abbott that within the next ten years "forty states had passed some
kind of Mother's Assistance laws; and by 1931 the number was forty-
five." [13] Alabama joined the forty-five during 1931. In the article just
quoted, the writer estimated the number of children under care because of these laws to be nearly 300,000. She further states that, according to some estimates, as many as 300,000 more children need help
from mother's aid. She gives the average grant per family during the
month of December, 1933, as reported by the Children's Bureau, for
twenty states, as ranging from $9.76 in Florida to $52.89 in Massachusetts. In comment, she further states that:

In many of the states, and especially those of the middle west, the monthly
grant varies greatly from county to county, the amount in the large urban

[13] Grace Abbott, "Mothers' Aid," *Social Work Year Book,* 1935, pp. 282–85.

centers being usually much higher than in the rural districts, while the grants in a large number of counties have been too low to provide the kind of care which it was intended that these laws should make possible for dependent children, they have usually been considerably higher than emergency relief grants, and there is much less uncertainty as to their continuance.[14]

In 1935, the year the above statements were made, the United States Social Security Act was passed by Congress. Under that act we are told that:

. . . 808,150 children in 335,285 families received payments in July, 1940. . . . The development of the program presents a mottled picture. In February, 1940, the national average grant per family was $32.35, so among the states the average varied from $8.13 in Arkansas to $60.13 in Massachusetts. If one considers such states as Texas, Mississippi, and Kentucky, which do not receive federal funds for aid to dependent children, the extremes might be even greater.[15]

However "mottled the picture," and however inadequate the funds may be, to anyone familiar with the juvenile court administration in Chicago or elsewhere if, as in Chicago, the court has jurisdiction over so-called dependent cases, it is clear that these mother's aid funds in the aggregate have kept thousands of children from being brought to the juvenile court as dependent, neglected, and even delinquent children. The reason, of course, is obvious: these mothers, usually widows, can give less time to earning a living for themselves and their children and more time to their children personally and thus prevent many children from becoming delinquent because of neglect.

Social Settlements

I have already told how Hull House provided one of the first probation officers for the Chicago Juvenile Court. The clubs and other facilities attractive to youth, not only in Hull House but in other settlements as they have been opened in all parts of the United States, have always welcomed youth.

The extent to which social settlements now contribute to the prevention of delinquency by giving various opportunities for wholesome

[14] *Loc. cit.*
[15] Geoffrey May, "Aid to Dependent Children," *Social Work Year Book,* 1941, p. 51.

activity to young people is suggested by these brief statements by Miss Lea D. Taylor, daughter of Graham R. Taylor, founder of Chicago Commons:

The National Federation of Settlements has 158 settlement members and 48 additional houses which are affiliated through the individual member-ship of staff workers—a total of 206 centers scattered from coast to coast, both north and south. The majority are in the east or middle west. A survey made in 1930 covered 160 of these houses, connected with which there were 1500 staff members and 7500 volunteers. In a study of activi-ties made in the same year 136 houses reported an enrolment of 153,268 people in 3,518 clubs and 6,192 organized classes, with the clinics, libraries, playgrounds, and general activities included, it was shown that these cen-ters reached 973,418 people, *80% of whom were under 18 years of age* [italics by H. W. T.].[16]

Recreation

Since the early days of the juvenile court, when the reporter previ-ously quoted, while on a visit, heard the judge of the New York Children's Court say to the boy who had been brought before him for playing shinny in the street, "Streets are for business—streets are not for boys to play in," the problem of a place for wholesome play has confronted juvenile court judges, probation officers, and all others concerned in the welfare and good citizenship of urban youth.

For example, here is a recent letter from a boy to the mayor of Philadelphia, putting the problem of a place to play ball up to the highest city authority. What was the final outcome? Philadelphia readers ought to find out. Here is the boy's letter:

DEAR MAYOR:
I want you to write me a slip that says these boys are alowed to play on this grown sign your signature please do it
                                                    your loving B . . . W . . . and the gang
PS my address is 2339 S . . . B . . . Street, Phila., Pa.

Investigation disclosed that Bert is nine years old and that a police-man had been chasing him and his football team off a vacant lot and the adjoining street which they wanted to use for a gridiron. Mayor Mackey invited Bert and his "gang" to visit him at City Hall and

---

[16] Lea D. Taylor, "Social Settlements," *Social Work Year Book*, 1935, p. 472.

promised to find a way to help them. There is no playground in their neighborhood.

A brief account of what communities had as yet done to meet this universal need of youth for wholesome play was written in 1929 by Howard S. Braucher, Secretary of the National Recreation Association of America. Here are a few items from this account: "The first children's playground under leadership was opened about 1886 in Boston." In 1906 the Playground Association of America (now the National Recreation Association) was started. By 1929 there were 747 cities reporting the use of tax funds for recreation and 134 the use of private funds only. Public funds were 84% of the total for both.

Only a few of the forty-one different statistical items of the article can be quoted here. For example, there were 7,681 playgrounds in 763 cities, 2,341 indoor community recreation centers in 255 cities, 1,709 athletic fields in 544 cities, 7,960 public tennis courts in 569 cities, 4,024 baseball diamonds in 639 cities, 700 outdoor swimming pools in 308 cities, and 310 indoor swimming pools in 122 cities; $33,539,-805.79 was the total expenditure in 890 cities.

Exclusive of laborers, caretakers, office and clerical workers, there are nearly 23,000 employed workers in the community recreation field, about 2700 of whom are employed on full time, the year round, in recreational leadership. . . .

120 colleges, universities, schools of social work and special institutions now offer courses in training for recreation leadership. The National Recreation Association maintains a National Recreation School which offers a post-graduate course of nine months for those who wish professional training and plan to make recreation their life work. . . .

Twenty-one states now have special recreation laws giving broad power to municipalities, school and park districts and counties to establish recreation programs.[17]

Details of further progress and also statements as to persistent inadequacies are given by E. C. Worman, who discusses recreation under twenty-two subtopics. From his summary introduction I quote:

Under conditions of modern life recreation (used herein as referring primarily to activities) has become an essential for the well-being of the

---

[17] Howard S. Braucher, "Recreation," *Social Work Year Book,* 1929, pp. 379–82.

people. The rapid growth of cities, the changes in working conditions due to the mechanization of industry, the speed of living, the changing home pattern, the *increase of delinquency,* a growing amount of leisure, and unemployment of millions of people call for new and varied types of activity through which the human body and spirit can be refreshed. Many agencies, private and public, have over the years endeavored to provide the means of recreation for the people; the home, religious organizations, boys' and girls' organizations, settlements, schools, industry, amusements, and sports organizations have all played their part. Since the turn of the century, government authorities, federal, state and local, have directed their attention to extending the movement. For thirty-five years, the National Recreation Association has been a powerful factor in the development of the recreation movement. The National Park Service, United States Department of the Interior, the Forest Service, United States Department of Agriculture and several of the emergency agencies such as the Civilian Conservation Corps, National Youth Administration, and Work Projects Administration have made great progress in recent years.

While much has been done, the task is far from completion. *Millions of children in city and country are not being served. The combined service of all agencies is not enough.* Few if any cities have enough playgrounds or city-owned recreation areas. School authorities are still reluctant to allow the use of school buildings for recreation purposes, although this attitude is changing for the better. Municipal finances in many instances prevent any worthy advance. Political patronage in some cities is still given consideration over the needs of children. [Italics by H. W. T.] [18]

As to what an adequate sparetime recreation program for the individual child would be I cite, in Chapter XII, a statement of my own perspective in 1918. For up-to-the-year progress in recreational possibilities, consult each yearbook of the National Recreation Association.

Other Organizations That Work Directly for and with Boys and Girls

Margaret Hodges lists twelve agencies under the title "Boys and Girls' Work Organizations." In the opening paragraph we are told that: "The organizations considered in this article are limited to those serving boys and girls under sixteen years of age." [19]

[18] E. C. Worman, "Recreation," *Social Work Year Book,* 1941, pp. 464–77.
[19] Margaret Hodges, "Boys and Girls' Work Organizations," *Social Work Year Book,* 1941, pp. 84–91.

For a brief statement of the kind of opportunity for wholesome activities each of these agencies offers to youth within the juvenile court age and for some resultant perspectives on the service of each for the prevention of juvenile delinquency, the article cited should be carefully read. The article closes with a valuable bibliography, which, with the publications of the various agencies themselves, would guide the persistent student farther on his way.

For their suggestion as to the total number of youth helped toward an abundant life by these twelve agencies, I cite here the membership in each, as given by Miss Hodges; in parentheses is the year in which the organization was founded.

Boy Rangers (1913) in 1940: 1,039 lodges in 47 states.

Boy Scouts of America (1910) during 1939: 1,230,716 enrolled as Scouts and 234,953 as Cubs. There were also 411,450 adult members.

Boys' Clubs of America (1906) in 1939: 348 such clubs, providing leisure-time activities and leadership for nearly 300,000 boys between the ages of seven and eighteen.

Camp Fire Girls (1911): total membership as of December 31, 1939, including Camp Fire Girls, Blue Birds, and adult leaders was 278,451.

4-H Clubs in 1939: 1,381,500 rural young people were members of 4-H Clubs. The members' age is ten to twenty years.

Girl Scouts (1912) in 1939: 573,254 Girl Scouts of all ages in about 5,685 communities representing practically every section of the country.

Junior Red Cross (American Red Cross, 1881) in 1939: membership totaled 7,556,306.

Pioneer Youth of America (1934) during 1939: 679 children were members of functioning groups.

Young Men's Christian Association (1883) for boys under eighteen, in 1939: 872 Associations carrying on work in regularly scheduled groups with 931,674 enrollments.

Young Women's Christian Association (1906): girls of junior and senior high school age are called Reserves, and during the year 1939 they numbered 340,000.

Jewish Welfare Board (1917): in the Y.M.H.A., Y.W.H.A., and Jewish community centers in the United States and Canada a total of 317 associations were affiliated with the Welfare Board in 1939; membership was 400,000, of which thirty percent were twelve years old or less and twenty-one percent were between thirteen and seventeen years of age.

Catholic Boys' Brigade of the United States (1916) in 1940: approximately 40,000 boys ten to eighteen years of age were members of the various local units.

Two persistent questions face each of us in our own communities: To what degree are members of their own groups and other children who are already at their crossroads of choice between the way that leads to delinquency and the way that leads to good citizenship invited to become members of the above-named organizations? And if invited, to what extent do they accept and enjoy membership therein? Only as these questions are asked and clearly answered in each community can we develop adequate opportunities and acceptable youth and adult fellowship for predelinquent youth.

Reformatories

As to the youth who have already chosen the wrong road, we ask: What do reformatories do for them? In partial answer, I give here extracts from an article by one of the leaders in improving the work in institutions.[20] This article shows two things, progress within such institutions and also something of the degree to which, up to the time the article was written, their work had not been coördinated with that of the communities from which boys enter the institution and to which they return.

As I have already stated, the first house of refuge in America was opened to receive boys in New York city in 1824. It was supported by private funds. Mr. Briggs says:

The first house of refuge was a prison: so were all those that followed it up to 1856 and so have been some institutions built since then. They had grated or barred windows, cells with grated doors, walls or stockades surrounded them, large numbers of boys were herded together without reference to their physical or moral welfare and yet these places were infinitely superior to the prisons for adults to which these same boys would have been sent had it not been for these houses of refuge and to which children of that class had been sent prior to the establishment of the refuges [namely, House of Refuge, Boston, 1826, House of

[20] Franklin H. Briggs, Superintendent of Thorn Hill School, Pittsburgh, "A Century of Progress in the Care of Juvenile Delinquents," paper read at the Conference of Juvenile Agencies which met in Boston, September 13–19, 1923. For further data on early institutions and their problems see Grace Abbott, *The Child and the State,* Chicago, University of Chicago Press, 1938, Vol. II.

Refuge, Philadelphia, 1826, and others, all from private funds up to 1846]. Expense was important and in order to keep the boys employed and have their labor contribute to their maintenance the unfortunate practice of contract labor whereby the labor of the boys was farmed out to contractors came into vogue. . . . The whole aim of the contractors was to get as much as possible out of each boy and to teach him so much as would make him most effective in the manufacture of brushes, brooms, chairs, chair caning, making of stockings, shoes and other articles in the manufacture of which such labor could be most profitably employed.

In 1846 New York State provided by law for the Western House of Refuge for Delinquents which was opened in Rochester in 1849. In Massachusetts a similar institution opened in 1848. The Rochester institution had contract labor, probably also the Massachusetts.

First cottage institution for delinquent boys in America was built in Lancaster, Ohio, in 1856 under the influence of George E. Howe, who located it on a large tract of land but built the cottages for *50 boys each*.

As early as 1783-89 a report says that at Mettray, France, their boys lived in families of 12 in a house, upon the land. The report stated that "Agriculture is the grand source to which the society looks for employment for its wards. Agriculture means natural life and is the primary spring of health and happiness."

The young French judge who founded Mettray is said to have found an earlier model in Germany. In 1888 the Western House of Refuge in Rochester threw out contract labor and inaugurated a complete system of manual and industrial work for its seven hundred boys. It was the pioneer in this respect. This system was introduced at a time when manual training in the public schools of the country was an unknown quantity and it existed only in a few private schools in the large cities [e. g., Dr. H. H. Belfield's Manual Training School in Chicago]. Military system was introduced and perfected, the cells were torn out and the dormitories made into open rooms. The bars were cut from the windows and they were enlarged. Its schools were re-organized and modernized and only teachers of the highest ability were employed.

F. H. Nibecker went to the Philadelphia House of Refuge in 1891 and soon moved it to a 500 acre tract in the country.[21]

The Rochester House of Refuge is upon the cottage colony system as distinctive from the cottage system, in that the cottages are placed more remotely from one another and each cottage is a complete unit in itself. This

---

[21] Briggs, in 1904, moved the House of Refuge from Rochester to a tract of 1,400 acres at Industry, New York. The paragraphs above, beginning "In 1846 . . . ," represent a condensation of Briggs's discussion.

separation of the buildings makes classification of the boys more effective, the family life more distinctive, places a greater amount of responsibility upon the boys and officers of each cottage group. . . . In the cottage colony system each group has its own supply of vegetables. It has its own fruit garden, its own playground, making it possible for a much larger number of boys to engage in play simultaneously than is possible where the cottages are more closely associated and several groups have to share the same playground. It also gives a greater variety of interests to keep the boys' minds occupied. They can have a greater number of pets without infringing upon the rights and privileges of any other cottage group. There is an opportunity for competition among the different cottage groups which is not possible where all the group work in a common field or common shop.

All the activities of the modern well-managed institution are directed to this end [the development of self-control], and whether at work, in the school room, on the athletic field or playground, the whole object is the development of self-control in the individual.

The progress of the century in the care and training of juvenile delinquents has been great. The pinnacle, however, is still far beyond and will never be entirely reached until the institutions come to be regarded both by their officers and by the public at large as sanatoria for moral diseases. . . .

The work of the institutions always has been, is now, and always will be the most difficult and the most heartbreaking work in the world, because it is dealing with that element of society with which all other agencies have failed and with which in some cases the institutions too must fail.[22]

Every generation has its shibboleth. We were certain at first that mental education would cure the ills from which we suffer. We enacted compulsory education laws, and still we had the delinquent with us. Then there arose the idea that manual training was the great remedy and still there are delinquents. Then the psychologist and the psychiatrist were going to be the agents by which delinquency would be ended, and we still have the delinquent with us.

Parental Schools for Truants

Some idea of the large part that dissatisfaction with school has in the past played in inducing truancy may be gained from the studies

[22] Briggs, *op. cit.*

of Dr. Healy and Dr. Glueck already cited. Dr. Healy says that in the total of 4,000 Chicago and Boston cases that he considered in writing *Delinquents and Criminals: Their Making and Unmaking* about forty percent of the boys and eight percent of the girls had been truants to such a degree that their "school nonattendance has been more than slight and for unjustified reasons." [23]

Of the 1,000 juvenile delinquents studied by Dr. Glueck, the extent of school retardation was learned in 935 cases. Of these *"only 145 boys (15.5%) were not retarded in school* [italics in the original]; 219 (23.4%) were retarded one year; 261 (24.9%) two years; 228 (24.4%) three or more years; and 82 (8.8%) were in ungraded classes. Thus a total of 790 juvenile delinquents (84.5%) were at least one year behind grade in their school work." [24]

In 1927 the relation of the work of the Chicago Parental School for truant boys and girls to the work of the regular public-school teacher, to the truant officer, to the juvenile court, and to the community was described in a paper by the psychiatrist Irene D. Milliken. The school had at the time of this article been in operation twenty-five years and had received a total of 10,000 truant boys and 600 truant girls. The writer said in part:

We have in Chicago a condition similar to that which most workers with juvenile delinquents have to face. The school teacher or principal, bceause of the variety of demands made upon them, has not the time to handle the problem child in their group. The child is turned over to the truant officer. Again, because of a large case load, if the child does not immediately respond, it is economy of time to bring him into court. The court gathers together the little information that is available and commits the child to an institution. The institution knows little of the case, save the details of the misdemeanor and has few resources to find more. In four months much is learned of the child but there is no definite person to carry that out to those meeting him when he is released and as a result it goes back into the inadequate memory of the institution. The cycle with the child begins all over again.

Who has failed with the child? If our own doctor ordered an operation for us, sent us to a hospital telling nothing of his finding, a surgeon operated on us and turned us over to a nurse without telling of his work, we then returned home to another doctor and another nurse who are told

[23] Pages 171 and 175.   [24] Page 87.

nothing of our previous treatment, whose fault is it if we die? The blame can be placed upon no inefficiency in any department but only upon the unwise decentralization of various organizations for treating the same problem. *How can this inefficiency be overcome?* [Italics in the original.] [25]

In October, 1931, four years after the above was published, William L. Bodine, Superintendent of Compulsory Education in Chicago, told me that there was then on trial a coöperative procedure to be used in each school. This procedure involved a conference, at the school, of the truant officer, principal of the school, and parent of the child in question, to adjust the problem of the child and thus obviate court procedure. He said that during the last year 769 cases of this kind were successfully adjusted, thus demonstrating, to his mind, the efficiency of truant officers as social workers and the value of a conference plan.

Later, in Chapter XII, I shall give further instances of efforts in different communities to coördinate community agencies to prevent delinquency. In the meantime, some questions for each reader are these: (1) To what degree is the foregoing description of the successive but noncontinuous, unrelated efforts to deal with the truant boy that were made in Chicago previous to 1927 true now in your own community? (2) What is being done about the situation? (3) What more can be done? (4) To what extent are the efforts of home, school, church, court, and other social agencies dealing with the same child in your own community made continuous, reciprocally informed, and progressive?

In this connection I can give a word of personal and professional testimony as to the prevalence, to a challenging degree, of noncontinuous, uncorrelated work with truant and delinquent children in 1917 in Cleveland, Ohio, in 1922 in Rochester, New York, and later in Hartford, Connecticut. Just before and during the early years of the twenties in this century, I made personal studies of the contacts between community agencies and lists of impersonally selected children who, between certain dates, had been brought into juvenile courts charged with delinquency. In the three cities named, each in a differ-

[25] Irene D. Milliken, *Chicago Parental School Report,* 1927, pp. 6–7.

ent state, I found that teamwork among the various community agencies involved had been sadly inadequate. In short, I found that teamwork in behalf of the juvenile delinquents whom I studied and teamwork for the families of these youths was, in all three cities, the exception rather than the rule.

The following is an extreme example as to the number of agencies involved in the case of a single family in one of these cities. It is typical in kind, though well toward the top in the number of different agencies dealing with one family. There were eight children in this family in 1922, and during fifteen years at least fifteen kinds of social agencies and institutions had attempted to give some form of service to the family as a whole or to some member thereof. These fifteen were: home; church; six different schools, three public and three private; out-patient department of General Hospital, for children's ailments; Rochester Dental Dispensary, tonsil and adenoid operation on one boy; attendance officers had father in police court three times; Child Study Department of public schools; visiting teacher for one boy; Police Court; Juvenile Court; Children's Aid Society; Department of Public Charities; Society for Prevention of Cruelty to Children; Social Settlement; and State Industrial School.

The impression made upon me by reading story after story of successive, ineffective efforts of different agencies with this family and with many other families was this: that there was in most instances a main road or direction in which the various members of a family traveled during a period of years, and that the efforts of successive agencies merely produced each time a slight detour in the road, taken by one and another member, only to lead the traveler back again into the original road toward delinquency and bad citizenship. What can communities do to meet such need of coördinated—orchestrated—services to delinquent children? In Chapter XII, I give such answers as I can.

Chapter XII: COÖRDINATION OF COMMUNITY AGENCIES

IT IS evident that there can be no solution of the problem of co-ordinated or orchestrated treatment of juvenile delinquency in any community so long as individual agencies continue to insist upon their right to perform their work as soloists. However limited in number and function in different communities are such agencies as have been briefly discussed, there are evidences of a growing recognition of the fact that the cure and prevention of juvenile delinquency cannot be achieved by the juvenile court and probation officer alone. But also there is evidence that they, working together with various other community agencies, such as I have already described, give ground for hope that one day we shall establish in every community a wonderful orchestra to perform symphonies of community service to children, to take the place of the somewhat isolated and ineffective solo performances of each of these agencies when its work was started. And, lest solo agencies feel alarm over the growing tendency to orchestration in their communities, they should remember that *in an orchestra there is also opportunity for an instrument to play a solo part, with the whole orchestra as audience, whenever such a solo is needed as an organic part of the symphony as a whole.*

Two Reports Which Show a Lack of Community Orchestration

A further challenge to inquiry as to the situation in our own communities is offered by testimony from Brooklyn and Chicago, as to the slight extent to which all the agencies I have named, and some I have not mentioned, are as yet practically helping in the cure and prevention of delinquency—in the development of good citizenship in youth. A survey made in Brooklyn by Neva R. Deardorff in 1931 states:

The accurate and decisive determination of neighborhood needs awaits the development of a much more complete system of social reporting than now exists. However, to the extent to which reliance can be placed upon infant mortality, boy delinquency, and persistent truancy rates as indicators of family conditions, areas I, II, III, IV, & VII, cited on the preceding page, would appear to be the districts in Brooklyn which have a comparatively great need for social-recreational service for boys. On the whole, they are of low economic level, delinquency rates were relatively high, with more than half of both the boy delinquency and persistent truancy cases falling within those five areas, and infant mortality rates were high. In 1927 approximately 38 percent of the total boy population of Brooklyn lived in these districts.

That the needs of the localities referred to have been recognized, in part at least, is seen in the fact that *30 of the 39 centers of organized boys' work in the borough were found to be stationed in these five areas.* While, in 1930, the same sections had approximately *165 Boy Scout Troops.* Yet on an estimate, *not more than 18,000 of the 87,000 boys living in this territory were being reached in any degree by the agencies, and there is no guarantee that among these boys there was included a fair proportion of those who give the community so much concern, namely the potential delinquents.* [Italics by H. W. T.] [1]

The second description of a community experience in coördination from which I quote describes an experiment in an area about one mile square, located south of the stockyards in Chicago. At the time the report was written, a project called the Chicago Probation Project had been carried on in this area for three years. Those sharing in the experiment were the United States Children's Bureau, the University of Chicago clinics, the School of Social Service Administration of the University of Chicago, the Cook County Juvenile Court, and other local agencies. Whatever its success, the fact that such an attempt at coördination was made is encouraging.

The area was selected because it seemed fairly representative of many poorer sections of large cities in respect to nationalities, native and foreign-born residents, churches, schools, economic status, delinquency

[1] Neva R. Deardorff, *A Survey of Work for Boys in Brooklyn,* Study 7 of the Research Bureau of the Welfare Council of New York City, 1931. NOTE.—For comparison with the above and with the next project to be described, see also Harold B. Hanson, M.D., "An Experiment in Child Welfare as Carried Out in St. Paul, Minnesota," in *The Child* [monthly bulletin of the United States Children's Bureau], February, 1942, pp. 177–92.

rates, and treatment resources that showed possibilities of development. The area was without a service club, an American Legion Post, a business men's association, a woman's club, or a community association of any kind.

The activities of the project have been two-fold: one, intensive work with individuals; two, extensive work throughout the community to develop treatment resources. In the case work program during the three years of the project approximately one hundred and fifty children, delinquent or with tendencies toward delinquency, have been referred to the project by the schools, the juvenile court, police or parents. These children and their problems were given intensive study and treatment, for which in addition to experienced case work personnel, psychiatric service was available.

Study of the records of these children and surveys of the neighborhood indicated lack of wholesome recreation, of satisfying contacts for children and unemployed youths and lack of cooperation among the many agencies whose services touched directly or indirectly the lives of these children and their families. It was on these two findings that the recreation program and the community organization experiments were undertaken.[2]

The report further states that, as the experiment could not be permanent, "The project set out to help the community—the lay citizens and the agencies dealing with young people—to become aware of the problems of delinquents and to provide incentives to right doing." This aim resulted in the establishment of small clubs for boys, with directors, in a center one mile from the nearest city playground; a girls' program director was later added and this center grew into a "small social settlement with an extensive program of activities and clubs supervised by a head resident trained and experienced in group work, with a small staff of paid and volunteer workers."

It was found that this work was too centralized and that:

. . . many young persons were not attending recreation programs because these were too far from their homes and because the trips back and

[2] Henry W. Waltz, Jr., "A Community Laboratory for Prevention of Delinquency by Probation," published by the Children's Bureau, U.S. Department of Labor, October, 1935. See also an article by Waltz, "Random Shots at Community Coördination," in *Probation* [the National Probation Association monthly], April, 1938. In this article Waltz discusses the problem of coördination in the light of experiments that had already been made.

forth were made unpleasant and sometimes unsafe by poor street light-
ing and by undesirable street idlers. It was decided, therefore, to stimulate a program of decentralized recreation activities, clubs and classes,
with volunteer leaders, and these programs were started in basements of
homes, in vacant stores, and in churches. Vacant lot baseball leagues were
organized. When relief workers became available as leaders the program
was expanded, and it then included baseball, football, model airplane
construction, dramatics, tutoring for children whose problems arose from
retardation in school, music, games, sewing and dancing (social, folk and
tap dancing). Excursions, trips, hikes, and picnics were arranged. With
this program it was almost always possible to have the activities under
the auspices of one or another of the established agencies in the areas.

A committee was formed out of the recreation leaders, workers in welfare and health agencies, churches, schools, the juvenile courts and the
police department.

From a committee this grew into a Community Council with lay members added, although it was found that these lay members were unwilling
at first to assume any responsibility for organization or direction of the
Council—still, cooperation in ideal and practice grew and committees
were formed to give special attention and leadership to different phases
of the community work. In the recreation field duplication was prevented
and demonstrated that existing agencies not only could improve their
recreation program, but by cooperative methods with pooled resources
could try out new ventures.

In one neighborhood where the recreation program was most detailed
and where there lived about 2900 children from ten to seventeen years
of age, the enlarged program increased the enrollment of children participating in organized recreation from 1000 to 2250. Of the 2250 in organized activities only 97 had police records during the three years.
*Many of those most in need of help were not reached, as is shown by
the fact that of the 650 who were not participating more than 280 were
arrested* during the three years. . . .

Again and again efforts were made to find some common interest
among these individuals upon which to build a class, a club, or some
other activity. These attempts, however, usually failed to adjust or re-
habilitate those young people. The common interest was often merely the
basic fact that all were "cases" or "problems." Difficulties arose within
the group when it recognized itself as "special" and came from without
when other young people tagged this group as the "bad bunch." . . .
When a rich and extensive program had been developed and it was
found that the bulk of the children known as "problems" were still not
included, the project again found it necessary to meet the particular

needs of many individuals. In some instances a child was taught a recreational skill individually which he could demonstrate later and through which he could win for himself recognition and a sense of accomplishment sufficient to get him started in some group activity.

These problem children very often avoided the wholesome organized groups because of some past experience in which they had been unwelcome because of their misconduct, or because leaders had used exclusion as the easiest disciplinary measures.

This exclusion from the group of the troublesome member is obviously no solution but merely an aggravation of the problem.

There remains therefore the task of developing further in the agencies, professional groups and laymen, a realization that the problems of delinquency can be solved only by the combined effort and interest of all. These agencies are often *handicapped by being so close to one phase of the problem that perspective is lost.*

Techniques for dealing with problem children are as many and varied as the children themselves—far beyond the ability and time of the social worker. *It is important then to convey some knowledge of these techniques to the legal, educational, religious, medical, family welfare, and law enforcement groups, and to the public at large. Such a plan requires meetings, discussions with representatives of all groups, and appropriate publicity.* [Italics by H. W. T.] [3]

I have quoted from this Chicago project at length in the hope that the reader may get at least a glimpse of an evolving process toward understanding, curing, and preventing juvenile delinquency in a given community. I hope that the contrast in processes between what was being attempted in this southern district in Chicago and what was attempted, or even dreamed of, during the first years of the Juvenile Court in that city, is challenging to the reader in behalf of his own community.

A Symposium on Preventing Crime

For information concerning details of a variety of current community projects in crime prevention, the reader should consult a 1936 book edited by Sheldon and Eleanor T. Glueck. In this book, of more than 500 pages, twenty-four different writers from eight

[3] Waltz, "A Community Laboratory. . . ."

states (Massachusetts, New York, New Jersey, Pennsylvania, Ohio, Indiana, Illinois, and California) describe concrete projects for crime prevention then going on in their twenty-two communities. After an introductory chapter by the Gluecks on "Philosophy and Principles of Crime Prevention," the remaining twenty-four chapters are grouped under these six headings: Coördinated Community Programs, School Programs, Police Programs, Intramural Programs, Extramural Programs, Boys' Clubs, and Recreation Programs. Their own conclusion from these reports on the actual work then going on in the eight states is expressed by the Gluecks in these words:

Reflecting upon the various articles contributed to this symposium, the student of crime and the practical worker in the field of crime prevention must be impressed with several hopeful indications.

First, there is evident an energy, enthusiasm, and intelligence that gives every promise of producing desirable results.

Secondly, there are signs of the awakening of the citizenry in various communities throughout the country to its responsibilities for many of the conditions presumed to be criminogenic and with this an awakening of a desire to participate intelligently in the amelioration of these conditions.

Thirdly, the crime-prevention programs being developed in different places indicate a rich variety of approaches without too slavish an adherence to any single cure-all. Related to this is a growing experimental attitude, together with a recognition of the value of the testing of processes by results, to the extent to which such evolution is possible.

Finally, there is evidence in these contributions of a growing recognition of the need of technically trained leadership, without ignoring the role that can be played by volunteers in the work of preventing crime.

Whatever may be the ultimate outcome of these experiments, evidence such as is found in this symposium justifies our looking to the future of crime control with at least some degree of optimism.[4]

What part should the juvenile court continue to play in an orchestra of community service to youth? Throughout the present book, numerous instances have been given of a recognition of the fact that the juvenile court could not alone cope successfully with

[4] Sheldon and Eleanor T. Glueck, *Preventing Crime,* New York, McGraw-Hill, 1936, p. 22.

the problem of treatment of juvenile delinquency, to say nothing of the problem of prevention. To supplement what has already been said, especially in Chapter X, I give now a few other specific opinions about limitations of the work of the juvenile court in the community, some of which also suggest possible solutions of the problem of juvenile delinquency by a coördination of all the community agencies for treatment and prevention.

In 1912, in a speech before a national audience of social workers, a Chicago man raised the question of placing the probation work of the juvenile court under school auspices.[5]

In 1914, another Chicago man wrote a book [6] in which he definitely argued that the schools, primarily, but assisted by other constructive agencies, ought to supplant the juvenile courts as centers of personal work then being attempted by probation officers. He also argued that all court decisions relating to juveniles should be made by judges in family or domestic-relations courts.

In 1919, in the *Survey,* two noted social workers took this extreme view in favor of shifting all work for juvenile delinquents from courts to schools. One paragraph reads thus:

The thing to do is to give up the juvenile courts we have and everywhere work for something else. If there are still states and counties in which no juvenile courts are in effective operation, so much the better; there will be no child welfare machinery to scrap and we can proceed at once to build new machinery that will be really up to date. This machinery must all be run from a central power station in connection with the public schools.[7]

In 1921 I argued that, while I welcomed the removal of all possible case-work service for children, even to ninety percent, from administration by any court, there would for an indefinite future still remain at least three situations involving the welfare of children which demand authoritative and legal decisions which can best be

[5] Willard E. Hotchkiss, "The Juvenile Court as It Is Today," *Annual Report of the National Conference of [Social Work] Charities and Corrections,* 1912, p. 450.

[6] Thomas D. Eliot, *The Juvenile Court and the Community,* New York, Macmillan, 1914. See also Thomas D. Eliot, "Welfare Agencies, Special Education and the Courts," *American Journal of Sociology,* Vol. XXX, No. 1, July, 1924.

[7] Henrietta Additon and Neva R. Deardorff, "That Child," *Survey,* May 3, 1919.

given in equity courts having access to the best possible case-work information and service.[8] These situations seemed (and still seem) to me to be these:

1. Situations where there are at least a few delinquent children to whom someone with community authority needs to say "You must."

2. Situations where parents, other adults, board of education, or other agencies and institutions dispute as to the custody or guardianship of children.

3. Situations in which parents or other adults should be subject to authoritative decisions and directions because they overwork, neglect, or abuse children. I cannot see how schools can render authoritative decisions in such cases without weakening all their other work as schools.

In 1937 Professor Eliot, whom I have already quoted, with new force, clarity, and conviction again discussed the problem of the best place and function of the work of the juvenile court in a community.[9] Not only this article but many others in the yearbook in which it was printed should be read by the persistent student of the future of the juvenile court. I cite only two paragraphs from Eliot:

My thesis is: (One) that there is functionally more in common between the case work services and treatment processes whether inside or outside the present court administration, than there is between the essentially and legitimately judicial services of the court and its case work offices; (Two) that social efficiency is promoted, and motivation and attitudes are clarified, when incongruous functions are not performed by a single agency; (Three) that essentially judicial functions are incongruous with functions of child care and treatment, and that this incompatibility is partly responsible for the shortcomings of the present system.[10]

Eliot, whose whole article breathes an urgent demand for more effective and better coördinated community services for children in every community, closes with this paragraph:

[8] Henry W. Thurston, "Is the Juvenile Court Passing?" *Survey*, October 22, 1921.
[9] Thomas D. Eliot, "Case Work Functions and Judicial Functions: Their Coordination," *Coping with Crime* [yearbook of the National Probation Association, 1937], pp. 252–66.
[10] Pages 255–56.

It will, of course, be necessary for judges to continue to route delinquents through the turnstiles of hell, but let it be with (or as) *an admission of society's failure* to provide a place and a reeducation for them within the community, not as a *solution* or *cure* of their delinquency. And let courts and treatment agencies alike bring pressure upon themselves and each other to devise ways and means to retain control of the offender *within the community*. [Italics in the original.] [11]

Before going on to a discussion of some actual and possible processes of community orchestration to treat and to prevent juvenile delinquency, I make here three citations to emphasize the fact that such orchestration cannot be wholly successful so long as there are such low standards of economic, political, and social life as are now often found in the community itself. This situation will receive further attention in Appendices A and B.

In the article by Eliot last cited, he makes this forthright statement:

Neither the court, the clinic nor the child caring system is to blame for the partial failure to check delinquency. Nor do I attribute the failure entirely to the mixture of functions in the present court system, for I believe *the total situation in our mal-civilized culture includes and implies delinquency; we are a criminal community* [italics by H. W. T.].[12]

With much the same implication in respect to the influence of adult example upon youth, Dr. William Healy says:

With the whole picture in mind, we can leave to our imagination what some new awakening spirit of good citizenship might bring about. Just for the sake of our national or local pride, to say nothing of the flowering of our civilization, what would it mean to have a general spirit of right social living in which delinquency would be generally condemned by young people themselves. No business-like war on crime by the Department of Justice, G-Men, a war that we find provokes youthful admiration for bravery on either side, and no more repressive measures for combating delinquency can possibly accomplish what a better type of general feeling for the values of socialized living might produce.

A reformative program for the defects in our national methods of living and in our ideologies would demand the acquirement of whole nets of new social values, of new personal standards and conceptions of responsibilities on the part of many of our citizens and particularly our *leaders in public life and in business—they who, whether they real-*

ize it or not, are definitely influencing the ideas and secondarily the behavior of our people, even of our children [italics by H. W. T.].[13]

Our third citation in this connection forms a connecting link between the former work of the juvenile court as a solo agency for dealing with juvenile delinquency and the work of community orchestration for the same purpose, which urgently challenges us now. After a summary of the work of the Chicago Probation Project, Miss Abbott develops her discussion under these headings:

1. The Juvenile Court—Success or Failure?
2. What Community Agency or Agencies Should Be Given Responsibility for Preventing and Treating Delinquency?
3. The Schools and Prevention of Delinquency.
4. The Training of Social Workers.
5. The Recreation Problem in Relation to Delinquency.
6. Economic and Social Security in Relation to Delinquency.[14]

Miss Abbott states that "No mistake was made thirty-five years ago in taking children and young persons out of the jurisdiction of the criminal courts and creating specialized courts for dealing with them. It was a necessary stop." [15] She further credits the juvenile court movement in these words: "The challenging and sincere idea which was back of the juvenile court was to cure, rather than to punish delinquency." [16] She then proceeds, however, to give three reasons why this ideal has not been realized:

First, because a judge with legal training only is not especially qualified to decide what should be done with perhaps ninety percent of juvenile delinquents for the reason that "The facts are not in dispute; there is no contest as to what should be done with or for the child." [17]

Second, she thinks that because juvenile courts do not afford opportunities for judges to decide many strictly legal questions, it is

---

[13] Healy and Bronner, *New Light on Delinquency and Its Treatment*, New Haven, Institute of Human Relations, Yale University, 1936, pp. 220–21.

[14] Grace Abbott, "The Juvenile Court and a Community Program for Treating and Preventing Delinquency," *Social Service Review*, June, 1936. See also a shorter article by Miss Abbott on "The Juvenile Courts," *Survey*, May 1, 1936.

[15] Abbott, "The Juvenile Court and a Community Program for Treating and Preventing Delinquency," *Social Service Review*, June, 1936, p. 237.

[16] *Ibid.*, p. 233. [17] *Ibid.*, pp. 235–36.

often hard to get the best lawyers to serve as juvenile court judges.

Third, she says that, either because the appeal to the court is made too late in the child's career or for psychological reasons, "In a large number of cases the authority of the court, instead of being of assistance, is probably a frequent factor in its failure to help the children and their parents." [18]

But the ten or so percent of delinquents for whom compulsory treatment is necessary she says "must, under our traditions, go to a court for decision instead of to an administrative agency." [19] On the other hand, for the ninety percent of children in the first stages of delinquency, and for the prevention of delinquency in other children, Miss Abbott argues both that more effective case work with psychiatric service available should be done by each separate agency dealing with children, including the school; and also that there should be established a neighborhood center for juveniles where parents and individual agencies not fully equipped may get the advice and coöperation of all the necessary specialists, such as those in health, psychology, psychiatry, and social case work; she does not believe that this neighborhood center for service to all children (for example, those in parochial schools, those children not now in any school, and those children whose difficulties are not primarily connected with school experiences) should be organized under school authority. Her reason for taking this position is that "Schools, as well as courts, represent 'authority' and often create fears that are contributing factors in conduct disorders. Moreover children who enjoy defying authority find defiance of the authority of the school interesting and exciting. In such cases the school's efforts at treatment may aggravate the disease." [20]

Miss Abbott also urges that adequate facilities for juvenile recreation be provided in every community, both to advise and to help the various agencies in their own recreation work and to supplement the work of all such agencies. And finally, we are reminded of a fact that should challenge us for decades to come: *"Progress toward greater economic and social security would greatly reduce delinquency"* [italics by H. W. T.].[21]

[18] *Ibid.*, p. 237.   [19] *Ibid.*, p. 238.   [20] *Ibid.*, p. 240.   [21] *Ibid.*, p. 242.

From the citations that have been made, the fact grows clearer and clearer that the problem of juvenile delinquency is unique in each community. Therefore, each community needs a unique coördination of its agencies to treat and to prevent juvenile delinquency. This fact will become still clearer as we continue our study.

To submit evidence of the inadequacy of the juvenile court alone or as a coördinating center for all community agencies to deal more successfully with all the problems of juvenile delinquency is comparatively easy. But this is not enough; the persistent problem of finding out for each community what coördination of existing agencies is best for that community and what further agencies are needed in that community for the creation of an orchestra that can perform a symphony of service to all the youth of the community must be faced by each community. As an aid to each community to study its own problem, I now cite evidence that these studies are already going on and give some suggestions as to the methods that are being used in such studies.

First of all, I recommend some of the reports of the National Probation Association. For example, in the yearbook of the Association for 1937, *Coping with Crime,* I find Section I, "Community Cooperation for Social Welfare," especially suggestive. The writers and topics of this section are: Eduard C. Lindeman, "New Patterns of Community Organization"; Ernest W. Burgess, Joseph D. Lohman, and Clifford R. Shaw, "The Chicago Area Project"; John F. Hall, "The Administration and Supervision of Community Councils"; Sara M. Einert, "Qualifications and Training of Coordinating Council Executives"; and Kenneth S. Beam, "Report of Coordinating Councils." The report by Kenneth Beam cannot even be summarized here. However, some idea of the amount of work that was done in preparation for writing the report, of the magnitude of coördination work now in process, and of the necessity for each community to study and solve its own problem may be gained from these citations:

A survey of various types of councils having as one of their purposes the prevention of delinquency was undertaken by the National Probation Association December 1, 1935, and came to an end in July of 1937.

During this period ninety-two cities in thirty states were visited, several of them more than once in the course of six transcontinental trips. Councils were found in cities and towns ranging in size from New York City to a village of five hundred people. Visits were timed for meetings of fifty-eight councils in regular sessions.

The preliminary report of this survey appearing in the 1936 yearbook of the National Probation Association, reported on about two hundred and fifty councils. At the present time we have some record of over three hundred, but this does not necessarily mean that fifty new councils were organized this year, only that fifty new councils have been discovered and listed this year, most of which are new.[22]

The closing paragraph of this 1937 report by Beam reads:

It would be difficult to overestimate the significance and the potential power of this movement. For a quarter of a century citizens' organizations have been growing in numbers and in strength. Now for the first time, they are coming together and are joining forces with social workers, public officials, religious and educational leaders. A power of influence for good is being generated which simply cannot be estimated. These councils are not far from the truth when they say "we can make of our communities what we will." [23]

Organization of Coördinating Councils

The National Probation Association also published, 1937, a fifteen-page booklet by Beam. From this booklet I quote these two paragraphs:

This type of organization does not and should not crystallize into one mold. The success of a coordinating council does not depend upon following a fixed pattern, but upon originality and ability in adopting a program to meet the needs of a community.[24]

No communities as neighborhoods are exactly alike! Therefore, no two council programs will be exactly alike. A new council should keep its eye on its own community, not on the program of some other council. It should work out its own original program as needs are revealed by studies and surveys. Success largely depends on study before the program is outlined.[25]

[22] *Coping with Crime*, p. 47.   [23] *Ibid.*, p. 76.
[24] Kenneth S. Beam, "Coördinating Councils—How Shall They Be Organized?" National Probation Association, 1937, p. 4.
[25] *Ibid.*, p. 12.

Those who object to the setting up of some new coördinating agency in a community, instead of relying upon the existing Council of Social Agencies for a new task, should note that the method advocated in the above citations would permit of such an expansion of the work of the existing Council of Social Agencies. A report made in August, 1940, by another association supplements the suggestions that we may get from the studies of community coördination made by the National Probation Association. This report is a "Survey of existing facilities based on answers to a questionnaire sent to cities in the United States of 35,000 or more." The General Summary of this report gives these data as to the variety of community programs and as to the number of cities (of the 150 having programs) having each of six types of program: [26]

Cities contacted	280
Cities that did not reply	91
Cities reporting no crime prevention program	33
Cities planning to establish programs	6
Cities with programs	150
I. Police Department Program	40
II. Police Departments in Cooperation with Juvenile Courts and Probation Departments	24
III. Programs by Courts and Juvenile Probation Bureaus	56
IV. Programs by Private Agencies	17
V. Programs by Departments of Education	3
VI. Programs by Miscellaneous City, County and State Agencies	10

The perspective of the police who were members of the committee that made this report is suggested by two quotations:

The causes of delinquency are many. The established institutions of society, the family, church and school, have undergone many changes which have had their effect on the emotional, moral, mental and physical make-up of our youth.

Scientific knowledge of the causes of delinquency must be encouraged. Existing social and economic safeguards must be strengthened. Agencies devoted to the problem must be made more effective and local responsibility must be stimulated.[27]

[26] The International Association of Chiefs of Police, *The Prevention of Delinquency and the Rehabilitation of Delinquent Minors,* New York, 1940.
[27] *Ibid.,* p. 1.

The second quotation is from a resolution that the committee submitted to a convention of the International Association of Chiefs of Police, in Milwaukee, Wisconsin, September 10, 1940, as follows:

Whereas, Communities throughout the nation are conscious of crime and delinquency problems in their respective areas and are familiar with the therapeutic resources available to them through public and private facilities, therefore be it—

Resolved that a permanent committee be appointed to make available to all municipalities interested, information on programs and procedures necessary to wage effective campaigns in controlling these problems. This committee to serve as a coordinating council to stimulate interest in this work and help in whatever way possible in the promotion of programs devoted to the *prevention of crime* and juvenile delinquency and the *rehabilitation of delinquents* [italics by H. W. T.].[28]

What Is Our Present Perspective?

In previous chapters and in this chapter, largely by the use of descriptions and statements made by successive writers, I have tried to suggest the most important changes that have been made in the treatment of juvenile delinquents from the days in England when the judge said to a boy accused of stealing, "Guilty—death," to the present, when thoughtful and observant members of all the agencies and institutions in the community—homes, schools, churches, business organizations, courts, police, and governments—are beginning to ask, "How in our community can we play an effective team game to treat and to prevent juvenile delinquency?"

Over thirty years ago, as I wrote one of my annual reports of the probation work in the Chicago Juvenile Court, I quoted some lines from Emerson that had been frequently in my mind as I looked into the faces of the procession of boys and girls who filed into the courtroom, paused a few moments before the judge's desk, and then filed out again, most of them to regard their court experience as little more than a brief detour from the main road on which their feet were set. These words have again come repeatedly to my mind since I copied for Chapter II the statements of Healy and Bronner as to the manifold frustrations of youth that cause them to seek satisfaction in ways that we adults call delinquent. And now, as a per-

[28] *Ibid.*, p. 19.

sistent challenge to both the reader and myself, as we seek more efficient ways to treat and prevent juvenile delinquency in our several communities, I pen these words from Tennyson again:

'Tis life whereof our nerves are scant
More life and fuller that we want.

What a change could be brought about in any community wherein a whole generation of earnest citizens persistently sought to provide for every child born into that community adequate opportunities to enjoy that fuller life for which his "nerves are scant" without becoming a delinquent and a criminal!

I believe that a growing purpose so to orchestrate our communities that every child shall live an abundant life results from our present perspective.

With regard to the different facilities and their orchestrations needed in a given community to give all the boys and girls an abundant life, and so to keep them from delinquency, I once asked two questions. These two questions, and my comment thereon, were written after I had made a study of the habitual spare-time activities of the delinquent youths who had filed through the juvenile court in Cleveland in a certain number of weeks. Instead of living an abundant life, I found many of them had been habitually hungry for something satisfactory to do in their spare time.

One. Are the facilities such that every boy and girl may choose for every day in the week a spare-time program that seems worth while to him or her, and that at least does not stimulate and invite delinquency?

Two. Does every boy and girl have at least enough of the sympathetic and intelligent supervision of some older person to guarantee early detection of wrong habitual choices of spare-time activity, and to provide suggestion, wherever needed, of better choices?

Surely it is a self-evident proposition that nothing less than giving the child a fair chance to choose a right use rather than a wrong use of all his spare time can lay any claim to adequacy. It is equally true that some older person ought to know whether each child's habitual choices are right or wrong, and, if they are habitually wrong, to help him as far as possible to make them more nearly right.[29]

[29] Henry W. Thurston, "Delinquency and Spare Time," *Cleveland Recreation Survey*, 1918, p. 143.

Soon after 1912, as a stimulus to probation officers to seek a more abundant life for their young probationers, I wrote a booklet. The parable with which this booklet ended closes this chapter.

PARABLE

Behold a certain probation officer went forth to his day's work among his probationers, and as he met them in their unlovely homes, upon the streets, lurking in the alleys, loafing on the corners, dodging the attendance officer and the policeman, selling papers, seeking for a new job, idly busy at messenger service, he found that some of the blind instinctive reachings of their natures toward a more complete life for their bodies were trying to take root among the thorns of personal and social immorality, appetite and passion. And these outreaching tendrils of their lives the thorns were already choking.

He found further that other gropings of the life within them had stretched out toward the stony soil of barren schooling, truancy, dead-end occupations; idleness and inefficiency in work; and unsympathetic, ignorant, and base companions at home and on the street. And these tender new out-growths of their natures were being scorched and withered in the fierce heat of a demand for competitive efficiency in industry and citizenship, for they had no depth of root.

And still other strivings toward at least a semblance of life and activity had struggled out upon the much frequented but hard paths of irreligion, theft, disorderly conduct, and opposition to law. And these the condemnation of public opinion, police, sheriffs, courts of law, jailers and hangmen were devouring up.

Then when the probation officer saw the blind, groping reachings after life of his probationers thus choked out among the thorns of appetite and immorality, scorched and withered by the sun of competition in the shallow soil of inefficiency, and devoured up by the officers of the law from the well-trodden byways of transgression, he sought out each aspiring, misguided, but growing tendril as it pushed its way out from the life of each of his probationers toward the thorns and stones and highways, and wisely guided them in the direction of the good soil of a healthy and clean body, regular attendance and steady progress in school, interesting and creative work, recreative and joy-giving play and companionship, better taste in dress, reading, music, and plays; toward a truer understanding of the worth of a real friend and of harmony with the Infinite.

And behold, when these blind, groping off-shoots of activity seeking a more abundant life, in places where there was no life, were thus guided to a good soil they began to grow and to store up health, intelligence, efficiency in work, joy in play, respect for law, and recognition of duty which give promise of self-supporting and self-respecting citizenship—some thirty, some sixty, and some a hundred fold.

And the probation officer, as late at night he daily lays his tired head upon his pillow, feels in his heart that his labor has not been in vain; and he breathes a prayer that on each coming day his eye may be keener to see the weak, straggling, misguided beginnings of life among his probationers and his hand quicker and more skillful to guide them toward places where the soil is good enough so that they can take root. And at the close of the prayer the persistent, aching, overwhelming burden of his heart finds voice in a great cry: "And Lord, if it please Thee to hear us, help me and my fellow-citizens of this town in the days that are soon to come to pluck up more of the thorns, to clear away more of the stones, to plough deeper, harrow longer, and to fertilize with a more generous hand, that straightway there may be good soil enough hereabouts to go around among all my probationers! [30]

[30] Henry W. Thurston, "The Probation Officer at Work," *Studies in Social Work,* No. 3, New York School of Social Work.

Chapter XIII: THE GIST OF JUVENILE
DELINQUENCY AS A COMMUNITY
PROBLEM

[NOTE.—I asked Mr. Mayo to write this independent chapter because of the unusual insight he has gained from his own life experience.

For most of his life, Mr. Mayo has had opportunity for direct observation of juvenile delinquents and of the efforts of both himself and others to deal with them. He was born and lived the first eleven years of his life at the Berkshire Farm School for Delinquents, of which his father was then superintendent. He says he has never yet been paroled from this institution.

After graduation from Colby College, Maine, in 1922, he held these positions in institutions for delinquent boys: Assistant Superintendent, Opportunity Farm for Boys, New Gloucester, Maine, 1922–23; high school instructor, athletic director, and director of parole, Maryland State Training School for Boys, 1923–24; Welfare Director, Dean of Training School for Institution Workers, and Assistant Director of the Children's Village, Dobbs Ferry, New York, 1924–30. From 1930 to 1935 he was a member of the faculty of the New York School of Social Work and gave courses on work in institutions and on delinquency. He has also lectured at the New School for Social Research in New York city. In 1935–36 he was Director of Personnel, Emergency Relief Bureau, New York city. Subsequent positions are: Assistant Executive Director (1936–40) and Associate Executive Director (1940–41) of the Welfare Council of New York city; President, Child Welfare League of America, Inc., June, 1939–; Chairman, Children's Bureau Commission on Children in Wartime, March, 1942–; Dean, School of Applied Social Sciences, Western Reserve University, July 1, 1941–.

As Assistant Executive Director of the Welfare Council of New

York city, there was daily thrust upon Mr. Mayo the problem, not only of understanding and helping to forward the work of separate social agencies, but the community problem of working out such an orchestration of all these agencies that they might render an effective symphony of service both to juvenile delinquents and to all others in need of community social work.

This is true also of his present positions as President of the Child Welfare League of America and as Dean of the School of Applied Social Sciences at Western Reserve University, Cleveland, Ohio. —H. W. T.]

DELINQUENCY is a legal term for a social problem; it is a reflection of conflicts and pressures in an individual, in his home, and in his surroundings. When delinquency is present to any substantial degree in a given geographical area, therefore, serious questions arise concerning the social health of the area, neighborhood, or city involved.

The approach of a community (here defined as any governmental unit, such as state, county, city, or town, or any geographical subdivision thereof) to the problem of delinquency must be based on the realization that what often appear to be deliberate antisocial acts stem from causes within the individual and his environment and that such acts are the outward form of inner difficulties.

In this connection it is perhaps necessary to review some of the more important principles relating to the individual and community aspects of delinquency as formulated during the past few decades. Physical sciences have moved forward on the basis of principles discovered and learned and laws established thereon, and the progress made in these fields is due largely to the fact that what has been learned has been recorded and used in the development of next steps. There has been too little of this scientific approach in the study and treatment of delinquency.

Although research, practice, and general experience have reminded us again and again of the cause-and-effect relationship between emotional maladjustment and delinquency; although we know that emotional conflicts emerge from and contribute to the pressures of family life; while we have abundant evidence to show the relation between individuals, their social groups, and the neighborhood in which they live; although we recognize all these as potent factors in determining conduct, we have not yet taken such data and experience to heart or put them into practice sufficiently in our philosophy and treatment. It is true, furthermore, that some students of behavior are so interested in individual causes of crime and delinquency as to be practically blinded to its many community aspects.

While the following principles may be expressed in numerous ways, a sequence and emphasis have been selected which point up the community aspects of delinquency.

1. Rooted in every individual is the need to develop *self*.

2. This development takes place largely through the *expression* of self in the family, the school, and the play groups and among other associates.

3. The early responses on the part of his groups to self-expression by a child tend to determine his later conduct; generally speaking, favorable responses elicit repetition of certain conduct and unfavorable responses tend to discourage repetition.

4. Furthermore, the total setting or environment in which a child lives tends to determine the *form* which his expression takes.

5. The ethics, mores, and standards of the group of which he is a part have a profound influence on his habits, his conduct, and the development of his total personality.

6. Thus it follows that delinquency is essentially *normal* rather than *abnormal* in the sense that given certain groups and communities it is almost a foregone conclusion that what we know as "antisocial conduct" will emerge.

7. The community in which children live is made up of neighborhoods, families, and individuals; of schools, churches, civic and political groups, and social welfare and health agencies. These groups are presided over by some unit of government. Every individual, therefore, every organization, and every unit of government has a stake in the treatment and prevention of delinquency, for the community itself of which all are a part is the larger group, setting, or

framework within which homes, schools, churches, and other civic groups must function. A common denominator or over-all factor in the community is *government,* and the pivotal point of government is the individual. The individual citizen then has in his hands the power to institute and maintain that quality of government without which wholesome and constructive community life is impossible.

The above principles, if they may be called such, complete a cycle, for we have seen that the community helps to shape the individual and the individual, acting through his groups, is the only instrumentality through which the community may be made a constructive force in the development of personality. Carried to its ultimate conclusion this implies that the roots of delinquency are not wholly in the individual offender, nor yet in the community in any corporate sense, *but in the individual citizen himself.*

Other units in the community, of course, in addition to government, must bear their share of the burden and need analysis and reevaluation in the light of what we have learned about juvenile delinquency in the last few decades. Foremost among these are the home, the school, the church, the court, and other social and health agencies. The following paragraphs will deal briefly with the community approach and the role of social agencies.

Social agencies and indeed the juvenile court were organized and exist for the primary and specific purpose of creating a more favorable individual and community situation from the standpoint of mental, moral, and physical health for those who have not "made the grade" for whatever reason. Unless their programs are based on a knowledge of the basic causes of delinquency, however, their efforts must fall short of the mark.

The seven principles listed above are a summary of individual and community factors and their relationship to the development of personality. What have we learned about the *individual manifestations* of delinquency which occur when the relations between the individual and his group (be it school or family or other groups) produce the conflicts which lead to the kind of behavior society designates as antisocial? It is to these manifestations that the health and social agencies and the legal machinery of the community should address themselves in seeking their part in the community attack on delinquency.

The following are perhaps pertinent and suggestive in this connection:

1. Our present knowledge of the causes of delinquency has taught us that its manifestations may be noted at an early age. Attitudes of very young children toward those in authority, toward the family and social group, and toward property often give early and accurate indication of the need for intensive treatment.

2. Excessive aggression or withdrawal during adolescence is a danger signal to be noted and dealt with skillfully.

3. Boys commit overt delinquent acts and give evidence of their maladjustment through the medium of gang activities and offenses against property. Girls are prone to emotional and temperamental difficulties rather than overt and violent acts against property and they seldom operate in gangs.

4. In so far as all young delinquents are concerned, crimes against property are far in excess of those against persons.

5. The typical or "composite" hold-up man in the United States today may be described as a young man nineteen or twenty years of age from an unhappy and probably a "broken" home. He is American-born, though his grandparents may have been born in Europe. He has no special vocational skills and has not finished elementary school, though he has average intelligence or better. He is fear-ridden, insecure, and in conflict. He and his family have been under the care of social agencies for years. He has spent from two to four years in a children's institution and perhaps a year in a foster family home. In almost every conceivable sense of the word he is "deprived," and as a burglar he is engaged in the business of supplying his conscious and subconscious needs in spite of all the laws on the statute books.

So much, then for some of the manifestations of delinquent behavior as we see them in our society. Are the social agencies, the courts, and the whole gamut of law enforcement agencies in the community building their programs around these concepts? If they are, they have culled out of their experience and observation the knowledge that the following must be kept in mind in any treatment plans. (These are suggested by the five foregoing points and are rooted in the philosophy of the seven principles listed earlier.)

1. Provision of opportunity for expression and *creative activity* of a satisfying nature constitutes sound treatment procedure.

2. The influence of a well-poised, objective personality is of more importance in treatment than any technique or method per se.

3. The principle of individual difference holds, and, though we must continue our studies of the individual and build treatment programs around him, we must not lose sight of the fact that children have certain *common needs* which cannot be dealt with on an individual basis. Among these are housing, protection against industrial exploitation and the ravages of disease, medical care, recreation facilities, and the like. The supplying of these on a community-wide basis will go a long way toward the treatment and prevention of delinquency.

4. Agencies should be influenced in program-making by the needs of special age or racial groups which need attention.

5. Courts and social and health agencies should therefore amass, analyze, and use salient economic, industrial, social, and population data of the neighborhoods or areas they serve. (Such material might well include known cases of delinquency and crime; the incidence of disease, the mortality rate, etc.) Such data would, of course, need constant checking to be kept up to date, but in the hands of competent persons they would constitute a more realistic basis for the development of sound agency programs than any other one device now known.

Basic data of this kind brought together by a local council of social agencies or a similar central agency, to a greater degree than now obtains as a rule, should be the starting point, chart, and compass for every group in the community dealing with the rehabilitation of delinquent groups and individuals. No one method could be more effective in focusing attention on the community aspects of delinquency and in encouraging a unified community approach to it.

Students in schools of social work and universities would gain a point of view from such material and its use which no other method can possibly give, particularly if the study of a given neighborhood were accomplished by a field-work assignment in the same area. Required reading in a course on juvenile delinquency should include such volumes as *A Social Study of Pittsburgh and Allegheny County* along with treatises on individual behavior and treatment procedures.

If we are to realize a fully effective community approach to delinquency on the part of social agencies, however, something more than basic social data is required. The essence of the treatment of delinquency on the part of the whole community lies first of all in every agency performing its own primary function more effectively, whether it be case work, education, or religious instruction. If agencies will do this and, at the same time, watch with a vigilant eye the "laps" and "gaps" between their work and that of other agencies, the way will be open for the quality and type of community planning and teamwork that will make deep inroads on the problem of delinquency. Among the present "gaps" in our services for children, for example, is our failure to act upon the early indications of delinquency now so well known to us and our appalling failure to set up adequate services for the adolescent.

In the face of this necessity for filling in gaps and avoiding duplication of service, social and health agencies face some rather sober questions, questions that should not be answered on the basis of what seems good for an individual agency alone but rather in the light of what is good for the community.

For example, with public relief agencies giving their attention primarily and almost exclusively to the distribution of relief and with most family agencies under private auspices operating on the basis of a highly selective intake policy, how shall we care for other families who desperately need the ministrations of the social case worker? Is it reasonable to expect that the public tax dollar can be stretched to furnish the relief agencies with an adequate staff of case workers to give this service, or should the private family agency *supplement* the public agency in this respect?

The reader may be familiar with the answers to these questions and the philosophy on which most voluntary family agencies base their decision to accept for the most part only those who seek their services and who they feel can profit by them. This decision has been reached thoughtfully and conscientiously, no doubt, but the problem of these other families remains unsolved and to some extent ignored, *in spite of the fact that most criminals, according to present research, emerge from families on or below the economic level of relief families.* There was recently prepared by a group of voluntary family agencies in one of our larger cities a statement of their main functions. In it there was no pledge to study the communities and the neighborhoods they served to determine where and what the greatest needs were. The emphasis was not even in that direction. It is encouraging to note, however, that in another and smaller town an experiment is being set up designed to "spot" for intensive and early treatment those families in the community which give indication of "social break-down."

A second and perhaps equally important matter that concerns social agencies in relation to crime prevention has to do with the relation between family and child-caring organizations. We talk of the unity and sanctity of the family, of strengthening family ties, of keeping a child in his family if at all possible, and then belie our words in hundreds of communities by building even higher the walls which separate agencies dealing with children from those engaged in family work. It is trite to say that the factors which these agencies have in common are stronger and more important than those that keep them apart, but it is true; and it is equally true that agencies which are attempting to build up a case for an isolated entity are not presenting a common front in the war against crime and its origin.

In conclusion, then, the gist of juvenile delinquency as a community problem rests upon:

1. The acceptance of those basic principles of causes and treatment of delinquency which experience has taught us to be sound.

2. The reëvaluation of the programs carried on by our schools, churches, and social agencies to determine to what extent they are actually based on and built around these principles.

3. The establishment and maintenance of honest and vigorous municipal, county, and state government.

4. The collation and analysis of basic economic and social facts

about the communities which agencies serve and in focusing attention on those geographical areas and special groups which most need care and protection.

5. The adequate performance by each social agency of its own *primary* function; its willingness to study the points at which its work impinges upon the work of others; and the extent to which each agency will enter into vigorous community planning.

6. In the final analysis, the main responsibility lies with the individual citizen, social worker, teacher, and clergyman to learn the social facts about his community, to face these facts and, through the instruments of a democratic society, do something about them; in this way and in this way only will communities be able to create a total setting within which children will be able to live with some hope of adequate development. Herein lies the essence of the treatment and prevention of juvenile delinquency.

APPENDICES

Appendix A: "ACTIONS SPEAK
LOUDER THAN WORDS"

A GOOD WAY for us to seek an answer to the question of whether adults set bad examples for youth is to make an honest observation and evaluation of the quality of our own actions and attitudes toward others in our family circles, in our business and professional relations, in our political affiliations and activities, in our interracial attitudes and activities, in our international outlooks, and in our religious antipathies and fellowships. Do we meet some or all of these social situations with a careless, selfish, or grasping attitude or, on the other hand, with a thoughtful, fair, and giving or sharing attitude? This question goes deep, and each of us must answer for himself. During the process of answering the question for ourselves we shall inevitably tend also to observe and evaluate what the actions of our friends, neighbors, and professional, political, and business associates are also teaching youth through their actions. If, in this quest, we have an honest desire to be ourselves judged, I believe we are justified in citing for illustration a few examples set by other adults, as well as those in which we have personally been involved.

Illustrations of Questionable Adult Example

One of my own earliest personal memories in this connection is that, when a boy, I heard a man who owned a sawmill in the town of Marshfield, Vermont, use a brutal oath while condemning his boy for swearing. I have since read the opinion of John Bunyan about this kind of adult example before our youth, as Bunyan's thought is expressed in a quotation sent to me by a correspondent:

Take heed that the misdeeds for which thou correctest thy children be not learned them by thee. Many children learn that wickedness of their parents for which they beat and chastise them. Take heed that thou smile not upon them to encourage them in small faults. Take heed that thou use not unsavory and unseemly words in thy chastising of them, as railing, miscalling or the like. This is devilish. Take heed that thou do not accustom them to many chiding words and threatenings, mixed with lightness and laughter. This will harden.

A few of the adult examples I have seen flaunted in the face of youngsters in the various neighborhoods of which I have been a part are these:

Some of us have been known to demand, at the cost of others just as old or needy, special favors in food, chairs, and places in the room in the sunlight, by the grate fire, or in the family car.

I have seen some of us, in time of drought, when there were town regulations against the use of water for lawns and gardens at certain hours of the day, watering our lawns and gardens during forbidden hours, keeping a watchful eye meanwhile for the policeman in the distance, so as not to get caught.

I have seen some of us cut in ahead of others in line to get our tickets for a movie, a concert, a lecture, or a train.

I have seen some of our cars parked all night without lights on the wrong side of the street, contrary to town regulations. During weeks of deep snow some of these cars occupy almost half the passable width of the streets, as it is too much work for us owners to shovel the snow away so that we can park next to the curb and thus leave the street clearer for travel.

Among those of us who drive cars I have seen some who disregard red lights, drive around curves on the wrong side of the road, and cut in on curves and in other situations where we cannot see if cars are approaching us from the opposite direction.

At various turnstiles admitting to subways and trains, I have seen some of us sneaking our children, of paying age, in under the turnstile; on trains, I have known some of us to lie to the conductor as to the ages of children, so as to pay only half fare or no fare at all.

I have heard of some of us who have a few dollars to leave to our heirs and who have been advised, by lawyers in such good standing that they are members of the local government, how to make our wills in such a way that our money may go to the same beneficiaries but pay less inheritance tax or none at all.

I have heard it said that there are some among us who, in making our income tax returns, have hired lawyers in good standing in the Bar Association to inform us as to certain temporary shufflings of ownership and accounts among relatives and friends to the end that, by various subterfuges as to the real amount of our income, we may reduce the amount of our income taxes. In such cases, we actually seem to prove false the tax part of that old saying, "Nothing is sure except death and taxes." Even though we succeed in dodging our fair share of taxes, we cannot really succeed in dodging the other part of the saying; *death— to our honor—is sure.*

"Yankee" Teacher and "Rebel" Student

A few years ago a young lady from Mississippi who was about to graduate from the New York School of Social Work, where she had been a member of one of my classes, came into my room to say good-bye. She said "I know that you were born in Vermont and so I thought that before I left the school I would tell you that I was a grown woman before I knew that 'damned Yankee' was two words." I could have retorted that in Vermont during my day the words "rebel" and "devil" were synonymous. Although we had become fast friends, these two labels had made the process of becoming friends more difficult.

An Example of Religious Prejudice

I was once an elder in a suburban Presbyterian church. My previous conections with several Protestant denominations were as follows: my mother was a Congregationalist; my father was a Methodist; I married a Presbyterian; my wife and I joined the Dutch Reformed Church in another suburb where we then lived. In a meeting of the Presbyterian elders, I heard another elder criticize the minister for permitting his assistant pastor, in his talks to children, to make frequent references to the good example of men and women in Protestant denominations other than Presbyterian, and once or twice even of Catholics. The elder's argument was that there were plenty of good examples among Presbyterians; why, therefore, lead the children to think of good people outside of this fold? After he had finished, I had an inner urge based somewhat on my own varied church experiences, and I asked him this question: "Mr. X, when you get to Heaven do you expect to find any people except Presbyterian there, and, if so, do you intend to have any dealings with them?" In reply, he said, "Mr. Thurston, that question is sarcastic." "It was so intended," said I.

It was this experience that reminded me of a story that I had heard of an upper-class Englishman who was once asked whether he thought anybody could get to Heaven without first becoming a member of the Church of England. In reply, he said, "I don't know, but I am sure of one thing. No gentleman would ever try it."

"Damnation by Label"

To such incidents as the above we can all add from our experiences, observations, and reading other incidents which show our adult attitudes of superiority to and disapproval of people of other races, colors, economic status, and political isms. In a wealthy suburban town I know, the Cosmopolitan Club, formed to help its fellow-townsmen, members of different national groups, to become acquainted with others, has never accepted any of its many Negroes into membership. In Vermont we used to call the French Canadians who came into our town "Canucks." We Americans have derogatory names for several other nationalities, for example, Italians and Poles. We, in our community, don't want anything to do with "those people" who live across the tracks, or down on the flat, or in the X ward of our town. We don't want such people to rent or buy residences in our neighborhood.[1]

In the nineties, when I was teaching in the Hyde Park High School, which was near the University of Chicago, I had the privilege of attending a University class in sociology taught by Professor Albion W. Small. Dr. Small had a name for this general disapproval of nationalities and religious, political, economic, social, and residential groups. He called it "damnation by label." He said that such condemnatory, thoughtless, indiscriminate use of labels was not only unfair to many individuals in the groups condemned, but that it also blinded us to the truth that there were usually some good qualities and phases of truth among the persons and programs that we condemned. Dr. Small's thought was not only that we were unjustly judging others but that we were ourselves kept from knowing the truth about our fellow men which we were once told by a high authority would set us free— "And ye shall know the truth, and the truth shall make you free" (John 8:32). How much honest regard for "the truth, the whole truth, and nothing but the truth" do we who habitually use "damnation by label" think our adult example tends to develop in the youthful citizens of our democracy?

An article entitled "Classes in America" was written from personal experience and observation by Charles Stelzle, who preceded Edmund B. Chaffee as pastor of the Labor Temple in New York city. Stelzle writes thus:

The latest Federal Census of Religious Bodies reports 213 denominations of which 155 are grouped in twenty-three families and fifty-eight are listed as separate denominations. For example, among the "families" are reported 18 kinds of Baptists, 17 brands of Mennonites, 19 groups of Methodists and 9 divisions of Presbyterians. Other denominations are also pretty well split up into segments.

Among these American religionists may be discovered many more classes than are found among the Jews, and most of their prejudices are absurd if not tragic. Roughly, the major denominations are divided into (one) Episcopalians, who regard themselves as the aristocracy of the church; (two) Presbyterians and Congregationalists, who flatter themselves that they are the intellectuals, and (three) Methodists and Baptists, who are said to constitute the "common people." Trailing along in all shades and degrees of alleged "inferiority" are scores of religious bodies which one regards with pity—and often with contempt if one belongs to the more powerful denominations. Just why, few seem to know, excepting that it is not religion that makes the difference—or the lack of it—but the economic and social factors that influence one's standing in the community.

---

[1] For vivid descriptions of racial prejudices, in this our democracy, against the people of at least ten different lands, read Louis Adamic, *From Many Lands*, New York, Harper, 1940.

However, this deplorable class distinction is not limited to the churches—if this is any comfort to them. It is found in much the same degree in fraternal orders, educational institutions and where one would probably least expect to find it, among industrial groups.

In the big machine shop in New York City in which I served a five years' apprenticeship and worked for three years as a journeyman there were at least half a dozen different grades of society. The draftsmen—who regarded themselves as professional men—felt that they were just a bit above the pattern-makers, who wore aprons instead of coats as they worked. The pattern-makers considered themselves superior to the machinists, because they wore white shirts instead of overalls and because they earned about half a dollar a day more. But the machinists had the notion that they were better than the molders because the molder's job was dirtier and in some ways appeared less "scientific." The molders looked down on the tinsmiths, and they all despised the "common laborer." They declined to eat their lunches and drink their beer in the same corner with him.

In a little railroad town there are three women's clubs—one composed of the wives of the engineers, another consisting of the wives of the firemen, while the third is made up of the wives of the brakemen. It is absolutely impossible for the wives of the firemen to join the club composed of the wives of the engineers, and as for the wives of the brakemen—they simply aren't in it. And all their husbands belong to the same brotherhood!

The average clerk in a drygoods store, let us say, regards himself as superior to the artisan and laborer. He does not want to be known as a "workingman." He imagines that he is in the same grade of society as the owner of the store. He tries hard to live the part, even though he sleeps in a dingy hall bedroom and dines on a chocolate éclair and a glass of milk.

In some of the big walk-up tenements in the poorer sections of New York the occupants of the lower floors look with disdain upon those who live nearer the roof, the lower floor dwellers constituting the aristocracy of the tenements—and how they like to show it.[2]

Adult Behavior on Halloween and at Football Games

Two illustrations of adult crowd behavior follow; the first is in a United Press dispatch from Chicago:

Rioting Halloween merrymakers wrecked large areas of the $55,000,000 World Fair in its closing hours early today, tearing buildings apart, throwing hundreds of benches and chairs into lagoons and tossing policemen in after them.

The mob, 300,000 strong, took complete possession of eighty-three miles of streets and concessions, drank everything in sight except Lake Michigan, and snatched everything movable as souvenirs.

Men, women and children fainted in the crush along the Street of Villages. Police were called to quell dozens of fights.

Plans to close the gates at midnight were abandoned after a screaming mob had battered through 200 police reserves and demolished a section of fence.

[2] *New York Times,* April 9, 1933.

The $500,000 Horticultural Building was almost denuded of rare plants by women who took home $200. plants as souvenirs. Some 300 persons, led by a group of revelers masked as witches, littered the Italian Village with wreckage. Dancers and models in peep shows fled and refused to appear after audiences repeatedly had torn down nettings and screens erected by censors.

Elevators to the Skyride observation tower, sixty-four stories high, were halted when empty bottles began showering down from above.[3]

The second example is a reference to behavior of college and town young men at intercollegiate games. The reference, according to a newspaper report, was made by President Angell of Yale in an address to about 2,000 graduates:

Persons unfamiliar with the real nature of the problem are prone to criticize college authorities severely for not preventing the insufferable disorder at various athletic contests, especially football. The destruction of goal posts by the supporters of the victorious teams has become an almost sacred ritual, to forego which would argue a lack of red blood and a true sense of loyalty to alma mater. Until recently the exponents of this cult were wont to wait until the game was over, but now they rush on the field as soon as they feel sure that the score cannot be materially changed. The whole business has become an intolerable nuisance.

So far as I know, no college stands wholly guiltless. Certainly Princeton and Harvard have both gone off with our posts in recent years and Yale has abundant mementoes of a similar kind gathered in Massachusetts and New Jersey. In the attacks upon the posts in the Bowl, there is always a liberal invasion of young men who show no indication of collegiate connections of any kind, but whose familiarity with alcohol is often flagrant.

Hockey and baseball spectators are the two other worst offenders against decent manners and good sportsmanship, although basketball crowds can put in some claim.[4]

Human Need as a Stepping Stone to Political Power

I quote some passages from a book by Jane Addams's nephew in which he interprets the views of Miss Addams, often with quotation from her own words. She makes clear the relation between a great variety of human needs and the political power of Alderman Johnny Powers.

No one who lives among the poor, she points out, can fail to be impressed with their constant kindness to each other. This kindness is heightened by the consciousness of each that he himself may be in distress next week. So he stands by his friends. To such a man "it seems fitting that his alderman should do the same thing on a larger scale." He bails out his constituents when they are arrested, or says a word to the justice when they appear for trial; gets them off with small fines, or sees what he can do to fix up matters with the state's

[3] *New York World-Telegram,* November 1, 1934.
[4] *New York Times,* February 3, 1936.

attorney when the charge is serious. He pays rent when no rent is ready, finds jobs when work is hard to get (one in five of the voters of the nineteenth ward were on the city payroll under Powers in 1896, and Powers asserted that two years before, in the "bad times," 2600 residents of the ward, more than one-third of the voters, had been on city jobs). He is at all family festivities the "simple friend"; gets up "benefits" for a widow or a sick man; spends ten times as much at church bazaars as anybody else, "murmuring that it's all right as long as the church or the poor get it." Above all, he is the simple friend in periods of sorrow; quite honestly "great at funerals," and always saving the very poorest from the "awful horror of burial by the county." . . . Even the direct purchase of votes is approved of by some of the community. A man who complains that he can get only two dollars for his vote, instead of five as in another year, seems less unethical to one who is aware that the same man's income for the previous nine months has been less than thirty dollars, and that he is in debt for more than that amount. As for the question where the money comes from, the simple answer acceptable to the ethics of the community is that the alderman "gets it from the rich," a process which tends to make John Powers as popular in the nineteenth ward, as the same theory made Robin Hood in Merrie England of old. With genuine pride the constituents assert that their alderman is backed by the head of the street-car company, a "swell," a man who had given a million dollars to a university, a man therefore as philanthropic, as upright, and as socially important as any "crank reformer" in Chicago. What then is the conclusion? That if we are to hold to the theory of political democracy, we must take pains to find a common ground of ethics and human experience.[5]

An Illustration of Political Relief

The makings of an old-fashioned holiday dinner were distributed yesterday by the Sheriff . . . to almost 3,000 families, residents of the east side of Yorkville. They came from every quarter of the Fourteenth Assembly District, of which he is the Democratic leader. There were men, women and children, from practically every block east of Third Avenue between Fifty-second and Eighty-fourth Streets. Sheriff . . . was waiting for them at the Club-house of the . . . Association, the regular Democratic organization of the district, with aides who helped him distribute the packages.

There were Irish and Germans, and Italians and Poles and Galicians and representatives of almost every other nationality, for the Fourteenth Assembly District is known locally as the "League of Nations." They came from 9 A. M. to 6 P. M., and left laden with heavy paper bags containing fourteen pounds of ham, from ten to twenty pounds of potatoes, a large loaf of bread, a can of lima beans, a can of pork and beans, a can of salmon, a can of syrup, 2 cans of soup, a can of apple sauce, a package of oatmeal, two pounds of sugar, six oranges, six apples, a pound of coffee and a pound of tea.

[5] James Weber Linn, *Jane Addams,* New York, Appleton-Century, 1935, pp. 172–74. Linn quotes Miss Addams's paper, "Ethical Survivals in City Politics."

And every bag contained the Sheriff's personal card of Christmas greeting. This is the twelfth year that the Sheriff has distributed Christmas dinners.

He began the practice when he became leader of the district. The dinners are his personal gifts, he explained, and given to all, regardless of political faith. Even non-citizens are included, he said, remarking that this year six hundred aliens were among those receiving the food-stuffs.

The only requirement is that a family be in real need. Applications for the dinners were made by letters and every case investigated by an election district captain. A needy person received a numbered card, to prevent duplication, and the card fixed an hour at which the recipient was to call. Thus the line before the clubhouse was kept within reasonable proportions all day.

The Sheriff himself, known as Daddy to the children of the district, who attend his annual May party 40,000 strong, and as Uncle Tom to the grownups, personally handed out many of the packages. With him, shirt-sleeved before the provisions, piled to the ceiling of the clubhouse basement, were Alderman . . . , Assemblyman . . . , Under Sheriff . . . of New York County and President of the Sheriff's Association, and the election district captains, all aiding in the distribution.[6]

Conflicting Standards of Political Ethics

A 1934 newspaper gives a letter by a Federal official to a New York local official and a reply by the latter, relating to the question of whether or not only Democrats should be appointed to park positions. The letter of the Federal official bore the date of January 27, 1931, and read in part:

My dear B . . . : I must confess that I don't agree with your method of selecting men which you indicate is done by a board of engineers. My attitude, B . . . , would be to appoint no one but Democrats to these laboring positions. The Democrats are in control of the State Government and have been for many years and we are not taking care of them in my judgment in the way that we should. I never yet saw a Republican office holder, giving any consideration to a Democrat.[7]

To this letter the local official replied in part (January 30, 1931), "I find myself in complete disagreement with you as to the method of employing men in the State Park System." [8] In the 1934 newspaper article that printed the 1931 letters, it is further reported that, when told that the local official had made the letter public, the Federal official smiled and said, "I never have been a hypocrite in public life and I have never been a hypocrite on any public question. The views I held in 1931, I hold today." I ask the reader, is membership in a political party, instead of

---

[6] *New York Times,* December 25, 1931.
[7] *Ibid.,* October 15, 1934.   [8] *Loc. cit.*

fitness for the particular public job in question, to be the basis for appointment to that job in our democracy?

Not with a belief that bad adult example among men as citizens, as businessmen, and in politics is universal, but as illustrations of persistent temptations to such bad examples as we read about so frequently in our twentieth-century papers, I cite these cases:

Thirty-one persons, including men and women, some of them physicians, were convicted in one of our cities for participation in a plot to defraud insurance companies through false proof of claims.[9]

In another city sixty-one persons were convicted of election and other kinds of fraud. The judge is reported to have said in court, "Most of them [defendants] were but helpless pieces of a game played by master minds."[10]

In a third city four officials were convicted of frauds and bribery.

The Chief Justice of the three judges who tried these persons is reported to have said in part: "The defendants in this case have been public officers. When we find that those who carry the very name of trustees betray their trust, we cannot complain much if the community holds in suspicion those in public office. We feel that the penalty for those elected ought to be as severe as the law allows."[11]

Of the attitude of citizens toward personal obedience to traffic regulations a newspaper reports a judge to have said in part:

It is surprising the pressure a traffic judge feels to violate his oath of office. Leading citizens do not hesitate to ask the court to dismiss certain cases or to show leniency.

When "fixing" is prevalent, the fellow who pays a fine in a traffic case feels he is a sucker. Few lack a friend in the police department, in the Mayor's office or in the Court personnel to take care of a ticket.

A survey in one large city showed 78% of the traffic law violators apprehended by the police escaped punishment.[12]

I close with statements by two men, one of whom had been director of a famous organization to fight crime, and the other a notable criminal. The first of these men makes his own statement and also quotes the second. Both men suggest the importance of good example by all adults.

One advantage of correcting the crime situation at its root is that working toward the diminution not only of known criminality but also toward the correction of all dishonesty which is technically not classifiable as crime. *All ques-*

---

[9] *New York Times,* March 17, 1937.
[10] *New York World-Telegram,* May 5, 1938.
[11] *Chicago Tribune,* February 6, 1932.
[12] William C. Larsen, Judge in Minneapolis Municipal Court, *Chicago Tribune,* October 4, 1934.

tionable business dealings as well as statutory crime would disappear if every one were actuated by an absolute and instinctive sense of morality. When Al Capone was asked why he did not leave off his career of crime he is quoted as replying with grim pride: *"Why the biggest bankers and business men and politicians and professional men are looking to me—to keep the system going."* [Italics by H. W. T.] [13]

[13] Alexander G. Jamie, Director of the Secret Six in Chicago, in article on "Industrialism and Mercenary Crime," in E. D. MacDougall, ed., *Crime for Profit*, Boston, Stratford, 1933.

Appendix B: YOUTHFUL AWARENESS OF BAD ADULT EXAMPLE

I ASSUME that the reader and I agree that our dominant family, racial, social, political, and economic groups pass on their characteristic forms of adult behavior to youth largely through youth's unconscious imitation of such behavior. To what degree such imitation of bad adult example becomes consciously purposeful and tends to lead on to behavior that adults call delinquent is a question that cannot be answered with any degree of mathematical accuracy. Nevertheless all adults who have to deal with juvenile delinquents as individuals should often ask if either unconscious or conscious imitation of adult example has, at least in part, stimulated them toward delinquency. I now cite a few instances of juvenile behavior, and opinions about juvenile behavior, which at least suggest rather definite conscious youthful awareness of bad adult example.

Junior High School Girls Draw a Cartoon of a Traffic Policeman

Three junior high school girls in a Middle Atlantic state recently published a mimeographed paper that they called "The Weekly News-sance" [Nuisance]. One of the cartoons, sent to me by one of the girls, consisted of four parts, as follows:

1. A traffic policeman is shown stopping a woman driver of an automobile. She protests in these words: "I had the right of way when this man ran into me, yet you say I was to blame."
2. Same policeman and same woman. The policeman says: "You certainly were to blame."
3. Same personnel and car. The woman asks: "Why?"
4. Same cartoon. The policeman says: "Because his father's the mayor, his brother's the chief of police, and I'm engaged to his sister."

Where does the reader suppose these girls could have got such ideas about "our policeman"?

"Prison Days and Nights"—Opinions of a Man Who Has "Been There"

The following statement is made by Victor Nelson, a man who had been in orphan asylum, reformatory, and state and national prisons off and on from the time his mother died in 1905 and he, at the age of seven years, was sent to an orphan asylum to 1932, when he was paroled from Norfolk, Massachusetts, to Dr. Abraham Myerson, Psychiatric Examiner of Prisoners for the Commonwealth of Massachusetts.

We are told that his release was for the express purpose of writing this book of opinions, because he is "articulate." We can give only a small number of extracts from this book, but the reader will note that these extracts include not only the opinions of Mr. Nelson but his report of the opinions of many other inmates, which show their awareness of the adult example of men outside prison walls and still generally regarded as good and respectable citizens.

Some of the statements by Mr. Nelson are:

Since the opinions and attitudes of rapers, murderers and one-time prisoners in general are largely those of the average law-abiding citizen they need not be reported here [italics by H. W. T.]. The attitudes and opinions which chiefly concern us now are those of the professional criminal.[1]

"Yeah," says No. 5. "They're all out for the old do-ray-me. Steal a million and you'll never hit the can. But get a pinch when you haven't got face money, and have to take one of them cop-a plea lawyers the court hands you and where do you get off? Look at me, with a sawbuck to do, and them Page and Shaw swindlers (they had plenty of dough) get off with a lousy couple of years down the Island. Guys like that get away with murder." [2]

"And what the hell do they know about prisons anyhow?" asks No. 6. "Most of 'em never saw the inside of one. They don't even know what one looks like, let alone what it feels like to pack away five or ten years in the can.

"They ought to make every one of the lousy crumbs do a six-month bit before they go to the bench. Then maybe they wouldn't be so goddam free with the years they hand out. And the likes of those guys—guys like this so-and-so, and district attorneys like . . . and . . . , and cops like this . . . , and all those guys, they're supposed to be guys for us to look up to and copy. Every other one of the bastards is a cheap grafter. And then they expect the likes of us to be honest." [3]

"Yeh," says No. 13, "and look at all these so-called business men—these bucket shop guys and stock swindlers and embezzlers. They swindle widows and orphans and poor people out of their savings and insurance money—but did you ever hear of one of them getting a bit like ours? Not on your life.

"They get a lousy couple of years, and when they come to prison, the warden and the screws fall all over themselves giving them all the good jobs and all the best breaks. In the first place, the *laws* don't let a *judge* give them the bits they can give us. No, the *laws* were *made* by *lawyers* and *business men* and *bankers* and the like of that. I think they are the lousiest bastards in the world.

---

[1] Victor F. Nelson, *Prison Days and Nights,* Boston, Little, Brown & Co., 1933, p. 21.

[2] *Ibid.,* p. 23.   [3] *Ibid.,* p. 24.

I may be a thief and all that; but, by Christ, I wouldn't steal my money from a widow or an orphan, or from poor people. Next to roping in a young kid, I think theirs is the lousiest racket in the world. Those guys do some real harm. They put banks and whole communities on the bum, while all we do is bust some guy for a few bucks that he can easily afford to lose. And all they get is six months, where we get years." [4]

No. 14 says, "And they get paroles and we don't."

Another says: "Lawyers, judges, district attorneys, welfare workers, ministers, mayors, and governors—they all are out for the dough, just like we are." [5]

Lincoln Steffens Tells How, When a Boy, He Became Aware of Bribery and Political Corruption among Adults

Next, the reader may well give attention to the words of Lincoln Steffens, who, in his *Autobiography,* tells how he, when a boy, first became aware of questionable adult example in California races, railroading, and legislation. Of his experiences with a boy named . . . who boarded at his home and was to be a page in the California legislature, Steffens says:

There was a long delay in his appointment, and I wondered why. The legislators were in town, Sacramento was filled with them, and the legislature did not meet. Why? . . . explained indifferently that they were "organizing." There were committees to "fix up" and a lot of fat jobs to be distributed; not only pages to appoint, but clerks, sergeants at arms, everything, hundreds of them, and yet not enough to go around. There were, for instance, three times as many boys promised pageships as there were pages, and a pageship was a petty job. The page got only $10.00 a day. Some places paid much more than this in salaries, besides what you could make out of them. "It all depends on who gets the Speakership," said . . . . "Let's go riding." "But aren't you afraid you'll get left?" I asked anxiously. He wasn't. His "member" was the San Francisco leader of the Republican R. R. crowd which was sure to capture the Speakership and then the whole organization of the House.[6]

After . . . had been appointed page, Steffens says that:

He found me a seat just back of the rail where I could sit and watch him and the other pages running about among the legislators in their seats . . . we learned the procedure, we became experts on the rules. . . .

"Where were the absent members?" Steffens once asked while a debate was in progress with many members absent.

I did not ask that question often; not out loud. The pages laughed; everybody laughed. . . . explained; "The members are out where the fate of the meas-

[4] *Ibid.,* pp. 27–28.   [5] *Ibid.,* pp. 31–32.
[6] Lincoln Steffens, *Autobiography,* New York, Harcourt, Brace & Co., 1931, p. 46.

ure debated is being settled." And he took me to the committee rooms and hotel apartments, where with the drinks and cigars, members were playing poker with the lobbyists and leaders. "The members against the bill are allowed to win the price agreed on to buy their votes." Bribery! I might as well have been shot, somewhere in my head or my heart. I was wounded deeply.[7]

Author of "The Gang" Says That Gang Boys Know Corrupt Politics

A more recent writer, who is entitled to an opinion on the fact and degree of youthful awareness of bad adult example, is Frederic Thrasher, who wrote *The Gang*. At a conference of social workers Thrasher said:

The Gang Boys in Chicago know corrupt politics. One of the boys I was interested in wanted to be a criminal lawyer, and we said to him, "Well, what would you do if you were a criminal lawyer?" Instead of saying, "I would prepare a good brief and I would look up all the evidence in the case, and I would know the law," he said: "I would go to the judge's house at night." How did that boy have that particular attitude? Because he lived in a certain area in Chicago where he knew that that kind of a judge lived, and he knew the political boss of the area, and he knew how you got out of jail if you got in. Some of these boys of twelve and fourteen you could not keep in jail in Chicago.[8]

Youth Are Aware of High Finance of an Illegal Character in High Places

This opinion is expressed by H. H. Clegg, Assistant to J. Edgar Hoover, at a dinner closing the Boys' Exposition, June 3, 1936, in the Hotel Commodore, New York city:

So-called high finance of an illegal character in high places is more dangerous in its consequences and influences than other offences against property. To reward the thief who stole millions and punish the thief who stole a mere pittance must not be allowed to become commonplace. Both must be labelled as thieves and should be treated accordingly. . . .

. . . youths, seeing bankers receive only nominal punishment for embezzlement of trust funds were encouraged to do likewise, and some move into respectable business and demand their cut.

It is necessary that the boy learn to make the law enforcement officer his hero, rather than to lionize the criminal. The boy loves a winner, especially when that winner has emerged victorious in spite of a multitude of disadvantages.

Three years ago boys were playing "John Dillinger" and "bank robbers," while today they are playing "G-men," "policemen," and "special agents." [9]

[7] *Ibid.*, pp. 47–48.
[8] *Proceedings* of the New York Conference of Social Work [Rochester, New York, November 12–13, 1928], p. 231.
[9] *New York Times*, June 4, 1936.

Does It Pay Youth to Be Honest?

A young man eighteen years old wrote a letter to a magazine asking the above question. He said in part:

This question is pretty important because I'm not the only one trying to decide it. A lot of other young fellows are, too. Not many choose to be dishonest because they can't help it. Most of them choose to be dishonest because they think it pays. Please understand that I'd rather be honest if I thought it would actually pay.[10]

As an illustration of an honest man who had had a hard time in business and was defeated for county treasurer by a slick liar, he cited his father; and of a dishonest man, or at least one not showing good citizenship, he cited his father's rival who succeeded in business and "ran for state senator and was elected with a bang. That's when he got really rich, altho state senators don't get a big salary."

The magazine offered prizes of $100, $50, and $25 for the three best answers to this young man's question. We are told that some 25,000 letters came in reply and that all of them had been forwarded to the young man who asked the question. The three prize-winning letters are also published, and in the one awarded the first prize is found this opinion of the adult generation that preceded him:

Since you and I (I'm twenty-three) and thousands of other young men are trying to decide how to succeed in life, I think we would be wise to solve our problems ourselves rather than to ask counsel of those who have produced the present state of politics and society.

Having failed to produce a social ethic, turning their backs to the good of all men, they are incompetent to advise us. *When we ask if we must be crooked to succeed, about all we get from our elders is a shower of moral precepts and pretty proverbs that are as useful as a wooden stick in shovelling snow* [italics in original].

And it is one of the colossal jokes of civilization that our elders, who believed in a Paradise in Heaven (and a Hell for crooked politicians), spent their lives grabbing all they could here on earth whereas the young people of today, who are not sure that a Heaven exists, seem more concerned with the welfare of their fellowmen.[11]

And among the paragraphs of advice this young man gives are:

Do something that most politicians have never done—learn the needs of the people you will represent. . . .

The Sun of Human Intelligence is peeping over the horizon. And the young people of this generation are awake and watching its splendors, while the old

[10] *American Magazine*, June, 1934.   [11] *Loc. cit.*

sleep, covering their heads and muttering, "It won't work. It's never been done before." See that you do not sleep too late.[12]

And now, as my last witness, I cite the words of Judge Ben B. Lindsey as to the awareness and imitation by youth of the bad example of adults whom they know.

Every citizen of a community who through dishonest political or business methods accomplishes what seems to be a success is "doing an injury to one of these little ones" of whom he may never have heard, but for whom he is morally responsible by his very acts and conduct as a citizen. Of such a one our Master said: "It were better that a mill stone be hanged about his neck and he be cast into the sea."

As much therefore as we are able to be congratulated upon the progress made, we are compelled to admit that some of the greatest injuries to children cannot be reached by law. I have been companionable with some of the boys in the children's court, and I have had bright boys of the street ask me questions, of which the following are fair samples:

"Judge, if So and So" (referring to an official holding a prominent position entrusted with sacred public duties) "can stuff the ballot box, why can't the kids play for money?"

This was the query of a newsboy who associated with a gang of crap shooters within a stone's throw of a gambling house protected by the police department, running in violation of the law and well known to these boys of the street who had often suffered the jail and degradation for doing what their elders did under the protection of their "pull" with the city government. A petty imitation of their elders made criminals of the boys, and the same crime on a larger scale made protected and even prominent citizens of the men. The great wealth they gained by crime seemed actually in some quarters to add respectability and political power to the men. It brought the policeman and his club to the boys. Another boy asked me how much money each alderman was to get for purchasing a certain site for a public building. He read in the papers of the open charges of graft against prominent citizens. Another boy once asked me if the saloon keeper let the boys in the saloon on Sunday or sold them liquor, and the policeman (whom he named familiarly) did not arrest the man, why it was the "kids could not swipe things." I have had a sixteen year old girl brought to our court for immorality, complain to me bitterly that the policeman who arrested her protected the dance hall or wine room keeper. She had no respect for the police department and saw no justice in law.[13]

I now cite a poet who interprets a child's awareness of and response to the adult world into which he has been born.

---

[12] *Loc. cit.*

[13] Judge Ben B. Lindsey in a report that he made as chairman of a committee on juvenile courts and probation after he had visited ten states and Washington, D.C. *Juvenile Court Record*, Vol. VI, No. 8, September, 1905.

To the Wise—a Bargain

Said the slum child to the Wise
To the people of place and power
Who govern and guide the hour,
To the people who write and teach,
Ruling our thought and speech,
And all the captains and kings
Who command the making of things;
"Give me the good ye know,

That I, the child, may grow:
Light for the whole day long,
Food that is pure and strong
Housing and clothing fair,
Clear water and clean air,
Teaching from day to day
And room for a child to play."

Then the Wise made answer cold;
"These things are not given, but sold,
They shall be yours today
If you can pay."
"Pay," said the child, "pay you?
What can I do?
Only in years' slow length
Shall I have strength,
I have not power nor skill,
Wisdom nor wit nor will—
What service meek and mild
Can you ask of a little child?"

But the Wise made answer cold;
"Goods must be bought and sold:
You shall have nothing here
Without paying—paying dear."
And the Rulers turned away
But the child cried to them; "Stay;
Wait, I will pay;
For the foulness where I live
Filth in return I give
For the greed that withholds my right

Greed that shall shake your might,
For the sins I live and learn,
Plentiful sin I return,
For lack in home and school,
Ignorance come to rule,
From where I sicken and die
Disease in your home shall lie,
My all uncounted death
Shall choke your children's breath—
Degenerate—crippled—base—
I degrade the human race;
And the people you have made—
These shall make you afraid;

I ask no more, I take
The terms you make;
And steadily, day by day,
I will pay." [14]

I close this book with excerpts from a twenty-nine-stanza poem in which a probation officer acknowledges his fellowship with the delinquent:

"I, Like You, Am on Probation"

We should always bear in mind
To be loving, fond and kind,
And not seek for faults to find
In the child upon probation.

Efforts use of every sort
For to keep them out of court.
That should be the last resort—
They're already on probation.

Hopefully you look ahead
With the child upon probation,
Yesterday is past and dead
For the child upon probation.

Many a dark and stormy night
Gave birth to morning calm and bright,
Dig up what's wrong and plant what's right
And merit public approbation.

[14] Charlotte Perkins Gilman in the *Public,* Chicago, February 22, 1908.

"As we do the children free
From their troubles, so should we
Help each other," for to see
The true meaning of probation.

If we would this course pursue
With the child upon probation,
Oh, the good that we might do
To the coming generation!

And when the day's work is o'er
Speak this kindly at the door;
Go my child and sin no more—
I, like you, am on probation.[15]

---

[15] This poem was written and printed at his own expense by Austin F. Minogue, one of my fellow probation officers in Chicago, who sent a copy to me three years after I had left the court. The writer was a middle-aged, deeply religious man who regarded his work as a sacred opportunity to help delinquent boys. The words of his verses are here literally copied.

INDEX

INDEX